E-mails to My Grandchildren

E-mails to My Grandchildren

Internet Mentoring the Next Generation

Once Removed

David Nagle (Grandpadavid)

iUniverse, Inc.
Bloomington

E-mails to My Grandchildren
Internet Mentoring the Next Generation Once Removed

iUniverse books may be ordered through booksellers or by contacting:

iUniverse
1663 Liberty Drive
Bloomington, IN 47403
www.iuniverse.com
1-800-Authors (1-800-288-4677)

ISBN: 978-1-4620-2202-1 (sc)
ISBN: 978-1-4620-2203-8 (dj)
ISBN: 978-1-4620-2204-5 (ebk)

Library of Congress Control Number: 2011908504

Printed in the United States of America

iUniverse rev. date: 06/24/2011

CONTENTS

SECTION 2: LIVING MY WAY

SECTION 3: LIVING WELL

Dedicated to my grandchildren

*You are what you are because of
the choices you have made.*

*Life is infinitely flexible.
You can make
new choices
anytime.*

*Mentor was charged with
the care and education of
Telemachus, son of Odysseus.*

*The most important bill in our whole [Virginia] Code
is that for the diffusion of knowledge among the people.
No other sure foundation can be devised for
the preservation of freedom and happiness.*

—Thomas Jefferson in a letter to Geo. Wythe, 1786

INTRODUCTION

"When an old person dies, a library has burned down." In his recent book, *Masque of Africa*, author V. S. Naipaul tells of having heard this saying among the people of the forest of Gabon.

At the age of eighty-five, I feel like a library, full of practical information, much of it not in the mainstream of the flow of information that is our present world.

I often awaken in the early hours of the morning, my mind in high gear about whatever happened to be the recent subject of current reading, far-ranging discussions with Mary, politics, or just about anything my mind had been mulling over that was calling out for cognitive attention. Several years ago, in those early morning musings, I found myself thinking of my grandchildren, wondering about their lives and wishing I could be to them what my own grandfather had been to me: a mentor and source of practical wisdom about living. And so this present project had its birth.

In our modern world, the easiest, most practical way to communicate is by e-mail. And so it has been with me. Expanding the e-mail pouch to include stories of my own beginnings, I mentored my grandchildren, electronically.

At first, I told them stories about our family, about my own growing up, and other intimate subjects that family members commonly share. Then as I added e-mails that were comments about life and living that I thought would be useful for them to know, one of them told me "I'm not reading them now, but I've put them away for later, when I need them."

That made me think: if these are being saved for future reading, as and when needed, the horizon of interest of my mentoring should be advanced to include information on a more adult level for their "later reading." Perhaps there are others who would like to have a copy of these communications, which are not strictly family-type stuff they could read when and as needed.

The collection that follows is not in any particular order. Stories are interspersed with serious attempts to offer advice that would be useful to the group of teenagers and twenty-somethings that were my grandchildren at the time of writing. Some are my own speculations about what life is and our place in it. My own life changed dramatically at about age seventy, and I began exploring and writing about what it is to age.

I have included some of the health information I discovered as a result of research, triggered by my first trip to Deepak Chopra's health clinic. During my week there, I absorbed some of the wisdom that Deepak, a superlative and magnetic teacher, unstintingly offered to those ten of us who detoxed together that week. I came away understanding something that, for my seventy years of living before that time, I had never thought about seriously: "Dying is a choice."

The basic life information subsumed within those four words is that everything we do is our choice. Not only that—who, what, where, and, especially, how we are is a direct consequence of the concatenation of choices we have made in the past.

That realization started a research project that resulted in a number of short essays on getting and keeping healthy—not exactly the kind of reading most young people would choose. But because I will not be around when my grandchildren will want and need that sort of health information, information that is not readily found, I have included some of those writings hoping they will "put [this] away for later, when [they] need them."

Because of the vicissitudes of life, choices of where to live, work, and raise a family, my children and I were never geographically close during their own childbearing and rearing years. So my grandchildren and I, while close as an extended family, have never been close in the sense of my being available to them to answer questions, give advice, participate in their thought processes, and generally have the relationship my own grandfather had with me.

Until I left at age eighteen to join the US Navy, I lived next door to my paternal grandparents, with effective daily access to both. Many of my own basic ideas about life were formed from conversations with my grandfather and the advice he frequently gave to me.

When we talk about how society has changed, the focus is usually on the many appliances and labor-enhancing devices we use daily without thinking. But the real change between the way life used to be and the way we live now has come with the changes of transportation. When we learned how to make efficient and widespread use of the inherent energy in petroleum and coal, we replaced the power of human and animal energy that had, since *Homo sapiens* started to walk upright, been the power humans used to transport themselves and their things.

During this enormous change—and it has only been over the span of the last twenty generations— society in the United States has contracted from a mostly agricultural construct into an urban-suburban-exurban way of life. The agrarian way of life and the villages and towns that supported that culture have mostly disappeared. It is not only in developed countries. Around the world, people have been leaving the grinding hard subsistence life of farming and moving to the centers of manufacturing and commerce—the cities.

This has meant the weakening, often the loss, of close familial ties. This also has meant the greater loss of the casual, everyday, living-together opportunity for older generations to pass on to succeeding generations accumulated useful information, not to say wisdom, about how to handle the challenges of living. For example, new mothers who once could rely upon practical advice and folk wisdom from all female family members, as well as a goodly number of neighbor women, about how to manage new baby problems now have a much restricted source of information because family members are often just not close at hand.

It used to be that family relationships, often contentious, were subjects that could be researched within extended family members, tips and sage advice passed down, generation to generation. Now for these very personal and intimate questions, we often must look for answers in books and on the Internet or, perish the thought, on cable and television.

Even up to the time of my childhood in the 1930s, people were born into a family that had roots in a community, and that's where they stayed—rooted in that same community, living near parents and siblings, having children who were really children of an extended family of uncles, aunts, grandparents, and sometimes even great-grandparents. Neighbors were friends. The whole community felt easy about looking after the welfare of the children of the neighborhood. People seldom traveled more than fifty miles from their place of birth. Truly, the "village" raised the child.

In my growing-up community, just twelve miles from Times Square, although very suburban in character, many times did I hear from a neighbor, when I was doing something foolish or slightly dangerous, "Your mother wouldn't like you to do that!" or "If you keep doing that, I'm going to tell your parents!"

Knowing that neighbors who would see whatever I might do were in every nearby house, I had a tendency to keep my actions and those of my chums within a reasonable range of societal approval.

My father's parents, Thomas Jerome Nagle and Elva Van Vechten Nagle, grew up within blocks of each other in Hollis, Long Island—a small community that became a town and later was incorporated into New York City. Grandma Elva's family lived on 194th Street; Grandpa TJ's family lived on 188th Street. When Elva and TJ married, they made their home on 196th Street, just a few blocks and a few minutes' walk away from their parents.

My family lived in a modest house next to the big house, where my father had grown up in Hollis. Grandpa had become disabled to run his business of selling paper and packaging materials when he was fifty. His sons took over until the business was sold in 1941. Because he was not working, during my years from age six until I left for the navy in 1943, Grandpa was always at home, puttering about the house or the yard, teaching me how to trim the hedges, till the vegetable garden, and rake the leaves. He had a store of aphorisms, short sayings that provided a commentary on life, and gave me his own brand of wisdom about how to meet and manage challenges that life presented.

Family gatherings in 16mm films in the 1920s picture three generations—the old, the middle aged, and the young—together for food and fun. I have memories of both Nagle great-grandparents—William, who had a goatee that was rough when he kissed me, and Nobie, of whom my only memory is that she smelled good. They both died when I was about six.

Of TJ and Elva's children, only my father, the oldest, and his next older brother chose to live close. They were, I think, in the last cohort of those whose mind-set was of that earlier social structure and who did not opt for the freedom to be away from family, which came with a rush during and after WWII. Four other Nagle uncles all chose to live away from their parents, scattering to Illinois, Florida, and California. My only aunt stayed close by virtue of economic necessity.

Perhaps it was WWII and the need for workers in making war equipment, weapons, and ships that speeded up the spreading out of families; but it was the automobile and cheap gasoline that allowed it. During the Dust Bowl era of the thirties, the flow of Oklahomans by truck and by car to California was a continuing national news event.

We continue to be a nation on the move. I am a particular example of that. Since leaving the navy in 1946, I have moved my residence twenty-four times, and at age eighty-five, I may move at least once more in this lifetime.

There are consequences in being a peripatetic society. The removal of mentors from the children of following generations is the most grievous. My grandpa was a mentor to me, and I greatly benefited from that relationship. I was able to teach my own children some of what I had learned in life from that time.

However, a young father is neither particularly experienced nor wise nor, in the present go-to-work world, with a lot of time for taking care of the teaching of his children.

By the time my children had arrived, both my parents were gone, but they benefited from the closeness of their maternal grandmother, who, for several years, lived in a "mother-in-law wing" of our home. After that, she moved to a home nearby with her retired schoolteacher sisters and was a frequent presence in the lives of her grandchildren. My grandchildren, though, never had hands-on mentoring from me. By the time they arrived, a lot of distance separated me from their parents. Our visits were a part of holidays and not much else. The e-mails that are the basis for this book were intended to be a mentoring experience for both sender and recipients.

For me, life has been one long and delightful learning experience. My earliest memories of school were of Miss Nancy's prekindergarten school, which she held in her large Victorian house that occupied a spacious corner lot at 191st Street and Woodhull Avenue, in Hollis, Long Island. Although by that time (1929, when I was four) automobiles dominated as they do now, it had not been long before that when a stable or barn was still a necessary outbuilding. Carriages and horses had been an essential part of every homestead, including Miss Nancy's.

Those early animals and conveyances had disappeared from Miss Nancy's barn before the lucky children in her day school arrived, but the barn was always a magnet for me, notwithstanding stern orders to keep out. I remember finding a board, the surface slick from decades of some kind of use which created a polished finish just right to make a short slide. I managed to position it near the barn entrance, and all my fellow preschoolers trooped over to enjoy it until we were discovered and the project dismantled.

In 1929, Hollis was a recently incorporated, very suburban part of New York City. Jamaica Avenue was the main road, starting in Flatbush in Brooklyn and laid out in an almost straight line to Montauk Point, the southern tip of the easternmost part of Long Island. It was paralleled just two blocks south by the Long Island Railway, which, in my childhood days, still had coal-fired steam locomotives in operation.

The railroad tracks, elevated about twelve feet above the surrounding area of homes and streets, defied anyone to trespass. The fill that lifted the roadbed so high was encased in straight flat walls of concrete. But they had not quite defeated the ability of small boys to figure out how to get up there to listen to the tracks to hear distant trains. Once, as a daring preteen, my friends and I purloined someone's ladder, climbed up, and carefully placed a penny on the tracks. Then we watched in quivering excitement and semifear as the smoke and fire locomotive thundered past, flattening the penny to our cries of accomplishment and delight.

When the tracks were electrified and a third rail installed, all parents warned repeatedly about the dangers of that advance in railroading. All too frequently there were reinforcing stories of children, animals, and some adults who touched the third rail and were immediately dispatched to the next world. My friends and I were all suitably impressed, and none of us ever dared again to get close to that seemingly safe but inherently mortal danger.

The point of these anecdotes is this: learning comes from living; part of living may be structured teaching and schooling, with books and classes and certificates at the conclusion to offer historical proof, if that be needed, of one's accomplishments. But learning is simply what one does in life.

As babies, we learn from observing and trying what we've observed. That pattern doesn't vary much as we grow and develop into maturity. We observe, and either virtually or actually, we try what we've observed. In the trying, we may modify our understanding of the process, refine it, and change it to better adapt to our needs and desires; but the learning process is much the same throughout our lives.

Thinking has been defined as the ability to see new relationships between facts. To be able to think, then, requires that we have a store of facts that we can use in this process of thinking. So stored memory plays a significant part in thinking as well as learning. The facts we remember are like mental bricks from which we construct thoughts. I have been blessed with a good memory.

My learning experience was expanded and refined during my years as a trial lawyer. Listening with great care to what a client or witness said and having a rapid recall of exactly what was said was important to be able to detect inconsistencies. The art of cross-examination consists of facing a witness with inconsistencies that may turn out to be misstatements of fact. Listening carefully to a client's recitation of facts determines the path a lawyer will take to help that person.

All of this is preface to telling you that much of the background for my comments about health and keeping healthy, maintaining one's biological age rather than one's chronological age, and other information I offer in this book is in my head. I offer little verification for statements that you may question, and I can only tell you that these are from my research, that my memory is good, my recall is good, and that I have said only things that I firmly believe to be true.

The sources include my studies as a trial advocate, in many cases involving claims of medical malpractice. I was fortunate to have nearby the University of Texas at Austin. The library there has a reading room into which pour the latest medical and scientific journals with the most recent studies involving cellular biology, nuclear and radiological advances, biology, disease, ad infinitum. What was less than current was in the stacks. All of this was available for hour upon hour of research into the subject of my lawsuits. Talking with and formally examining numberless doctors and scientific experts in their fields about the broad range of matters in my lawsuits added facts that I otherwise might not ever have encountered.

When I closed my practice in 1995, before I went to Deepak Chopra's clinic, I read everything I could find that he wrote and listened to his tapes and DVDs. After that first mind-blowing week, I attended his seminars and investigated on my own the virtues and benefits of sesame seed oil and the important herbs and processes prominently involved in ayurvedic healing. I've attended many ayurveda intensives at the Chopra clinic with teachers allied with him and lectures and seminars with Deepak Chopra himself.

In addition, I experienced ayurvedic Panchakarma and other healing protocols at Maharishi Mahesh Yogi's Center for Ayurvedic Medicine in Lancaster, Massachusetts, read extensively from the library there and continued my investigation into ayurvedic healing concepts in preparation for a book on Ayurveda.

I have written and rewritten a book about how to make the best use of the herbs, nutritional nostrums, and healing practices that I am firmly convinced have helped me stay relatively well and active to my present age. But I offered the latest version to friends and others to read, and their comments have led me to put it away as too preachy and too lacking in authoritative citations to be credible with most readers. I have included some writings here that comprise knowledge I gleaned from many sources about caring for the body. From those, you can draw such wisdom as you find there.

The e-mails in this book are divided into sections, with a rough concordance of the individual writings to a general subject matter. But in the originals, there was no attempt to create ideas in groups nor to follow any particular pattern of mentoring. While individual stories and comments will be remembered, this organization of individual e-mails is not something my grandchildren will recognize. My thoughts to them followed no set pattern nor were e-mails grouped into any sort of logic, as I have attempted here. What I intended were stimulants to thinking, pushing and urging young minds to risk thinking differently.

Thinking often consists of establishing new relationships between known facts. One does that in one's head. Facts have come from sources that may be long forgotten, though the facts remain in the brain as building blocks for new ideas.

Formal education has provided a matrix on which I have built, but learning is still individual, still just me and my ability to take in and remember facts that then become the basis for just about every product of my brain, including this book and the information I have offered here, all of which I intend to be of benefit to the reader.

I have been fortunate to have had the advantage of studying philosophy and history at the University of Virginia and then law at the University of Houston. But the thoughts that make my brain synapses snap and crackle are composed of the mosaic of experiences I have had, including the experiences of listening to and reading the thoughts, ideas, and experiences of others.

This book is a collection of some of the e-mails I have sent to my grandchildren, over a period of years, on a broad variety of subjects. Those included are similar to what one might find if one sampled the shelves of a library. There is a mix of stories about my own life, comments about society and the way we live, and about the way things used to be. I have tried not to be preachy, but inevitably, giving advice can trend toward preachiness. I apologize for those lapses and assure you I have edited these ruminations to try to keep them to a minimum. I have included less commonly known methods of keeping healthy that I have found particularly advantageous in my own life, because that sort of information is not easily found.

To paraphrase Will Rogers, I ask the reader, as I counseled my grandchildren, to not let your schooling get in the way of your education.

In this book, my hope is that as you read, you will enjoy the stories I have told my grandchildren, that you will allow your learning to proceed with information and mind-questions that are new and interesting to you. I know you will test what I offer against your own experience and knowledge. I hope you will not suspend your learning simply because there are no footnotes to confirm that others have or had thoughts similar to mine.

The vital role provided by mentoring is fulfilled when the mentored accepts the mentor's challenge to learn. If any of this book impels you to such, the mentor's intent will have been fulfilled.

No one could make a greater mistake

than he who did nothing because he could only do a little.

—Edmund Burke

SECTION 1:

LIVING TRULY

#1 Rules to Live By

The navy sent me to the University of Virginia in 1943. There I first learned of the code of conduct that Thomas Jefferson set out for students at his university. It was simple, straightforward, and useful.

The *honor code*, simply put, had a basic presumption that all who attend the University of Virginia (then an all-male school) were gentlemen, defined by three elemental rules of conduct—"A gentleman does not lie, cheat, or steal."

That's it!

Those still are simple, basic, and useful rules for living. Don't lie, cheat, or steal.

The code did not only apply to the relationship between student and faculty. This was a code to live by, in school and beyond, when the student moved into the world of being a citizen, husband, and father.

The code permeated the life of the university. One did not lie to one's professors or to one's fellows or to anyone within or outside the university's walls. One did not cheat on exams or at cards. The code provision about stealing was looked on as just another aspect of cheating: one must not take anything from another where there was not a fair exchange, whether of money or goods or energy.

My growing up had been in a family that regarded truth and honor as bedrock principles of living. Tales of King Arthur and Robin Hood, read to me as a child, and my later readings of the adventures of D'Artagnon and his companions taught that the world considered certain activities honorable and others not. Those stories had inherent in their plots, character descriptions, and dialogue that honor and strength of individual character were to be valued and emulated. As a child, raised on such trenchant literary fare, cheating, lying, and dishonoring the fair sex was established in my mind as the basest of craven behavior.

Emotionally, I was primed to accept the honor code as a self-evident statement of what all men (and women), let alone gentlemen of the sort who attended Mr. Jefferson's university, should accept as a guiding principle of conduct.

The world of that day was just beginning to open up to the primacy of women in our society. Before that time, literature, mores, and generally accepted truths about who we are and how we live presumed that men were strong, women were weak, and that the fundamental duty of strong men was to protect and defend the person and the honor of weak women. The code did not speak to that distinction. Neither did it mention women or the obligations of women to society and to each other. Of course, the code must be taken as a statement of unisex principles.

The opposite of lying is speaking the truth. As I learned, truth is not immutable. The truth is not necessarily the same for all people at all times. That is because what we regard as truth is simply our human understanding of reality. In contrast to humans, animals likely have no need to make a distinction between truth, what is, and lying—a conscious, intentional telling of what is not.

In our lives as they are lived, we generally equate truth with reality. Reality is what is. As we find so frequently, agreement on what is can be difficult to achieve.

If we are emotionally healthy, we recognize that living in a pretend world, living as though the world is different from reality, is an indicator of mental or emotional instability or both. Seeing the reality of the circumstances one lives in, as they truthfully are, is essential to making both casual and critical life decisions.

Lying is pretending the world is different than it really is. It is like creating a small stage play. The lie may be one pretend fact or many, but telling any pretend facts as true requires that you live in a pretend world, the play, rather than the real world. The real world is complex, and each truth interacts with all other related truths. In the pretend world, you must remember the pretend facts and, usually, make up more pretend facts to keep the play from falling apart into truth. It's hard work.

The practical aspect of always telling the truth is that you don't have to remember the script of a story; you don't have to live in a pretend world.

Being truthful with others helps you to be truthful with yourself. Seeing the external world as it really is creates a pattern of thinking that fosters truthful acceptance of who you really are. Being honest with oneself is more important than being honest with others.

Living in a pretend external world is difficult. Living in a pretend inner world is madness.

If you look at life as a journey, a long path from birth to death, the quickest way to lose your direction along that path is when you know not who you are.

So lying has enormous potential downsides and nothing to recommend its use.

Cheating is related to lying because it is a form of playacting, of pretending something is different than it really is.

Cheating in school has to do with pretend learning. Learning is always a subjective activity. In the scholastic environment, there may be a teacher to provide information in the form of facts, to offer the student vicarious experiences about the subject and to encourage the student to learn. Always, it is the student who learns. The end result of learning is to create knowledge and, perhaps, wisdom. Scholastic tests are reality checks to see if that is actually occurring.

In the context of learning and taking exams to exhibit your understanding and comprehension of the subject, cheating on an exam is depriving you of the reality check of what you have actually learned. Understanding and comprehension are not improved one whit by cheating. Reaching back to the reasons for not lying, while cheating, the student is pretending to be learned. Pretending is playacting and not accepting and living in the present reality. Cheating is a self-deluding, self-defeating activity.

Cheating and stealing are related in that both cheating and stealing deprive somebody of something without a fair exchange of energy in the process.

Emmanuel Kant was a man whose thinking on the subject of human behavior is a part of our heritage of philosophy, the Greek word for "lover of wisdom." His concept of *categorical imperative* is a useful shorthand version of how to understand and evaluate what is happening when a person steals.

"Categorical imperative" was his term for a screen for judging whether any action taken was ethically good or bad. This criterion for judging action is simply for determining in advance the practical consequences of the action. Good is supportive of the social purpose and function of society. Bad is the opposite. The screen is for all people, everywhere, in a similar situation. If everyone agreed that all could do "it" and all would find it acceptable behavior, it was good.

To understand the force of this screen, imagine if all people lied or cheated or stole. Would all people agree that everyone could do this, and the result would be "good" for all? Obviously not!

When using the terms "cheating" and "stealing," we generally refer to tangible property taken without permission of the one who is accepted to be the owner and then treated as the owned property of the taker.

You should not ignore that nontangible aspects of life can also be taken from by cheating and stealing. In many ways, nontangible losses are experienced as more severe than the loss of tangible property.

It would be impossible to consider a society livable, much less just and fair, if everyone took for themselves whatever they wanted from the possession of another. There would be continual disruption of life if, when one reached for an object, the object was missing, permanently taken without permission by another.

As toddlers, we learn that both physical and emotional fighting creates discord and pain in our lives. When as children we fight for control of possessions, for control of a place or activity or thing, that others think imposes on their perceived rights, we create for ourselves a more difficult way to live. There develops the opposite of harmonious social relations.

Peace and harmony are equated with "good." Violence and controversy are equated with "bad." These are simply distillations of human feelings created by universal reactions to experienced conditions.

For most of us, these lessons impel us to find ways to avoid such unpleasantness. We find ways to act, which often becomes habitual, that allow us to enjoy a peaceful, nonthreatening, and nonthreatened existence within our social structure.

Strife and social discord would inevitably follow if stealing should be universally regarded as an activity that any person could engage in at any time, in any place.

Lying, stealing, and cheating selectively, only when compelling circumstances arise but not otherwise, is not better than if the categorical imperative allowed such activity universally and at all times.

Living with people who lie or cheat or steal, even if they do it seldom and only when they think it useful for their purposes, is very disconcerting for those around such fabricators. It is useful to realize that they are so afraid of the consequences of facing reality that they feel compelled to develop a fictional parallel set of facts, which more suits their state of mind.

There develops a distrust of all information received from such people. One cannot ever be sure that the information they offer is a description of what is real or a description they are inventing to help them cope with their fear of what is real. Such conduct is, then, a manifestation of serious disconnect from reality.

Whether using the screen of the *categorical imperative* or simply a test of what is practical and allows you to be in continuous contact with reality, lying, cheating, and stealing are each unacceptable conduct.

Live a good, honorable life.

Then when you get older

and think back,

you'll enjoy it a second time.

—Anonymous

#2 Choose to Change

One of the most useful things you can do for yourself is to understand and accept that you are responsible for everything that happens in your life.

Believe it or not, just about everything in your life really is, or has been, your choice.

Most choose not to believe that. It is too easy to believe one's life is under the control of some outside force, something that limits or even denies one's own individual right of control, control of the who, what, how, and where they are.

But it is true. Everything we do is a result of our choice, either immediately before or, as with habits, at some distant time in the past. We control our bodies by choosing the nutrients we put in them and the activities we engage in on a daily basis—where and how we spend our time. We control our destinies by choosing what and how much we learn, by choosing those with whom we work, by choosing those with whom we live, by choosing where we live. Accepting responsibility for your condition, whatever it is, for the who, what, how, and where you are, is a part of being adult.

As a child, you were pretty much under the control of your parents. Although they no doubt gave you much freedom to make choices and helped you evaluate the likely consequences when there were multiple choices available, it was not until you moved out to go to college that the real adult responsibility of making choices on your own became a pressing reality.

I don't remember much from my childhood attendance at the Episcopal Church my family attended, but we had a very gifted minister. He mixed metaphor with homely stories and quotes from the Bible when useful. One that I remember, and that has stayed with me all these years, goes something like this: "When I was a child, I spake as a child, I thought as a child, I acted as a child. But when I became a man [or woman] I put away childish things."

You have all grown past the stages of childhood and are now women and men. One of the marks of being adult is actively taking responsibility for your life. And that's what I'm most interested in here.

There are, obviously, natural phenomenon, earthquakes, weather, or economic forces that might involve you and about which you will have little say. These are ever present and simply form a part of your life environment. Over these sorts of things and many of their consequences, you, admittedly, have little or no control.

But those events are rare. Most of the choices you will make are about mundane things; living and attending to the needs of living involve making choices, and that's a good place to start thinking about choosing. I'm not counseling you about what choices to make. I am only prodding your awareness so that you don't, consciously or unconsciously, choose without being aware that that is what you are doing.

Be careful, as problems develop in your lives, that you don't make the choice to shift the responsibility for your choices to someone or something outside yourself. Parents, siblings, place in the family pantheon, spouses, bosses, God—these all provide plausibility to your inner conscience seemingly allowing you to avoid accepting full responsibility for your obligation to manage your life by the choices you make. Be careful not to abdicate your power over your own life by giving away any of your power to choose for yourself any part of the life you live.

The choices you make each day, large and small, are the pavers you lay on your own path to the tomorrows of your lives. Each choice involves some sort of change to the direction you had previously been going.

My choice in these e-mails is to ramble freely among the subjects that interest me and I hope will interest you. Particularly, since nutrition is not a subject that you will have likely encountered in school, I want you to know some of the important truths I have discovered about that. There are more. One amazing truth I have discovered, and that I hope you will keep as a subtext of your life, is this:

Aging is a choice.

We may think of aging as inevitable, but the only inevitable in life is death. And although the choices we make that lead to dying are over such a long period of time and are so attenuated from the outcome of the choosing we do that we commonly fail to make the connection, dying is also a choice in the sense that it is the result of many choices. Too, there are multitudes of anecdotes of people who make conscious and deliberate successful choices to remain alive in the face of grievous illness or injury in order to attend an important event or to delay the actuality of death until an absent one returns.

Aging is how we describe what happens to the cellular structure of our bodies in the chronology of time. How these marvels of cellular evolutionary engineering react to time passing is something over which we do have a lot of control. Aging, in the sense of describing a condition of the body, is truly a consequence of choices we make.

Examples in your life will leap to mind as you read the personal parts of my own journey of discovery that have prompted me to want to share what I have learned with more than the limited group of people that are my immediate world.

Much of what I have discovered you will find adaptable to your own life, with, I am confident, many happy results.

I expect you will be convinced, as I have become convinced, that everything we do—everything—including intangibles, like thoughts and beliefs, have consequences that affect some sort of change that affect our individual lives.

I do not intend to persuade you to make this choice or that choice. I simply offer information about choices that can be made and the changes those choices can make in your life. That's what a grandparent is supposed to do. I am your friendly advisor but, mostly, your friend.

If you take away nothing else from these pages, I sincerely hope that you will develop a greater understanding about how much real control and direction you can exert over your own life, particularly over your own body.

The health and the energy level of your body is, to a major extent, the controlling factor of not only how you feel but also how you feel about the life you are living.

The choices you constantly and continuously make inevitably determine who you are, what you are, and whether your life is really the way you want it to be. Perhaps the most important part of choosing is to realize, with each choice you make, that the change that will come about from that choice has already started once your decision is made.

Your intention informs your choices that, in turn, inform and set in motion the energies that will make changes in your life. Your choices can make those changes you really want, really happen.

With the new day comes new strength and new thoughts.

—Eleanor Roosevelt

#3 Living in Harmony with Nature

I'm sure you have noticed by now that humans are pretty arrogant about themselves and their place on the earth. The Bible and its interpreters have done a super job of making people feel they are really something special to the extent that many humans have decided they can plunder the earth of its resources without having to take into account other species or even other members of their own species.

It has helped make us think we don't have to respect nature and the way the earth works. It is far too common to find that our fellow humans think that they can do anything to the earth and to themselves and think that there will not be any consequences. Let me be sure you know that there are consequences, most of them unpleasant, to ignoring nature and the way it works. I urge you to stop once in a while and listen to the music of nature. The way everything fits together into a harmonious whole is breathtakingly complex. But if you listen and pay attention while you listen, you can learn many things that will make your life easier, better, and more fun.

Living in harmony with the rhythms of nature, rhythms of the earth, is what I am talking about. And just why is it better to do that?

The cells that make up our bodies have developed over an estimated six hundred fifty million to eight hundred million years, from simple single-cell creatures through the evolutionary path to the present. Whatever else we are, we are physically a collection of cells—complex descendants of single-cell creatures that first appeared in some primordial soup of minerals, water, and amino acids that first collected in pools around the earth.

Until quite recently in historic terms and for 99.9 percent of human existence on earth, we have been dependent on the sun for light to define the day and moonlight and starlight to ameliorate dark skies at night. The basic cellular rhythms of our bodies have developed in response to that experience. We crave sleep when it is dark and feel energized when it is light.

When we speak of our bodies, we tend to not acknowledge that our bodies are but a collection of cells. The ancestors of those cells began developing the DNA helix that programs cell life, cell function, and cell death, long, long before cells collected into groups and called themselves human.

Mankind, the human genus, seems to have made its quantum leap from some sort of apelike hominid to *Homo sapiens* near the equator, in eastern Africa, some twelve thousand to fifteen thousand generations ago. Recent studies of DNA found in female cell mitochondria indicate that Eve, mother of all present humans, existed probably circa 250,000 to 300,000 years ago.

The cells of the creatures from which we (and our cells) descended developed their stratagems for existence by adapting to the rhythm of each day, each season, and each cycle of seasons, where they then lived.

Although signs of man's pithecanthropus ancestors are not confined to Africa, they have all been discovered within a narrow band of latitudes of the earth close to the equator. Much of our physical adaptive responses to light and dark originated during the fifty thousand or so generations of development of pithecanthropus and hominids before the first *Homo sapiens* appeared.

Even now, when we humans inhabit regions far from the equator, as in the most northern latitudes, our cellular structure takes its most visceral cues from the light hours of the day. During the time from spring equinox to fall equinox, when the nights shorten relative to the other half of the year, our bodies find it natural to sleep less and be active more, the light and dark sequences somehow impacting our pineal glands to modulate sleep requirements.

In equatorial regions, daylight is a fairly constant number of hours as the sun traverses to its northern and southern equinoctial points during the seasons of the year.

Our genetic predecessors lived (and adapted their living) to regular periods of light and dark. Adapting their living, for our purposes, translates into cellular adaptation. Physiological adaptation to any condition or situation necessarily means that our cellular structure and the processes of our cells have adapted. Because that's what we are—a cooperative cellular community adapting to the environment in which we find ourselves in an evolutionary way.

Humans have spread around the world and now can be found living and sometimes thriving at heights of twelve thousand feet and more, in extremes of heat, cold, humidity, and aridity and with extremes of little or no sunlight for months at a time and more months with little or no darkness. All of these extremely diverse conditions speak to the ultimate adaptability of humankind in its individual quest for survival. It does not alter the underlying programming of the cells, which is the human body.

Human cellular structures respond in predictable and observable patterns to the presence and absence of light. Populations in the extreme latitudes seem to feel good, getting along on substantially less than eight hours of sleep during these periods of near constant light. Conversely, when the light disappears for months at a time, suicide rates climb, and psychiatrists report an increase in a condition they have named SAD (Seasonal Affective Disorder). Even in the far north, when light is effectively absent for most of the day for months at a time, sleep needs for most people do not usually exceed one-third of the day. No matter whether north or south hemisphere, winter sleep needs seem to not increase greatly over summer sleep needs. But summer sleep needs do seem to greatly decrease during extended periods of daylight.

What is true is that natural human cycles of sleeping and waking do vary with the amount of daylight. What is also true is that during the dark hours, many of the body's cellular functions exhibit a quite different pattern of behavior and activity than during hours of light.

During sleep, our bodies not only put many of our systems into a sleep mode, where the activity is substantially less than during waking hours, such as actions of the heart, respiration, metabolism, kidney and liver functions, but the initial period of sleep is a time for the body to complete metabolizing the food nutrients taken in during the day. During sleep, the mind will also attempt to metabolize and integrate the emotional content of events that happened during daylight hours. A very useful compartmentalization of the day's hours and human physical responses to the twenty-four-hour cycle of our days is found in an ancient Indian discipline, *ayurveda*. Ayurveda time segments beautifully mirror and illustrate how your body manages its workload.

Ayurveda divides the day into six four-hour segments. There are traditional vedic names assigned to each segment not necessary to state here. The important thing is the logical division of time segments that reflect how human bodies actually function during the day and night. These ayurveda time segments correspond to observable dominant physical energy levels we each uniquely express in times of the day.

The least energetic and least action-oriented waking hours start at 6:00 AM until 10:00 AM, when the body, coming out of the sleep period, is calm, relaxed, and generally slow moving.

From 10:00 AM to 2:00 PM is the time of the greatest available energy and the most complete digestive powers and metabolizing processes of the body.

Afternoon time, 2:00 PM until 6:00 PM, is a period of slower activity and frequently an expenditure of nervous energy.

The second cycle of the day, again divided into four-hour segments, begins in the evening, at 6:00 PM; it is a time of taking it easy, for the body to slow down from the day's activities. Food digestion is slower then, and if heavy foods are eaten at supper (or dinner), they will cause the body an extra burden at this time.

During the time that follows, 10:00 PM to 2:00 AM, metabolism of digested food is in high gear, with the body creating energy to undertake repair of damage that may have occurred to cells and systems during the day. Emotional events that happen during the day may also be metabolized during this period as dreams. REM sleep often occurs toward the end of this time.

It is during this time that those who call themselves night people find that they get their second wind, their energy level rising as they draw upon the energy the body was intending to utilize in repairing its systems.

A spurt of human growth hormone, often shorthanded as a bolus of HGH, which usually helps produce the first periods of deep sleep, may also be kicking in again to create a feeling, often intense, of well-being. Playing (or working) into the night and spending the energy which the body usually uses for repair of itself may explain why after such a night we often have puffy eyes and wrinkled skin in the morning.

Finally, the twenty-four-hour cycle is complete. During the hours of 2:00 AM to 6:00 AM, there is lighter sleep and REM dreaming. The nervous system further metabolizes the emotional events of the day and works to restore balance to all the body's systems. And with that, it is time to get up and do it again, first light or before.

Paying attention to the traditional activities during the several time periods does not mean giving up any of your right to decide how you will manage your body or your time. It is merely recognizing and taking advantage of what generations of people, before you were born, have recognized as how the human body works and what works best in this earth environment.

Everything that we take in as nutrients has chemical energy—components that the body either metabolizes into energy forms it can use or passes on through the intestinal tract as waste and eliminates. As young people, still developing emotionally, you need to know that every sensory event that occurs to your body creates an electrical potential within your body that has to be metabolized as well.

In the case of sensory events that evoke no emotional response within the body, metabolism is usually swift and complete. The energy of light, sound, taste, smell, or touch is converted by the senses into electrochemical energy, which is processed by the body for its benevolent effect or damaging potential, which the body then accepts, moves to get more of, or moves to avoid; and the incident is completed at that.

The exception would be any sensory event that creates a dislocation of energy or of molecular structure, such as any trauma to the body that causes injury to the cellular structure with which the body has to deal and either accept and integrate or repair.

When an event occurring to the body creates an emotional response within the body, that event has its own unique content—an electrical-chemical mix that is stored as memory, able to be retrieved at will and, perhaps also, that comes roaring up from some unexpected stimulation, usually at a most unexpected time.

Feelings of love, compassion, joy, exuberance, exhilaration, and other emotions we generally categorize as positive create hormonal responses that flood the body with good feelings. We can feel these emotions all through our whole system. The body metabolizes these emotional responses, seemingly with nothing but positive lingering effects.

Fear, anger, hate, disgust, despair, panic, and other strong negative emotions also send hormonal and information messenger molecules flooding through the body. If these emotions evoke feelings of alertness to potential danger, a weak or strong variety of the fight or flight pattern of bodily response and a change in blood flow will occur. There will also be a slowdown of major systems, such as the digestive process. When the situation has passed and the hormonal flow has returned to normal, there still may be lingering effects of this internal disturbance, with which the body must deal.

The body stores unmetabolized emotional events in a manner similar to the way it stores unmetabolized food. Some emotional events which have negative components become energy blocks, either in a major organ, such as a kidney (being pissed off is more than just an expression), the neck and shoulders (he gives me a pain in the neck), or perhaps along an energy pathway which results in a block of energy flow and some condition of disease at that place in the body or, more likely, at some distant organ or confluence of muscles that we designate as referred pain.

That emotional event can be resolved by release of built-up emotional tensions through our natural release mechanisms of yelling, screaming, crying, fighting, physically hitting or kicking (kicking a pillow or other substitute for the object of the anger creates a valid release), or some form of strong physical activity, such as running, jumping up and down, or twirling until dizzy. Each of these is a valid and useful way of releasing (metabolizing) negative emotions. If not metabolized at the end of the event or soon thereafter, the body may attempt to metabolize the lingering effects of the event through REM dreaming.

Recent psychological and psychiatric techniques use a form of REM to help patients access and resolve emotional problems in a usually expeditious way.

The body may also just store an emotion for future action. These future actions often take the form of unexpected tears, a flare of inappropriate anger, and sometimes as a burst of energy channeled into tasks we want to accomplish. However, once the body has stored the unmetabolized emotion, it may just keep it where it is—in the tissues—forever.

Ayurveda healers say that *ama* is a sludgelike substance found in the tissues of the body that is a combination of both unmetabolized food which the body has stored and the consequences of unmetabolized emotions, also stored in the tissues of the body. The objective of Panchakarma, a detoxification routine highly valued in ayurveda healing, is to dislodge that *ama* from its place in the tissues and encourage it to move into the bloodstream, where it will be carried to the kidneys and the liver and thence to the bladder or large intestine, there to be moved out of the body as waste.

Natural healers tell us that cancers are the consequence of angers the body has stored and failed to metabolize. Arthritic personalities are recognized by orthopedic specialists. These are people who are martyrs and long suffering. They internalize their angers that then localize in their joints.

Since anger is a form of fear and fear generates stress akin to a fight or flight response, the adrenal glands of a person who lives in a state of fear stay active and productive, even though the fear is mild and controllable.

Understanding that you seldom have real control over external events that affect you and your loved ones, that life is what it is, is a long step toward allaying fear of life and the damage to your cells that such fear creates.

At this time in your lives, the information I have just added to your knowledge reservoir is likely more than you care to know. But at some time, in some relationship or other transactional event, you will wonder, "What's going on?" Keep this around, and you may find that the path to an acceptable answer starts with what I have told you here.

Knowing yourself is the beginning of all wisdom.

—Aristotle

#4 A Life Full Of Interesting Potentials

If you think about it, this life is full of interesting potentials for each of us.

As I write this, the ages of you, my grandchildren, range from seventeen to twenty-six. Most of you have had strong preliminary thoughts about what you would like to do, where you would like to live, and who you want to be. These will change as you grow, learn more, and see other choices available to you.

The truth is, we each can use thought power to choose and to make both broad and narrow details of our lives any way we want them to be. In twenty or so years, when we stop to look back, many, perhaps most, of those things we thought of doing, being, and having, will appear in one form or another in our rearview mirrors. We will have thought of them but not taken the next step, choosing actions that would bring them into our lives

Putting first things first, we generally accept thinking, i.e., ratiocination, as sort of an automatic process. Everyone thinks, right? Well, yes and no. Everyone walks, too, and runs and eats and does all the other semiautomatic things that every human does. But surely you have observed how differently we do these things. Some do everything with grace, as though born to the skill of walking with their head up, back straight, and legs going forward with the balance and poise of a natural athlete. Others do not.

The same is true of just about all aspects of your active life, including thinking.

Take a moment to ponder thinking as an activity. Thinking can be as simple as noticing the milk container is nearly empty, realizing that there will be a future need for milk, and concluding with a determination to get more milk. It can be as complex as Einstein thinking through the theory of relativity to a conclusion that changed the world.

Recent research has determined that thinking stimulates the brain to create more neurons (brain cells, sort of) and to create more connections, more synapses, between neurons. We know from our own experience that with use, muscle cells grow, expanding in size and strength, enhancing their ability to perform the tasks we ask of them. In much the same way, recent studies have established that thinking enhances our ability to think. We apparently influence both the speed and scope of thinking, by thinking. Thinking begets better thinking.

This is one of the reasons that as we age, specialists in the problems of aging recommend that we take on projects that require thinking. Doing crossword puzzles, for example, is a highly touted method of keeping brainpower from diminishing. But any type of thinking that challenges us to work at thinking and to exercise our brain neurons will do.

Thinking is also measurable. The electroencephalogram and now the functional Medical Resonance Imaging (fMRI) are both devices that can measure the existence and intensity of energy produced by the brain both in repose and in action. If the thinking of one individual produces measurable energy, imagine what could happen if groups of people all focused their thoughts on the same thing at the same time.

Followers of Maharishi Mahesh Yogi, the Indian teacher who brought Transcendental Meditation to the United States, in fact have tried that. ("Maha" means "highest" or "best"; "rishi" means "teacher." The favored pronunciation is "M'har-shee.")

I met Maharishi in 1973, when a friend on his staff called and asked me if I would do him a favor and come to a welcome reception. He said it was about a very new thing that would change the world. He didn't disclose any more, saying that I would find out when I came. I was intrigued but would have said yes anyway. Gould Beech was a longtime good friend from my time with Roy Hofheinz, one-time mayor and flamboyant promoter of the Astrodome and other landmarks of Houston, Texas.

The reception was a very intimate affair in an office building where one of the empty suites had been arranged to host Maharishi and his entourage. About fifteen of us assembled at the rear of what turned out to be the reception room, a longish room with no decorations except banks of cut flowers and greenery of potted plants. A red carpet runner, four feet wide, led from the door to a low dais at the far end of the room on which more flowers were arranged in a circle, around a quite small clearing in the middle, within which there was a very large white pillow.

Maharishi entered, followed by three petite Indian women in colorful saris. Maharshi barely topped five feet in height. In the stark white robe he wore, his stature seemed even smaller. The women were all shorter than the Maharishi.

There was a very soft polite applause as he swept down the red carpet, mounted the one step to the dais, seated himself on the pillow in the lotus position, faced the waiting group, and immediately closed his eyes, his face in complete repose in a meditative state.

After several moments, he opened his eyes, his face presenting a beatific smile and said a few words of welcome.

This was my first introduction to Maharshi and meditation. Before that, if I had ever heard the word "meditation," I don't remember it. Maharishi Mahesh Yogi, trained as a physicist in India, had received a message from the universe that his role in life was to make the world aware of the benefits of ancient Vedic arts of healing and societal organization, including the use of mediation.

He had been to many countries around the world and was now bringing his message to the United States, a focus of particular concern.

He regarded the United States as the preeminent force in the world. He conceived it his responsibility to use his energies to help direct that force for the good of the world.

When he first came to this country in 1959, he was met with a big yawn by most of those with whom he came into contact. Yet there were some who heard and agreed with his message of bringing peace, providing all people inexpensive health care and, imfluencing the powers of government to the goal of creating a good environment for its citizens. To that end Maharishi intended to use the simple expedient of training large numbers of people to meditate.

Focusing the meditation energies of 0.001 percent of the population in a given area, according to his concept of how focused energies of the mind work, can influence the state of mind of the population of that whole area. He tried on two occasions to attempt to bring a more peaceful atmosphere to the seat of our nation's government, Washington DC. A story about one of these efforts and its result is below.

Meditation, particularly Transcendental Meditation, the brand name he gave his method of meditating, is both practical and utilitarian. Those who do it regularly report both mental and physical health benefits as well as improvements in their business activities. An explanation of mediation, how to do it, and the potential results are the subject of another e-mail, so I will just leave it at that here. If you do not know how to meditate, it will be well worth your time to learn.

One more word about Maharishi—before he died in 2008, he headed a vast worldwide organization from the headquarters in the Netherlands. He promoted his original goals with frequent large ads in the *New York Times*, advising the progress on his plan to create an Ayurvedic Health Center in each congressional district in the United States. This was to advance his idea that all people of every economic condition are entitled to health care they require and to promote Vedic principles of enduring good health. His ideas are being carried on by his disciples, both in the United States and worldwide.

I learned about the following story during one of many stays at the Maharishi North American Center for Health in Lancaster, Massachusetts. The library in the center has a wealth of information not generally available about meditation and Maharshi.

In 1988 (I believe that was the year), violence in Washington DC was out of control. Citizens were being accosted, assaulted, and robbed on the streets, often in daylight, in places that had been thought of as safe areas of the city. A congressman was knocked down and robbed not far from the steps of the Capitol building. Violence was rampant. The authorities seemed to have lost control of the city.

Maharishi believed that this was an intolerable situation in the capital of the greatest nation on earth, and he called upon his disciples of meditation to assemble in Washington and meditate for peace. He organized a program of meditation for the participants that started at nine in the morning until noon, broke for lunch, reassembled at one o'clock, and continued until four o'clock every afternoon of each day for nearly nine weeks.

Maharishi's theory was tested: he theorized that one-tenth of one percent of the population in any given area following his guidelines for meditation and focusing on an end result desired by the group could, by force of their meditative thoughts, influence the behavior of the population of the whole area. One-tenth of one percent of the population of Washington DC at that time was approximately four thousand people.

From the middle of May, when the effort began, until the end of July, when the process ended, there were varying numbers of meditators. The group that first responded numbered about 2,000 and soon grew to over 4,600 and then varied between 3,500 and 4,000 until they disbanded and went to their homes in other parts of the country and the world.

Their meditation focused on creating a peaceful environment and inducing peaceful behavior among the population. During and following this period of intending to influence population behavior by group thought, the DC police reported a significant reduction in violent crime (words of the then Chief of Police). The statistics also showed that during several occasional extremely hot summer nights, when all crimes and particularly violent crimes would have been expected to peak, those numbers went down.

In jails, meditation trainers have taught Transcendental Meditation to inmates, following which the incidence of violence in those jails reportedly dropped measurably.

In each of these instances, conduct changed. In each instance, the change was intended. The process intended to create change was deliberate and well thought out. In each, the power used to change behavior was the energy of thought.

Some years ago, a book by Norman Vincent Peale, *The Power of Positive Thinking*, was very popular. In it, the author argued that one's life could be changed by thinking positively—that is, by thinking thoughts focused on the result one wished to occur.

The book was not by some edge-of-reality writer. Peale was a Catholic prelate, steeped in the doctrines of Roman Catholic religious thought and doctrine, and offered straightforward advice about how any person, using positive thoughts, could greatly improve his or her life situation. Many testimonials spoke to the effectiveness of using one's own thoughts to direct and advance one's path through life. It was and is as he wrote—thoughts do indeed have power.

To use thought energy to direct and power one's life, one has only to understand the basics. Thought power does exist; it is available to everyone. Thought power can be increased in the same way any other faculty or skill can be increased. Practice and use are the simple, effective methods of making your own thought power stronger. Perhaps you have heard the expression, "The thought is parent to the deed." That simply says what humans have recognized from time immemorial. Before we act, we think. Taking the time to think in our present societal craze of fitting more and more activity into smaller and smaller time frames seems like asking the impossible. But it is this conscious allocation of time that will make the difference in your life.

What kind of thinking will actually increase the power of your thoughts? Meditation is one way and the "how to do it" of meditation will be described in another e-mail. For now, know that before you take the first step in any journey, you must have determined the direction you wish to go. Without a direction, you will not be able to take the first step. Having a goal, as in so much of life, helps make clear the path to that goal.

The intermediate goal of meditation is to have the muscular structure of the body completely relaxed and nontense. Once that is accomplished, the next goal is to completely relax the mind. The end goal of meditation may be simply accomplishment of the two intermediate steps.

But having an end goal of meditation beyond relaxing the body and mind will focus the energies of your mind to direct your body to accomplish that end goal. Simply determining what you intend is enough of a task to take on at the start. An example of a simple goal might be the healing of an injured knee.

Think about what you want to be, what you want your body to be, how you want to act, how you want your surroundings to be, and how you would choose to spend your time each day.

Once you have made decisions about these aspects of your life or life path, write them down. Don't be shy about changing any or all as you go through the process of thinking about them. They will change as your thoughts become more and more focused and you find yourself and your ideas changing until you determine what you really think. But know that nothing about thought is truly permanent. Everything is, and should be, fluid, in motion and subject to change.

When you have written them down, after awakening and before sleeping each morning and night, review these writings and think about them. Imagine how you could achieve each of the goals you have set down. Exclude all sensory stimuli. Allow no noisy media, no music, no extraneous talking, nothing, to distract you from what you have set as your immediate goal—that is, to focus your thoughts solely about each item on your list.

What you will be doing is sending thought energy to your cells as well as out to the Universe. Not that every choice you make will automatically come about. Other forces are at work in the Universe, and your energy may bump against energies that are stronger, have been there longer, and are impossible for you to change. Nonetheless, if you persist in your thoughts, if they are organized and consistent and reflect your determined intent, you will find that remarkable coincidences happen with great regularity, moving you toward your goals. (But then, as I've pointed out elsewhere, there are no coincidences. The Universe really does operate in marvelous ways).

Equally important to communicating your goals to the Universe, you will be talking to yourself, informing yourself of your decisions, desires, and intentions. Nothing is more important than all your being be directed to the goals you have decided on.

Every choice you make in your daily life will either take you closer or keep you further from your goals. To make better choices, it is vital to have thought in advance about what it is you really want.

As mentioned at the start, exercising your mind is more than just a saying. It reflects the reality of life, everyone's life, yours included.

At every point in your life, every part of your life *from that moment on* is pure potential. All is *to be*. It can be the way you want it to be. The first step is to think about it with clarity and purpose.

Note: Maharishi Mahesh Yogi died in 2008. The organization he founded and led continues his work of helping mankind live better, fuller, more healthful lives through the teachings of ayurveda.
Find out more at <u>www.wikepedia.org/maharishi</u>.

Human beings, by changing the inner attitudes of their minds,

can change the outer aspects of their lives.

—Proverb

#5 Habits/Choices

For most of us, when the desire to change our bodies strikes, the immediate reaction is to buy a book on diets or how to look gorgeous in a week or some other advice on what to do to make the external changes we wish for.

What is usually missing in all of the advice books is the first important step—that of visualizing what it is we want to be when the process is completed. The body is indeed the vehicle in which we live and function in this world, but the thinking part of the brain, the mind, is where the command center is and where whatever changes are going to happen need first to be programmed.

We are what our deep driving desire is. As our will is, so is our deed. As our deed is, so is our destiny.

Our life is shaped by our mind, for we become what we think.

Both of these clear statements about how we humans truly work in this world are from India, centuries ago.

The first is from the Brihadaranyaka Upanishad, circa 2500 BCE, the longest and oldest of the Upanishads (Br. iv.4.5). The second is a quote from Buddha by one of his disciples, contained in the opening verse of the Dhammapada, circa 520 BCE

We live by habit so much of the time that to change who we are, how we are, and what we are absolutely requires that we change our habits.

Changing a diet for the purpose of changing our looks is hard enough. Changing engrained habits takes significantly more effort. Which is why, notwithstanding good intentions, we often fail to really change.

It takes paying attention to activities that, by their very definition (i.e., "habit"), we do without paying attention to them. It takes work just to pay attention. It really takes work even after choosing to change to do it.

And like the joke about how many psychiatrists it takes to change a light bulb—only one, but the lightbulb really has to want to change—we really have to want to change and must have that as a deep driving desire if we are going to delete old habits and create new ones.

It is important that we have clarity in our thoughts about change. Our bodies, our cells, must know exactly what it is expected of them.

And this applies so often not only to the changes we desire to make in our bodies, but also has to do with every aspect of ourselves and our lives: *who* we are, *how* we are, *what* we are, and *where* we are. It also has to do with *when* we are, for life itself is decisional.

I'm a great fan of Thomas Jefferson and often apply one of his sage bits of advice. He said, "Always reach for the smooth part of the handle." The smooth part of the handle in the task of changing habits is the part that experience has taught us most often works.

What most often works when we want to change a habit is to decide to do it when our environment is different than the usual. Somehow this gives the mind more freedom to change routine behavior. Change is easier when our ability to focus on what we really want to do is not clouded by familiar stimulation to keep doing what we have always done.

We develop many patterns of behavior in conjunction with recurring events in our environment, recurring patterns in the behavior of people we live with, our own activities, and even smells and sounds. These are called anchors and have much more to do with the patterns of our lives than we consciously know.

To change habits, we often have to remove or, at the least, suppress the effect of these anchors. Changing environments and, with that, changing routines is reaching for the smooth part of the handle to do this work

Changing routines can be as simple as taking a weekend break at a friend's home. Anything that takes us out of the expected, the comfortable, the familiar old patterns of living, allows us to better focus on change.

The undeniable success of weekend seminar intensives advocating change that often dramatically change living patterns has to do, in large measure, with the fact that participants are outside of their usual habits of living and have the freedom to place all the new information coming at them onto a clean sheet, so to speak, a tabula rasa, relatively uncomplicated by old patterns of doing or thinking.

Decisions for change under these conditions have the advantage of starting off with clarity of intent and purpose. Frequently, anchors for new ways of being are provided by the speakers to help solidify decisions to change.

The constellation of habits we live by at any given time is the result of personal choices we have made at some time in the past. Though we often deny our ability to choose, we always have a choice of what habits we allow into our lives. It is true that some forces (weather, economic) are not under our control. But as to the most important aspects of our lives, the nonmaterial aspects of our lives, who and what we are is all up to us every time.

Childhood and family circumstances, siblings, spouses, occupations, and monetary needs all have helped create the environments that shape our lives. Yet these forces are not the ultimate causes of who we are and what we are.

We, ourselves, once we have achieved adulthood, bear the responsibility for who and what we are. Everything we do, every habit we create, every place we live, everyone we live with, work with, play with is a part of our life because we have agreed it can be that way.

But that's not how we usually think about who or what is responsible for who or what we really are. When we casually shift how we understand our responsibility for ourselves away from ourselves, we greatly increase the difficulty in making any substantive changes.

Our beliefs are a matter of choice too. After all, beliefs are simply a habit of thinking a certain way. But beliefs, once in place, may be more difficult to change than any other habit.

Bernie Seigel, author of the best-selling book *Love, Medicine, and Miracles*, says that we become addicted to our beliefs. His observation is that when one challenges the beliefs of another, they act like an addict.

The Catholic Church has long known and taken advantage of the difficulty of changing belief systems. Their asserted motto, "Give us the child until it is five and then . . ." expresses their certainty that once the child's mind has been inculcated with the precepts and beliefs of Roman Catholicism, little that might happen after will change that state of belief. And that has been the case until very recently, when the Catholic Church has become more demanding of its members and many more educated parishioners have rebelled.

That is currently (2009) the case with the base of the Republican Party. Those who are the *true believers* (to borrow a term from philosopher Eric Hoffer) of what has been loosely termed as Conservatism act like addicts whose minds have been warped to a belief that only their concept of governance should be followed.

Current problems the Western world has with Muslim extremism is another in-your-face example of a substantial portion of humanity that has decided that their belief is the only belief that should be tolerated. They are truly addicted to their religion. The threat of this for the rest of us is alarming.

The psychiatrist Eric Berne, in his book *Games People Play*, proposed the idea that we each continuously choose to keep busy, in both mind and body, in order for there not to be empty time in our lives.

If that is true, and the idea has achieved a ready acceptance in most psychiatric and psychological disciplines, then many of the choices we have made and habits we have developed have not been made with a serious intention to establish a specific pattern of life but as a consequence of an innate desire to keep busy. It is no wonder that so many habits do not serve us.

As adults, unless some crucial event has taught us the value of making all choices with care, many of us follow the path suggested by Eric Berne: we make the choices necessary to keep from having what we think of as empty time in our lives. These choices, too often, become habits. Once habit becomes addiction, changing gets to be very hard indeed.

Smoking is an example of a habit that is begun by many youths just to do something to fill time. Peer acceptance and wanting to be cool certainly add to the mix of incentives, but at base, kids are filling time with actions of their hands, lips, mouths, tongues, etc. Adults who have quit and take up the habit again are frequently using cigarettes to have something to do with their hands, just like kids starting to smoke.

But even addiction is a choice. The body is choosing to have a certain kind of pleasure, ignoring the long-term, sometimes fatal, consequences. The mind may, and often does, understand the dangers; but the body, demanding addictive satisfaction, opts in favor of near-term pleasure.

When the mind determines to convince the body that the long-term pleasure of living disease free is a higher and more valuable pleasure than the short-term kick from nicotine and satisfaction from time filled with trivial action, then the mind will ultimately triumph. When the triumph is complete, the body will be convinced and will no longer crave either the nicotine molecule fix or the trivial action which smoking provides for the hands and lips.

It all happens in the mind. We become what we think. Those who casually deplore their own cigarette habit and in the same breath say that they do actually enjoy smoking affirm that they have a strong habit they have no wish to change or that they really are addicted and have not the will to change.

What has worked for me has been self-hypnosis or autosuggestion, which has allowed my subconscious to take over and reprogram my choice-making process without my having to work hard at it.

Stopping smoking was hard for me and took almost two years. But eventually the message got to my choice-making process that I was no longer a smoker. When that happened, not smoking was easy. I simply no longer wanted to smoke. That occurred in 1974. I have not wanted a cigarette since.

The "Yes, but . . ." response to any suggested change of habit, such as the smoking habit, is a signal that the mind is rejecting change. Until the decision is firm and there are no "buts" involved, the intention is wavery at best and probably noncommittal overall. Without commitment, there will be no change. Without the mind being unidirectional on the intent to change, there will be no change.

I have offered a bit of information about your natural energies and how these natural phenomenon can be marshaled to help you change habits, how you can enlist your own energy for your benefit, in another e-mail (#38 Using One's Energy to Heal).

Habits are much like the autonomic system of your body; autonomic functions are basic and essential to life, like breathing, oxygen absorption, and heart rate. Not only do most of us have no control over these systems, but we also don't even think about them. They are, in fact, automatic and they go on, waking or sleeping so long as we live. Habits can become like that.

Yet, there are those who learn to exercise control over this autonomic system of the body. The great magician, *Houdini*, for one, was able to control his heartbeat, his breathing, his metabolism, all as a necessary part of performing his "magic" tricks. He would allow himself to be wrapped in locked chains and then placed in a cabinet that had more chains around it and lowered into a tank of water, from which he would then escape in a matter of minutes. Not only was the feat of extricating himself from the locks and chains that bound him a remarkable display of skill, the escape time was much longer than would be possible except for his control of his autonomic system.

You do not have normal control of your autonomic system, but the example is to show that what seems almost impossible is, in fact, possible. Habits, too, seemingly impossible to break, can be changed. If control over the autonomic system is possible, the same dynamics can be used to exercise control over habits that have become addictive in nature.

Identify the habits that promote good health and good feelings and those that do the opposite. Most of those that oppose the health of your cells are ones that, for a variety of reasons, feel good, at least some of the time.

Then focus your energy on creating a mind image of how much better your life would be if an injurious habit were ended or replaced by a habit that promoted good health.

Your own intentions are the place to start. You can change yourself into the *you* you want to be. It is just a matter of . . . when do you want to start?

Time is a built in eraser for most things in our lives.

Time changes us at its own speed whether we will or not.

You can, though, direct your own change with every choice you make.

—GPD

#6 Would You Really Put That in Your Brain?

If you have been listening to your parents, you take some care in selecting the food you eat. At home and at school, you have learned that there are foods that serve you well and contribute to your well-being, and there are foods that we properly call junk foods. So I expect that you pay some attention to what you put in your stomach. But do you know that there is a close analogy between what you take into your body as physical food and what you take into your brain as mental food?

Your brain is marvelously adapted to the way you live. Not only is each body different, but each brain within each body is different. Each brain adapts to serve the mental and physical needs and activities of the body in which it is located. Like a faithful servant, while it is functioning and doing the tasks asked of it, it is also constantly observing the input, selecting synapses to strengthen. Synapses used over and over, because of same or similar experiences (physical or mental), signal the brain to strengthen those connections. Some are purely mental; some are related to motor actions. The names of family members and the skill with which one uses an eating utensil are examples of strongly developed synapses in each category.

With lack of use, synapses gradually become less strong, less accessible, and assume a sort of reserve status—available but often not as quickly or as strongly. The name of a person met just once may fade and become difficult to call up; over time, it may become irretrievable.

What neurologists and neuroscientists are discovering is that the brain is malleable. Your brain has plasticity. Each brain adapts to fit the uses to which it is put by the person it serves. More importantly, recent work has shown that specialized parts of the brain, when damaged or destroyed, can be reactivated, in the repaired sections or in new sections taken over for the purpose, by physically taking the body through the processes that developed that skill in the first instance. In much the same way, a child repeats words, phrases, and motor skills to advance its ability to function in the world it finds itself in; repetition is critical to this rebuilding of skills in a damaged brain.

Apparently, new cells in the brain are alerted to the body's needs and somehow adapt to perform the new functions. New synapses of these cells develop, and the synapses strengthen with repetition. In many instances of focal brain damage to soldiers, lost skills, such as using a spoon or fork to convey food to the mouth, have been rebuilt. Therapists guide the hand and arm with infinite patience through motions the injured brain has lost the capacity to do voluntarily until the new synapses are established and the skills return. A child's brain may learn this in days. A brain damaged by trauma may take weeks or months to reestablish lost abilities. But therapists, working under the direction of neurologists, are showing the brain can relearn many things never before thought possible.

The Iraq War, with its unfortunate abundance of brain-injured soldiers, has provided neurologists and therapists a substantial source of raw material to work with. The work they have done givers us proof; determination and long hours of very hard work, using the same activities the body went through initially to learn a lost skill, encourages the brain to shift the responsibility to do those skills to a new area.

An example: the loss of the motor skill affecting the ability to use one hand and arm because of shrapnel damage to the portion of the brain that controls those motor movements can be restored by, first, helping the nonworking arm and hand to do simple tasks and then, when use begins to return, by the person involved demanding of his or her brain (through repetition) that it refine the skill of making those movements. Through innumerable repetitions of therapeutic movement of flaccid muscles, the brain is presented with the body's need to be able to do something.

The brain as a unit somehow gets a set of undamaged cells to agree to either change the functions they presently perform, add the new needs to their existing repertoire of control signals, create entirely new cells to take over the new requirements of the body, or affect some combination of these. Then uncounted repetition of the desired movement creates the connections necessary to restore function and then strengthens the synapses until the body is able to respond to a desire to move with the movement itself.

The brain may start out as a jumble of neurons in the fetus, but with each experience, synapses begin to form and form and form until there are, literally, hundreds of synapses connecting each cell with other cells. For cells that occupy the most active centers of the brain synapses likely number in the thousands.

Synapses are created with each new experience. Do these synapses remain intact? Are they strengthened? Or does the brain make the decision to allow them to lapse and fall away? The actions by the brain to either amplify or diminish the synapses are apparently guided by and are the result of the demand for the synapse to be firmly established by recurring use, or it is disestablished because of disuse.

It is important to remember that the brain not only controls motor skills, speech, memory, and other voluntary activities but also emotional experiences, the feelings we have that make us happy, sad, angry, fearful, and so on.

The practical effect of this understanding about the brain, developed from the experiences of teaching injured soldiers to establish new neuronal pathways in the brain to do work that damaged and destroyed cells previously had done, is that we now have proof of the plasticity of the brain, that it has the ability to transfer tasks within its cellular community, and that repetitive experiences are a signal to the brain to strengthen synapses for responding to the body's need for action.

It is not a leap of great faith to assume that what the brain does with control of voluntary functions of the body, it also does with emotional and mental aspects of brain activity. Repetition as a key part of learning a poem, for example, is a common experience. If our brains are subjected to any stimulus on a regular basis, it is reasonable to conclude that synapses will develop that are the same as or similar to the response of cells which control motor skills the body requires.

If one reacts to a perceived insult with anger, each repeat of that strengthens the anger response. If one has a response to a perceived insult that is a tranquil acceptance that the perceived insult is of no consequence, that response of equanimity becomes the norm.

Knowing that, being careful about what we allow to become repetitive is only prudent. The brain will establish priority based on repetition. How we respond to events that occur in our environment establishes how we will likely respond to the next similar event. Violence will beget more violence. Fear will beget more fear. Deliberately being confident and calm will increase the likelihood that we will usually respond to the world with confidence and calm.

We mostly have control over what we see. Some things of a horrible nature are thrust on us, and we cannot avoid experiencing them. But those are rare. Recurring nightmares and posttraumatic stress disorders that shocked the mind and the brain of soldiers in Iraq, from being forced into experiences that aroused deep and uncontrollable feelings of fear, are excellent proof of the effect there can be on the brain from seeing and hearing, much less being involved in, events of this sort.

We voluntarily and vicariously experience horror in books and movies. Notwithstanding, we are not actual participants or actual observers of the events we take in through our eyes and ears; these experiences are real and physical in the sense that the brain receives the input and synapses are created, which, once established, either become reinforced or allowed to become dormant. These experiences affect our thoughts, our moods, and our level of contentment with life.

This is true because the brain doesn't distinguish between what is actually physically going on outside the body and what is presented from what we read and hear and experience solely within our brain. Both situations are real to the brain.

So the question you must ask yourself is, when offered the chance to voluntarily see, hear, or otherwise experience a violent, horrific, or degrading event, is that something you want to put into your brain?

If you would not voluntarily put into your stomach a toxic substance that would adversely affect your health and well-being, why would you allow into your brain any experience that you could control, which would be other than something to increase your contentment with life?

When you go to sleep, there is a period soon after the body's systems slow down when you start breathing heavily and enter REM sleep. That signals a time when a bolus of human growth hormone flows from the pituitary into the blood stream. The effect of this HGH is to help the DNA of each cell repair any damage or dysfunction of that cell.

Seeing or reading about violent events triggers a reaction in the body, notwithstanding the event is experienced vicariously. The reaction to violence is a mild (sometimes not so mild) fear that triggers the adrenals to produce cortisol, the fight or flight hormone. Cortisol does not metabolize quickly. It lingers to keep the body alert as the danger may not be completely past. When not needed to promote safety, cortisol is toxic in the sense that it takes over and controls many bodily functions, including heart and circulation. Keeping the body on extreme alert, when such is not necessary for life, is exceedingly stressful.

Now that there is empirical proof that the brain adapts to and supports the lifestyle of its owner and learning what is important and reinforcing neuronal pathways from repetitive impressions, you can more intelligently direct experiences to your brain in order to encourage its development to be what you want it to be. You can use care to have a brain that develops more empathy for others, that accepts compromise, and understands the value of cooperation over conflict. Your brain can help you promote for yourself a more peaceful and contented life.

The question, "What? Are you going to put that in your brain?" is a serious question. It is a question for parents who are guiding the evening TV viewing for their children or allowing their attendance at violent or scary movies. It is a cautionary question about what you will do or experience before bedtime.

It is a question for all at all times. What you put into your brain helps establish what your brain considers important. Ultimately, because of the brain's malleability and plasticity and through the process of reinforcement, what you put into your brain determines who and what you are.

First say to yourself what you would be; and then do what you have to do.

—Epictetus

#7 Balance

Keeping balance in your life is hard. It takes effort. It takes focus, and it takes persistence toward your goal. But all the major healing disciplines of the world regard balance as critical to a successful life. But balance is a slippery term. It is hard to know what balance is, except that we seem to know when we are out of balance. Things seem not quite right, sometimes awfully wrong.

I want to pass on some ideas about balance that I've found from various sources, with the hope that at some time, one or another of these may help you find your way out of an uncomfortable emotional or unhealthy physical situation.

Except for Western allopathic medicine, the major health maintenance systems of the world, such as ayurveda in India, herbal and acupuncture healing in China, osteopathic, chiropractic, naturopathic, and homeopathic medicine in the Western world, all devote substantial amounts of life process information to keeping healthy. By life process I mean what is commonly called folk wisdom.

And the principles of maintaining health found in all of these have to do with maintaining balance among and between the various physical and etheric aspects of our humanity.

Ayurveda, a healing tradition from India, regards everyone as being endowed with a basic constitution, termed a *dosha*, which describes the primary personality type that you possess. Physical or mental illness and disease are viewed by ayurveda as being the result of an imbalance in your basic *dosha*. Putting your *dosha* back in balance is the ongoing health maintenance goal of curative ayurvedic medicine. Keeping the *dosha* in balance requires attention to diet, daily living routines, meditation, yoga, and periodic cleansing rituals (panchkarma) to rid the body of toxins.

Chinese medicine regards balance of chi, the Chinese term for the body's energy, as the principal goal to be achieved in the maintenance or restoration of health. The Chinese system of health care has a three-thousand-year history of using herbal and acupuncture treatments to do this. Physical and emotional trauma and stress, as well as opportunistic bacteria and viral invaders, all can interfere with the free flow of energy within the structure of the body. Reestablishing the body's natural balance is the goal of Chinese medicine with good health naturally following.

Both ayurveda and Chinese medicine view the body with different eyes than Westerners. Their seers and sages, as well as their healing teachers, tell us that there are major and minor centers of energy as well as pathways along which energy flows throughout the body.

The seven major chakra centers of ayurvedic healing are described in Chinese medical literature as major chi centers. More numerous points of ayurvedic healing (marma points) are included in acupuncture energy points of Chinese medicine, points which are not chi centers, but which connect to major organs or where energy pathways cross or merge.

Ayurvedic traditions in India have a history of more than four thousand years. It is thought that ayurveda was taken to China sometime during the first thousand years of ayurveda development, perhaps the second millennium BCE and, with Chinese modifications and additions, forms the basis for both Chinese herbal and acupuncture healing as it is practiced today.

The Japanese variant of acupuncture, shiatsu, uses the traditional Chinese and ayurvedic points of major and minor energy centers for the unique shiatsu type of pressure application. The goal of shiatsu is the release of blocked energy, the stimulation of the internal organs, and the balancing of energy flow throughout the body.

Hatha yoga breathing technique of alternate nostril breathing (sometimes called *pranayama* breathing) has, as its goal, the balancing of the two hemispheres of the brain. We seldom are aware of the way our body does its own balancing, without our conscious control, by causing each nostril to alternate as the dominant source of *prana* (life force) intake for about thirty minutes at a time. You see, the body works to keep in balance. We need to be sure not to interfere with that process.

Balancing the two hemispheres of the brain is an important prelude to meditation in order to allow the natural activity of the mind to settle down, with the further goal of quieting all thought processes to the point of complete absence of mental thought processing, at the same time that the mind remains alert and aware that it is still.

Your emotional and physical bodies have difficulty staying in balance when your lives are as frenetic as they have become in the Western world. That seems also to be a condition the Eastern world lives as well, at least so it appears from the TV snapshots we see on the news about the lives of both the ordinary person and the aggressive business personalities in Hong Kong, Korea, Singapore, China, Taiwan, and India today.

Keeping in balance requires that you frequently take time to counteract the external world that forces itself upon you. Work-play, family-self, home-society, action-quietude are just some of the contrarieties you must deal with many times every day. Keeping these external and internal needs in balance is no mean feat. And when competing forces get you out of balance, the trick is to put them back in balance as nearly as possible on a continuing basis.

Establishing contact with the Universe regularly at least once, preferably twice, a day is the way to accomplish that. Meditation allows you to get into harmony with universal energy. In meditation, you move from the present moment focus of self and your surroundings to a transcendent focus of universality. In meditation, the body slips into a state of calmness, which causes heartbeat and respiration to slow dramatically; blood pressure, systolic as well as diastolic, to drop significantly; and mental activity, measured by EEG wave records, to shift to alpha as your body and the brain tend toward balance.

You live in a maelstrom of energy. Some of it you are aware of as the energies of family, home, society, and work pull at you. Other forces surround but are invisible to you, but they are there nonetheless. The energies that produce responses in your sophisticated radio and TV sets are some of the energies always around and passing through you. Scientists have cosmic ray counters that let us know that there are other energies, not created by us but in which we are immersed nonetheless, that pass around and through our bodies every second of every day.

Our sun, the center of our relatively tiny solar system of planets, satellite moons, and assorted cosmic debris, man-made and natural, puts out billions of units of energy every second—some visible, some not—that envelopes our earth and we humans who are on it.

Every human on this planet is an energy source. You are affected by the energies of those close to you, both physically and figuratively. And since energy is nonlocal and can be everywhere at once, you live in a surround of energy the effects of which are not yet known. You may be affected by energies of those you don't even know exist.

Those who love you can send loving energy or nourishing energy. People with whom you have disagreements can send disruptive energy that, for good health, needs to be neutralized. It is important to be aware of and use meditation and concentration to block negative energies that others may send.

Meditation is the practice that can put you in harmony with universal energy and keep you there, focusing and using that energy to protect and enhance your lives. Whether on a tightrope or in the normal course of living, balancing requires both attention to your circumstances and conscious effort if you are to maintain a balance. Without balance, the tightrope walker will fall. Without balance, your lives also may falter.

Along with the simple act of meditation, balance can be achieved with moderation in diet, avoidance of toxins like sugar and chemical sweeteners, avoidance of more than very moderate alcohol consumption, avoidance of foods that cause allergic reactions, avoidance of environments and relationships that are toxic, and constant attention to your emotional and physical health, taking steps to restore balance when it seems to have slipped away.

Balance in your life is a result of the lifestyle you choose to live.

You are the only person on earth who can use your ability.

—Zig Ziglar

#8 Education-Everything in Your Life

If you think education is not all that important, consider the following:

The two immigrant ethnic groups in the United States that place education of their children above all else and encourage their children to excel in academic challenges are Jews, who make up about 2 percent of the total US population, and Asians, who make up about 4.4 percent.

These two ethnic groups are represented in greater numbers than their total population would predict at the top of many fields of endeavor, including *medicine* (research as well as practice), *engineering* (also research and practice), *architecture*, *art* (both fine art and graphic), *finance* (banking and brokerage), *writing*, *entertainment* (acting and producing), and *music* (performing and composing).

These two groups are, proportionately, more affluent than the general population.

The personal trait that distinguishes those who achieve from those who merely get along, or even fall behind, is *discipline*. Recent experiments in education, including KIPP schools, have demonstrated without challenge that discipline is probably the single most important factor in a successful education. This does not diminish the important role played by an outstanding teacher or a teacher who inspires. But over the years of schooling, discipline of mind and body is the engine that propels the student into excellence.

For example, in KIPP schools and others like them that emphasize discipline in appearance and time scheduling, as well as learning, children coming into those schools with test scores lower than national averages leave on track for college.

One can learn from the experience and knowledge of others. One can also become his or her own teacher. Attending a prestigious school is not an important consideration in learning. Having a superior teacher is. Ultimately, though, it is the student who learns. It takes work, but we can each become our own best teacher. With the desire to learn and the discipline to use our time to that end, we can educate ourselves in the activities that we love. Good consequences are closely linked to the discipline of the student who wishes to learn.

While attending a prestigious school is not necessary to learning, there are advantages going that route not to be denied. Friendships formed at university are often lifelong and may have a great influence on your life after formal schooling.

Know that there are at least two stages of learning anything: first, accumulating information and establishing the interrelationships of that information so that one understands the subject matter and, second, being able to explain the subject to another so they will understand it.

To get to the second level of learning requires focus of the mind on the subject, determination to learn as many facts about it as one can, and exerting the necessary effort of both mind and body to gain an understanding of the subject. All this requires discipline. Discipline is the key to learning and the satisfaction of life that follows. It is not without significance that categories of human activity, such as art, and engineering, are called *disciplines*.

As you must by now understand, money is not everything. But it does open many more options for those who have it, and that can be important to the overall contentment with your lot. In this country today (2010), it is estimated that those with professional degrees have average lifetime earnings of \$4.4M; BA degree, \$2.1M; high school diploma, \$1.2M, examples of the monetary effect of education on your life.

It hurts to find out that what you wanted doesn't match what you dreamed it would be.

—Randy K. Milholland

#9 How Do You Get There?

When I worked in radio and, later, in TV, I was often asked how I got into the business. I often told my questioners, "You just have to want to do it badly enough that you keep looking for an entry point." And that's true. The rules are much the same in any business or trade. First, you have to really want to do what it is you think you want to do. One way to find out is to apprentice yourself to the object of your fantasies. Do not look for compensation. Your compensation will come in the form of knowledge about your chosen activity. What may look from a distance like the ideal way to spend your energy may, upon closer contact, be not such a good fit at all.

This applies to people too.

If your initial experience confirms the challenge is right for you, the path to entry will open. And it will likely come totally unexpected.

When Joyce and I married in early 1947, I was just back at the University of Virginia after a three-year stint in the navy in WWII. To get my degree and keep my life moving, I took a full load (fifteen hours) of courses. With a family started soon, I needed more money than the GI Bill provided.

I had done some announcing work in high school and had a teaching job in the navy that involved talking before groups. I thought I could do announcing at the local radio station and make the school and work schedules fit in a way I could manage.

Of course, the local station had no need for another announcer, and they sniffed at my thin experience in that field.

So I started going to the station and just hanging out. I worked to make friends with the staff. When something needed to be filed, I volunteered to help. When something needed to be obtained from some local store, I volunteered to go get it.

I became a real gofer, offering to help with whatever was going on. I confirmed I really liked the people and the whole atmosphere of that radio station. I really wanted to work there.

Within two weeks, the early Sunday morning announcer was sick and the program manager asked me if I thought I could handle that schedule until after his church service, when he would come in and take over. That was it. That was the path. I saw it and I took it. I must have sounded okay because a part-time job offer came before that Sunday was done.

I got the job by wanting it and by showing that I wanted it.

So I worked twenty to twenty-five hours a week at WCHV, went to school, studied, and, during the next three years, learned how to be a real husband and a real father to our first and then second baby. Life was busy. But I found time to fit other things in too. I took on (sequentially) the role of Nanki Poo in a local production of the *Mikado*, stretching my baritone voice to that delightful tenor role. In 1950, I worked for three weeks as a US census taker in a strip of land that stretched about ten miles south of the Charlottesville city limits. I don't remember being tired or stressed, although, in retrospect, I couldn't have had much time to sleep.

In fact, sleep, deep renewing sleep, while absolutely necessary to allow cell repair in your body, can be postponed during times of intense need to keep awake and keep alert.

I learned to make time to allow my body to rejuvenate from Rod Hofheinz, my employer at KTHT, a radio station in Houston. Roy was also the inspired owner of a baseball franchise, the Houston Astros, and his imagination and leadership led to the creation of the Astrodome, the first completely enclosed sports pavilion.

Roy had been a boy wonder in local politics, a profession that can sap one's strength. He had tapped into his enormous energies to simultaneously develop his political career (he was the youngest mayor of Houston), raise a family, and start a business.

As he taught me, he learned to drop down on a couch, close his eyes, and, within a minute or so, be completely relaxed—asleep but not deeply asleep—returning to consciousness twenty or thirty minutes later, refreshed and ready to continue whatever undertaking was then at hand.

In this manner, he was able to remain clear headed and alert in his dealings with often devious political opponents, business adversaries, and others wanting to gain an advantage. Roy's ability to engage in long negotiations without flagging was legendary. He kept up his energies by simply staying aware of his body and giving it downtime when he read the signs that said such was necessary.

To accomplish this nearly immediate retreat from the present and make the most of precious time set aside for energy renewal, Roy had developed a routine for relaxing the musculature of his body. By the time I knew him, his descent into complete relaxation was near instantaneous.

When first he lay down, he took three deep clearing breaths, mildly oxygenating his system so that he could then allow his breathing to become very shallow very quickly, without stress to oxygen-demanding cells. Then he focused on each muscle group, from his feet to the top of his head, quickly tightening and releasing the tension in each. His routine of these actions took less than a minute, and he would be quietly asleep. Having set his internal clock for the amount of time he wished to allot to this, he would awaken at the time he had mentally set, alert and ready to continue.

During my lifetime, the world has become a bit more of an intense place to live and work. Multitasking is a term of great currency. But it seems to me that the tasks and energy demands of today are merely different in nature, not different in total demand upon the individual, than they were when I was young and finding my way.

For example, today, a granddaughter and her husband are both working, building a family, and studying at a local university. This sounds like a replication of part of my own experience.

While working for a TV station, KPRC-TV in Houston, I became aware that the role of the executives in TV was very much like being older teenagers. Their thought processes did indeed sometimes involve business decisions, but in my experience, their days were spent in endless discussions of sports figures and teams, Hollywood-type gossip, local social tidbits, and the like. To me, it all was very vacuous and unsatisfying. I didn't want to spend my adult life being like those men.

I decided to go to law school. I was thirty years old.

When I went to visit the University of Houston Law School, established just a few years before, the dean told me that I was too old, too busy with my work in TV, and an unlikely candidate for any of the limited student positions that their classes could accommodate. They were aiming at building a school of full-time students, and of course, I could only go part-time, or so I thought then.

At that time, the whole of the law school was in the basement of the university library building; classes were numerically small because of the cramped space and were being taught by four full-time faculty and an equal number of practicing local lawyers.

Here again, "wanting to" proved effective.

I gathered several letters from a local pastor and others, who offered their opinion that I would probably make a decent lawyer. I created a daily timeline showing how I could fit school into a work schedule. And I started hanging out at the law school, monitoring classes and talking with the teachers.

The combination proved effective, and I was allowed to become a part-time student.

The Houston Bar Association had a review committee that evaluated all law student applicants for suitability. Generally, they said they were interested in screening out applicants who had a criminal background.

They asked what kind of law I wanted to practice, and I said I wanted to do trial work. That provoked a great laugh around the table from the six lawyers who then proceeded to tell me I was too old, there were only a limited number of lawyers who did trial work, and on and on.

Of course, my ambition was set, and that's what I became, notwithstanding their scoffing.

I spent two semesters taking nine hours of night classes each semester and then switched to daytime, adding classes and getting my degree in the usual three years. I did have help from my employer. KPRC-TV allowed me to work weekends and nights and accommodated my school schedule to free my daylight hours for classes.

Sure that I was pursuing the path I really wanted, I just did not accept that it wouldn't happen. When those who held the power of decision about my future became convinced of the certainty of my intentions, doors opened, and I walked through. These experiences do not make a categorical imperative for others, but I offer these examples to you as food for your own thoughts about how you get to do the thing you really want to do, when you have nothing to offer but the desire.

As Woody Allen has sagely remarked, "Ninety percent of success in life is simply showing up."

I offer you another truism on this from the mists of time:

We become what our deep driving ambition is.

Here's a bit of wisdom from our African American culture.

To get what you're not getting,

you need to do what you're not doing,

think what you're not thinking,

be what you're not being.

#10 Lessons from Gran Torino

Recently, Mary and I went to see the Clint Eastwood movie *Gran Torino*. I came away with much food for thought about two aspects of that production, both very well done insights into human behavior.

The first involved language and how some parts of society have adopted and adapted one word for extraordinarily expansive use. In the story, several different groups of teenage ruffians are shown, sometimes as gangs, sometimes as merely participants in carrying along the central story line. The impression one gets is that they have left school before their education was completed. Yet they communicated information and emotion directly and forcefully. Though their language is that of the streets, they used their limited vocabulary in very inventive ways.

The word that is the most used by these young toughs is also heard on television, in movies, appears in magazines such as the *New Yorker* and other major publications that feature writers considered best in their craft, in boardrooms, and on street corners. It is not heard in school classrooms but is in common use in our population. I am referring, as you all probably have guessed by now, to the vulgar word for copulation, "fuck."

What struck me was not so much the constant, repetitive use of this good old Anglo-Saxon word. What I ended up pondering was how a word that is basically a verb was also used as an adjective, adverb, and gerund. By inflection, these street toughs used one or another of various possible permutations of that word to expresses the gamut of emotions—from disgust to delight, from friendship to hostility, from a casual comment to intent to act, from amazement to outrage, from derision to admiration—to add invective to epithet and, of course, as a universal expletive.

Fifty years ago, the common word for excrement was the most used expletive but was much more limited in its scope. "Fuck" has had such a universal application in our language because it is so adaptable to so many situations and so useful to those with limited vocabulary to simply, clearly, and forcefully add emotion to any verbal content. It seems unlikely at this writing, that "fuck" could become a word accepted and commonly used by all segments of society. Yet the experience of the English language in the United Kingdom alerts us that many words and phrases, once thought vulgar and not to be used in polite speech, like "bloody" and "bugger"—clearly understood euphemisms for, in sequence, menstrual discharge and anal sex—are now common parlance in England.

The many possible uses of "fuck" as a part of one's vocabulary allow breadth of expression to those who do not know other words to use. "Fuck" may, at some time, be replaced by some other word or combination of words. For now, its dominance is impressive. Within the lifetime of most of us, this word has come to form a large percentage of the vocabulary of the American common man. There could hardly be a more compelling example of how words in our language evolve and are evolving by common use than was presented by the characters in this movie.

The second thought-provoking part of the story is the way the central character, a retired autoworker named Walter Kowalski, responds to people of the Muong, indigenous allies of the United States in Viet Nam, who were brought to this country after that war. In the film, Muong immigrants have taken over Walter's staid middle-class neighborhood, much to his dismay. At first, he expresses his outrage at the feelings of injustice he has at this invasion of foreigners into the sphere of his life by physically defending his property lines and demanding everyone keep off.

Seeing an altercation on the front lawn next door, which bleeds over onto his property, he intervenes, using an old military weapon as a threat. The young son of Muong neighbors, who has been getting the worst of the fight, is rescued and the toughs dispersed by Kowalski. The gratitude of the neighboring Muong family and that of their Muong friends is immediate and effusive. Much to Kowalski's chagrin, flowers and food are brought in superabundance to his front steps. Thus begins a thawing of the animosity of Kowalski toward the Muong and, in particular, toward the rescued boy and his family.

The story builds on the progress of understanding, friendship, respect, and, ultimately, love between the crusty American who, at first, would not even acknowledge the humanity of his new foreign neighbors. The story ends with Kowalski making a final dramatic act, acknowledging his acceptance, defense of, and deep love for his new Muong friends.

I'm sure that Eastwood did not intend a morality tale in *Gran Torino*. Nonetheless, there is a moral forcefully advanced by the story line. The lesson here is the same that the Buddha, Jesus of Nazareth, Gandhi of India, Rev. Martin Luther King, and others have been offering to the world for eons. Treating one's neighbor as oneself is really the best way to live one's life.

The lesson is one that finds its essence in the homely proverb, "You catch more flies with honey than vinegar." A corollary is that violence is nonproductive. Peace can be achieved by nonviolent means. The way to understanding, acceptance, and peaceful coexistence is in nonviolence. When love of others is introduced, things change.

In the Middle East, in 1948, the Jewish terrorist organization, Irgun, shelled Jaffa, an Arab city. After three days, nearly all Arabs (72,000 of 75,000) fled, joining a total of nearly 750,000 Arab-Palestinian refugees displaced by the military actions of Jews.

Farms, businesses, houses, property both personal and real were violently seized from Arabs, who then formed the majority of inhabitants of Palestine. Throughout what is now Israel, Arabs fled or were forcibly sent out of the claimed Israeli borders. Not every Arab property was taken. There is now, still, an Arab minority population in Israel. Their lives are peaceful, but Israelis have greatly limited the rights of those in this Arab minority.

An American commission, under President Truman, recommended a two-state solution that would have established both an Israeli and an Arab country, coexisting in the territory that was Palestine. That concept was rejected by the British and the UN.

Instead, the UN General Assembly approved the concept of an Israeli state within the region of Palestine. Great hordes of Arab refugees were sent fleeing to fetid refugee camps in Jordan, Lebanon, and the West Bank, and then a part of Syria. In these camps, Palestinians were overcrowded, underfed, and miserable for losing their identity as well as their property.

The resentment and rage against Israel, now nearly universal in the Arab world, derives from this physical and emotional humiliation of Palestinian Arabs, displaced from home and homeland with no compensation or relief except inadequate charity from a disinterested world that felt sorry for the Jews.

Arabs now exhibit a generalized desire for revenge against Jews, the Jewish state, and against those who were seen to have helped create the State of Israel.

Since the UN's acknowledgement of Israel as a sovereign state in 1948, the United States has given Israel huge sums of money with which, in large measure, they have bought munitions and built factories to make war materials and equipment. Israelis were afraid and had good reason to be afraid their neighbors would be angry. The Israeli response to fear was to arm.

But suppose they had reacted like the Muong in *Gran Torino*, who came into and took over a neighborhood, buying homes and displacing the white middle class that had long been residents there. Suppose the Israelis, instead of making war on the Arabs in the first instance, in order to create their state, forcefully appropriating Palestinian land and assets, had peacefully bought their way into control of that land and then, with majority control, had created their Israeli state.

Suppose, after creating their own state, Jews had used the prodigious amounts of money given them by the United States to build, for themselves and also for displaced Palestinians, hospitals, electric plants, farms, and schools—especially schools—to teach the then largely illiterate Arab population how to govern themselves fairly and equitably, how to be productive, and how to develop their own economy in the West Bank and Gaza. Because the Israelis did not help those they dispossessed, the West Bank and Gaza, as well as areas of Lebanon and Jordan, became sites of overcrowded refugee camps with low literacy, high rates of disease, and high rates of mortality.

Had the Jews bought their way into Palestine and then overwhelmed the Palestinian Arabs with practical economy and society-building gifts, the Middle East would likely be a far different place today.

Gran Torino does not pretend to be a story with a moral. Yet, to me, it has a powerful message from which we can learn: giving to one's neighbor defuses anger and encourages friendship. The lesson of present-day Israel's problems with her neighbors is that violence breeds long-term anger and more conflict. Those who would most benefit from being peaceful neighbors in Palestine have unnecessarily become enemies engaged in constant and destructive acts of violence against each other.

Did it really have to be this way? I think not. For me, the second lesson of *Gran Torino* is that gifts of friendship and love, as well as gifts of practical usefulness, stimulate responses in kind. I suspect that is a nearly universal response of humanity.

What if, for little more than the effort of giving, we could experience the benefits of that response in all our lives? It would be a great experiment in living together if the world would focus on giving instead of fighting.

Here's something to ponder:

Even when chance plays a role,

our lives do not happen by chance alone.

—GPD

#11 More about Language

I wrote to you a little about language in "Lessons from Gran Torino." There I was drawn to examine how one particular vulgar word has come to be both ubiquitous and universal, performing as a modifier, expletive, and substitute for nearly every emotion that those with limited vocabulary feel the need to express. The operative term here is limited vocabulary. Limited vocabulary not only limits the ability to express oneself, but it also limits the ability to think and be mentally creative.

You must understand that words are like building blocks. With words, you build thoughts in your mind and, using words, express those thoughts in your communications. In your mind, you use words to think with. In speech you use words to communicate with others. In each case, a limited vocabulary can be and usually is a serious impediment to expression.

Nouns are like the stones of a wall. A good supply of those is needed to build anything of any substance. So learning nouns, learning about things, learning the names we give things, memorizing these names for recall when you need them as a part of thinking is like gathering stones together before building a wall.

Since you need words to convey thoughts, the more words you know, the more thoughts and the more intricate the thoughts are that you can have and express. Having an expanded vocabulary offers fabulous opportunities to both think creatively and to express those thoughts to others.

Of course you know by now that society has some rules about using words. There are some words that describe intimate sexual contact, human excretory functions or the product of excretion, and some bodily functions that society has agreed are not generally acceptable to be used in mixed company or with children or in other ways that one needs to determine by careful attention what is happening around one at various levels of society. These rules are better taught to children early in their lives so that they will not be embarrassed by blurting out a word that might be okay in one group but not in another.

Actually, it is far better to teach children that nothing they do should embarrass them, rather than what I just said, but that's for another time.

My own childhood was in a much different time than the one in which you have grown up. During my childhood and up to the time I went into the US Navy at age eighteen, the home I lived in was right next door to Grandma's. She was to me the essence of every idealized description of a grandma. I loved everything about her except one thing.

She washed my mouth out with soap and water every time she heard me say a word that she considered dirty. As a child, words are often just sounds and have no substantive meaning for the immature mind. I have no recollection of what words prompted her to use such a drastic cleansing technique, a pretty good indication that punishment of that sort was not very effective.

No matter. When I said a word she thought was dirty, the way she remedied this breach of good manners was to remove the dirt from my mouth with good old Ivory soap and a clean, wet washcloth. With one finger wrapped in that soapy cloth, she would make sure no part of any dirty word lingered in my mouth.

It didn't just happen once, a tribute, perhaps, to my urge to experiment with words even at a quite young age. And since I remember more than one occasion of tasting Ivory soap, it apparently had little deterrent effect in my experimenting with language I used in her presence.

It also had no deterrent effect on the language I used during my teen years. Going to Brooklyn Technical High School put me in contact with boys attending that school from all over New York City. Italian, Puerto Rican, and black male student friends from every class and section of New York City provided a pretty good assortment of dirty words in several languages. By the time I graduated, I had simply learned to be careful and not use common and accepted male teen language where it could be heard and misinterpreted by teachers, parents, or Grandma.

Reflecting on that time, I am convinced that experimenting with language is not dissimilar to other experimenting that we all do as we shoot through our teen years. As life becomes more and more structured, compressed, and demanding, it becomes important to find outlets for the frustration, anger, impatience, and all the other rapidly passing emotions that bubble up each day of our teen lives. So I accepted words into my everyday vocabulary that adults (at that time) considered dirty. To me they were not words that expressed thoughts so much as exclamations that allowed me to innovate in expressing emotions.

At one time, I really did think I was using too many words that my grandma would disapprove of, and I consciously developed an expression, "Aw poots," as a substitute for swearing. "Aw poots" was intended to be innocuous but could be said with enough strength to convey the way I felt at the time without (I thought) offending anyone.

What I didn't know is that, in Italian, "poots" is an onomatopoetic slang expression describing the act of defecating. I said it at my best friend's home one day (his family was Italian) and was roundly denounced by his mother, who happened to be near. She was only half convinced that I had made up the word that, to me, was completely inoffensive.

The language of seamen is pretty salty. Officers maintain decorum in front of those they command but, among themselves, are just as likely to use colorful language as their men. The US Navy lexicon of dirty words is rich in content from many languages. When an old navy chief decided to vent, in my experience, the surrounding air could take on the complete spectrum of hues of powerful expression. My youthful three years in the US Navy greatly expanded my knowledge of the world supply of dirty words. But knowing them had the effect of changing my behavior. When I moved from the navy back to the University of Virginia and thereafter, I consciously used as specific a word as I could recall to express whatever I intended at the time. What I discovered is that even small dictionaries have lots of substitutes for the kinds of words that propelled my grandma into soapy action.

Since about 1970 or so, I have been surprised at the expansion of the vocabulary heard in TV and radio media. When I was in radio and television, I was constantly on guard to not inadvertently blurt out a word the FCC considered unsayable on the air. If there are limits now on what is an acceptable word or expression (in English) and what is not, I have not seen those limits published. Advertising for many pharmaceutical drugs intended to affect and modify basic human functions, such as elimination or sexual activity, have also helped push the limits of what is considered nonsanctionable language on TV and radio.

Such words and expressions in print, both descriptive and expletive had, in my experience, been mostly found in fiction and avant-garde publications. When I first saw the word "fuck" in the *New Yorker* magazine, I stopped and read more carefully to be sure I had seen correctly. As time has gone on, the number and use of words that previous generations of society had avoided in mixed company and in the media has only expanded.

I am reminded of an essay in a short-lived publication in the 1960s, edited by the American poet Ezra Pound. The premise of the essay was that the same words not only are used differently and mean different things to different groups in our multifaceted society, but the same words within a given group of people, depending on inflection, can also convey a variety of different meanings and intentions.

The example used was "motherfucker." In various permutations and with selected modifiers, "motherfucker" can be a term of extreme derision, as in "He's a *mean* motherfucker!" or a high compliment, as in "He is *some* motherfucker!"

I don't generally watch television. The other day I was waiting for results from an election to be presented and watched the beginning of a prime-time show in which one of the ancillary characters said repeatedly to his office friends, both male and female, that he had "lost his cherry." It did not advance the story. It did portray the speaker, a male of twenty-something years, as sexually inexperienced. But my take on it was that this repeated statement was written in for shock effect. My own response was, "So what?" It was simply bad writing, bad storytelling, and not worth my attention, so I turned the TV off.

In examining the phrase "lost my (his/her) cherry," it is interesting to note this phrase has an ancient pedigree of usage as a shorthand rendition of a visual event. When used centuries ago, it simply told interested friends and neighbors that the marriage bed of a new bride showed proof of her virginity. The phrase described an important social and economic circumstance. Failing to be sure of her own intact hymen, the bride (or the bride's mother) used the juice of a ripe cherry to provide visual proof of expected virginity. The payment of dowry generally depended on such proof, which is no small matter to the family of the bride. It also was a sly admission that, by convention, the red stain on the marriage sheet might not have been real blood. It seemed an inappropriate bad joke when declared in a modern TV show by a mature male about himself.

Although the examples I have suggested may raise the inference that there are no limits anymore to the language one can comfortably be used in mixed company, in fact, limits on language usage do prevail.

Even though words that my grandma considered dirty are really just words that are commonly and, in some circumstances, usefully uttered, unspoken guidelines tell us that the conditions of use of those words are limited. What one says in the company of oneself to vent an emotion may not be said to a mixed gender group without being thought a boor. It is unquestioned that using dirty words to help convey thoughts or ideas is an admission of a lack of vocabulary to express oneself. Of all the indicators of intelligence, the ability to state an idea or instruction using words that clearly and succinctly convey the information intended is the most persuasive. To do this, a broad knowledge of words and what they mean is essential.

Most of the words that are descriptive of elimination or sexual activities or sexually specific portions of our bodies, in our English language, have Latin, Greek, or Anglo-Saxon derivations. Latin or Greek derivative words are found in the medical dictionaries and are in everyday use in the language of medicine and health care. Those words can be fairly termed technical. They have very little force beyond their ability to narrowly identify or describe body parts and functions.

Anglo-Saxon words with sexual or excretory context, on the other hand, the four-letter words that are said with an expectation of a snicker or a titter, are the dirty words of our day. When they are used, they are usually freighted with emotional content. They are strong words, whereas words that technically describe body parts and functions are simply words.

Being able to convey thoughts with words that are clear, concise, and informatory is still the mark of a mind that attracts respect from one's peers. While on a purely academic level, all words are equal and none is less useful than another, in the real world of spoken language, there are social credits to be gained by those who take the time and effort to expand their personal lexicon of words, words they know and can use without having to look them up in a dictionary, words that my grandma would approve of.

Indulge your imagination in every possible flight.

—Jane Austen, *Pride and Prejudice*

#12 Self-Interest and Greed

Milton Friedman and the Chicago School of Economics are considered to be the progenitors of the phrase "market force." Actually, they simply took what every gambling casino operator knows (and what allows the house to always win) and converted it into a concept that had the imprimatur of academia.

It is that, in the human species, greed trumps nearly everything.

In the case of Friedman and his followers, they cleverly renamed this most basic and controlling of human characteristics. By not calling by it what it really is—greed—they were given a pass by economists and allowed to call it by a less objectionable term. Friedman gave the concept a spin to make it more acceptable and called it market force.

Basically, what is at work is the primal force of self-interest. According to this breed of economics, if everyone is given the greatest latitude to exercise his or her own decision-making process in a market free of constraint or control, self-interest will sort all costs in the fairest way possible.

Many of our present-day economic gurus, apparently the long-serving head of the US Federal Reserve, Alan Greenspan, among them, were favorably inclined to the then quite radically conservative ideologies about "market force" and "free market capitalism" of Ayn Rand as expressed in her novels *The Fountainhead* (1943) and *Atlas Shrugged* (1957). Her ideas of a world without restrictions on the energetic entrepreneur's ability to amass monetary fortune form the core of the present political conservative movement of individualism. Society, to Ayn Rand and to present-day conservatives, exists simply to provide a venue in which wealth can be pursued and consolidated, without concern for fairness, equity, laws, or regulations.

Her books glorified the law of the jungle as it might inform social structures, where every person looked out for themselves and there was no "social conscience" to ameliorate the devastating consequences to ordinary people of not being as clever, conniving, or ruthless as more powerful others, who would effectively rule the world.

Ultimately, when all the academic language obscuring the true basis of *market force* is stripped away, it parallels the ideas of Ayn Rand, who hypocritically, ended her days aggressively fighting for social security and other government benefits for herself that she had vilified in her writings.

"Market," in this concept, does not simply include tangible things like food, housing, and consumer goods of all kinds; "market" includes intangible things (ideas) as well. Each individual decision to accept or reject a product will theoretically contribute to a decision mass, the effect of which, in turn, will determine what products and what ideas—in short, everything we as humans need and use in our society—will survive the test of usefulness and desirability.

Market forces theoretically do not speak to determinations of what is good or bad. Even so, the inferred outcome of market forces at work is that the end result for all will be good if market forces are allowed to work, and the end result for all will be bad if they are inhibited (by law, regulation, or custom)—i.e., what the market supports is good and what the market does not support is not good.

This is not exactly new. Socrates, Plato, the Hedonists, and others in the golden age of Greece, twenty-five hundred years ago, recognized that, if allowed, greed would dominate human behavior. These thinkers described the decision-making process by the simple and honest term "self-interest." They did not suggest that self-interest be put aside. However, they added the modifier "enlightened" to the concept, which makes an enormous difference, changing emotionally dominated greed to cool, rationally based true self-interest.

Resolving the ever-recurring questions life presents each of us on a daily basis, using the screen of enlightened self-interest, brought into the thought process several important considerations that are not obviously at work when only market force is the measure of choice.

"Enlightened" meant enlarging the scope of what was being rationally thought about, to take into consideration known or expected ancillary and subsidiary factors along with the probability that these factors would impact our choices, and extending the decisional horizon from that of immediate gratification to that of long-term benefit.

The control of greed over events has been more obvious at some points in the history of this country than others. In our post-civil war period, for example, rampant greed racked the country. Industrial and merchandising monopolies flourished. The intentional flouting of safety and health of workers in manufacturing and marketplace in nearly every endeavor, for the purpose of increasing profit, was accepted as reasonable in the quest for wealth.

From the humblest immigrant to the most powerful families, everyone reached out to grab for themselves the material wealth of this land in as many forms as can be imagined: minerals, timber, seafood, new technologies, cattle, land itself; all were seized and utilized to create vast individual and family wealth.

The end result of the over six-decade scramble for personal material wealth, roughly from about 1875 through the stock market collapse in 1929 (and collapse of other markets as well) was a serious disruption of the entire concept of marketplace that seems likely to have contributed significantly to the country's Great Depression starting in the 1930s.

Economists tell us that public malaise and unwillingness to spend and take a chance that the future would be better extended the years of the Great Depression. Those same public responses to the aftermath of the 2008 financial bubble burst are prolonging this present recession.

President Roosevelt apparently understood this underlying problem that had to be overcome to move to growth and prosperity. His famous speech that included the phrase "We have nothing to fear but fear itself," is an indication of the concern of those ruling the country, that the buoyant optimism of the previous decades had been lost. The *New Deal*, President Roosevelt's designation of multiple programs intended to help the country out of the Depression, interfered with, but only briefly, the plans and actions of the then wealthy to accumulate and hold more and more wealth.

From about 1936 to 1980, the social concepts put in place by the Roosevelt administration were dominant. Some few among those with money and power understood that their self-interest required them to consider the condition of the working classes in this country, if only to preserve their own wealth. Most of the very wealthy considered President Roosevelt a traitor to his class. But he was applying the most practical of judgments.

What will work for the most benefit to the most people? If public policies work for the multitude, the wealthy will also benefit. It was political pragmatism as much as an understanding that the wealthy, by their concern with immediate goals, had lost sight of their enlightened self-interest.

Roosevelt intended to make this a country where all people had sufficient means to provide for themselves and their families comfortable housing, abundant food, and suitable clothing. This would necessarily create a country where the shrewd, the talented, the canny, and the lucky could reach the top of the economic ladder.

He laid the basis (1941) for a meritocracy by substantially increasing the federal estate tax on inherited wealth (to 77 percent). Oncoming generations would have to work for their wealth and not be coddled by inherited family wealth, at least not beyond a certain level.

And the country prospered with those laws in effect.

For the country, these decisions of Roosevelt and the democratically controlled Congress he dominated were decisions of enlightened democratic self-interest that benefited all our citizens, the wealthy, the middle class, and the poor. Social security also greatly helped the elderly, who, at that time, were overwhelmingly poor, many actually destitute.

When the financial markets of this country collapsed, we collectively recognized the dangerous destabilizing effects of allowing greed to govern without some limitations and controls. In-depth congressional investigations into public and private fraud, which played a large part in allowing the financial bubble to swell and burst, was the basis for public clamor for regulations that stayed in place for several decades. Even the ultimate Republican, President Nixon, for the most part, did not attempt to undo the social and financial regulatory structures put in place during the Roosevelt presidency.

But with President Reagan, in 1980, the assault by the moneyed class on restrictions that prevented them from following their Ayn Rand philosophy came into public view. President Reagan famously said, "Government is not the solution. Government is the problem!" With that as a war cry, the very wealthy in this country rallied to the conservative Republican banner. For thirty years now, they have mounted an assault on government and taxes. With clever use of their great wealth, they hired journalists and academics to change the political climate in this country to their benefit. And it has worked. The wealthy have succeeded in convincing great numbers of worker-wage earners, the so-called lower middle class, that the philosophy of individual greed is better than the political philosophy of a community of shared responsibility.

The mantra that the wealthy have been able to propose and have stuck in the minds of those voters they wished to attract was this: "You know better how to spend your money than the government does. So cut taxes and you will have more money to spend as you decide!"

It is hard to imagine a more blatant appeal to greed. But it worked.

Looking back to the first two decades of the twentieth century, the intent of the wealthy in this country was quite obviously to create personal and family wealth of such magnitude that it would perpetuate itself. The net effect was the creation of a class of plutocratic families, who would come to dominate the political as well as the economic forces of the United States.

Among the most prominent of those families were the Rockefellers and the Mellons. These two families are significant for the diverse way they have used their wealth to influence and affect the country.

The Rockefellers opted to invest their personal and family energies and money in useful endeavors, both public and private. They created large commercial developments in New York City that benefited them but also incidentally brought great wealth to the city and its people. The Rockefeller Fund investments and programs have enhanced the lives of great numbers of less advantaged people, especially in the New York City area.

The Mellon family, heavily imvolved in banking and the manipulation of money, continued to create wealth for themselves, but some members of that family used their wealth to exert influence on the national psyche and to promote legislation to bring back the days when greed ruled.

Mellon-Scaife money has been used to finance academics that wrote essays and articles advocating the ultra right-wing M-S point of view in publications that Mellon-Scaife sponsored and supported financially, as well as in journals that favored the M-S philosophy. These academics also went on the speaking circuit, expounding the M-S liturgy in favor of "free markets" and against even modest government regulation. They adamantly opposed taxing wealth or the high incomes that wealthy people inevitably had. M-S money was also used to fund journalists to research, write about, and disseminate the M-S doctrine, churning out periodicals and books supporting the M-S conservative viewpoint and generally, openly intending to convince America that greed is the standard to which this society should adhere.

Mellon-Scaife money is the most venerable of these family funded efforts to influence public opinion and thereby influence/control election results. In the news more recently (2011) are the Koch brothers, of Koch Industries of Oklahoma, whose asset wealth derived from the exploitation of petroleum and other energy products is such their annual income, each, is in the billions of dollars.

Think tanks, such as the Heritage Foundation, the Cato Institute, and others are mainly funded by money from these plutocrats who fervently support the creation of laws that favor the wealthy and allow the wealthy the greatest ability to protect, preserve, and extend their wealth.

The federal estate tax, first established in 1916, is a thorn in the side of those with first-generation great wealth. Most of the old wealth of this country has been put into trusts and other economic vehicles that essentially allow those who live on inherited wealth to not be subject to federal estate taxes, except as their own efforts have created new wealth. For the newly wealthy, and many of those have accumulated wealth in the billions of dollars within very few years, the federal estate tax is an impediment to their desire to add their family names to the list of the immensely wealthy of this country.

Money from conservative donor sources has been used to vigorously oppose spending tax moneys on government programs characterized as socialistic. Included in programs they oppose are many designed to provide support for the disadvantaged, especially the elderly disadvantaged. Social Security has long been a target of the wealthy. All sorts of stratagems have been tried to undo this bedrock social program that allows the elderly to live out their lives without the threat of descending into grinding poverty. So far, the attacks of the wealthy have not succeeded, but they have not given up.

It has recently been disclosed that money from the billionaires of this country have funded many innocuously named charitable organizations, so-called because they are not set up as profit-making organizations. These exist solely to fund and support anything and everything—authors, speakers, political movements (like the Tea Party), and anything else—that will help mold public opinion in this country and direct its laws to their purposes.

When Ronald Reagan was elected president in 1980 and popularized the idea that government was the enemy of the people, the argument was made that government taxes funded programs for people who were not contributing their fair share of work and money to support the country. The spoken complaint was that this was unfair to the majority who worked hard for their living. For conservatives, the strongest and most bitter complaint was that taxes interfered with their pursuit and accumulation of wealth.

The idea that any tax on income or wealth building inhibits economic growth for this country has been dominant as an icon of Republican dogma and political speech for thirty years. It doesn't matter that this position has no support in empirical evidence. Financed in large measure by M-S and other inherited money, as well as by others who have accumulated great wealth recently, such as the Koch brothers and parroted by conservatives in both political parties, the assault against taxation on the grounds that it weakens the economy is strongly embedded in our urban political myth history.

The election of President Reagan marked an observable turning point when greed and self-interest, unalloyed by concern for others, again became the driving force of the country. The concept of enlightened self-interest was pushed aside in the rush to become really rich.

And that's where we find ourselves today (2011).

It is interesting to examine the sixty years from 1950 to 2010. In terms of social change, they divide equally into two thirty-year segments, each of which exhibits clearly a different philosophy of governance and each of which offers historical evidence of results such governance causes.

In the first thirty years, taxes were relatively high, but incomes rose rapidly and at about the same rate across all income levels. In this country, roads and bridges were built and well maintained; impressive new infrastructure was built. People were optimistic. Government was seen as the friend of industry and business and took the lead in many new arenas of commerce. A multitude of new products came from government activities, particularly military R & D.

Taxes on income were high—55 percent on very high incomes. It was not advantageous to have a high yearly income. CEOs of major US companies earned, on average, forty-two times the average wage of their employees. Other perks there were, but actual earnings were not high. Yet corporate leaders and their staffs felt well paid and enjoyed a high level of creature comfort as well as general public respect.

Federal estate taxes were also relatively high. In 1935, the top rate was set at 70 percent. The size of estates to which that rate was applied was also high, particularly when the value of the dollar is considered. In 1935, the top rate applied to estates of $50 million and up.

In 1981 federal income tax rate on the highest incomes was 70 percent. President Reagan began a concerted (and successful) effort to lower taxes on the wealthy, which Republicans (and some conservative Democrats) have continued to this day. Income taxes on the highest incomes are now 35 percent.

President Reagan also reduced estate taxes. In 1984, the top rate was set at 55 percent and applied to estates of $5 million or more. Special provisions of tax laws further allow the richest to effectively avoid any estate tax. Now, in 2010, the top rate is 25 percent.

By 1998, the richest 1 percent of families in the United States owned 38 percent of all household assets, the richest 10 percent of families owned 70 percent of all such assets, and the least rich 40 percent of us owned 0.2 percent. In 2009, 16 percent of all the dollars earned in our country were reported by less than 1 percent of those who filed tax returns.

In the second thirty years, starting in 1980, Republican politics began to demonize government: taxes were too high and the government was too intrusive and regulative of business. President Reagan famously declared that government cannot solve the problems of the country—government is the problem.

Taxes were reduced, mainly on the rich, with the explanation that they would spend lavishly, invest magnificently, and there would be a "trickle down" effect of their massive spending of the money they saved from not having to pay taxes that all would benefit from. It didn't happen.

In fact, serious changes in income and wealth distribution in our country have occurred that continue and seem now, in 2010, to be getting worse. For example, economics professor Robert H. Frank of Cornell University wrote about this in the business section of the *NY Times* on Sunday, October 17, 2010. According to statistics developed from his research, over the past thirty years there has been a rising inequality of income between the very rich and the rest of the country that seems to have had measurable deleterious effects.

Based on the census data for the one hundred most populous counties in the United States, those counties where the income inequalities were the greatest, there was also the largest increase in bankruptcy filings, the largest increases in divorce rates, and the greatest unwillingness on the part of the public to support basic maintenance of public infrastructure such as roads, bridges, railroads, dams, and ports.

The inequality of income is partly due to changed tax laws but is also due to a change in public acceptance of the idea that some people are entitled to make very large sums of money as income. The long-term goals of those with great wealth—to change public ideas about wealth—have apparently been achieved. Certainly the changes in public policy that have come about during these last thirty years have had a major influence on the economic health of this country.

Not only have CEOs in this country received incomes several hundred times the pay of the average worker they manage, but bankers, brokers, and traders of stocks and companies, in 2006, were also paid multimillions during the year with additional year-end hundred-million-dollar bonuses, which is more than most workers can expect to earn in a lifetime of work. For these munificent incomes, the financial industry does not manufacture, produce, or create one tangible useful thing. All of the money earned has been from cleverly trading intangible assets. Much of it is taxed at the lowest favorable rate of 15 percent; even billion-dollar incomes get this advantage.

High taxes on high earnings is simply the fair way to force those high earners to pay for the advantage they have in living in an environment, a society, that we have all created that has provided them the ability to earn well. While they have used their skills and ingenuity to earn well, they used what we all have created in the doing. Taxes are their payment for this privilege.

From 1994 through the 2006 national election, the recent Republican-dominated Congress has gone along with the idea that we should borrow what the country needs to operate in order to reduce taxes on those who have or are in the process of accumulating great wealth. Great wealth compounds over generations. The wealth, usually managed by professionals, simply keeps on growing. One cannot spend it all or lose it all. It just grows and grows and grows.

That result is not good for the country. Only a meritocracy will provide the bright people we need for this country to maintain its position of leadership in the world community. Inherited wealth in relatively modest amounts will not interfere with the concept of meritocracy, with each generation earning its place and its wealth. The experience of the world is that large inherited estates greatly interfere with this important goal.

In Congress, we already see the effects of great inherited wealth. Many congressmen, children of great wealth, attended Yale or Princeton together, schools known for high cost of attendance, difficulty of entry, and the practice of making room for the children of graduates.

It is not only that the rich get to go to the best schools. There they form lasting friendships and associations with other rich kids. Those friendships, in turn, influence political appointments available during their lives as well as investment and earning opportunities that the rest of us just never even hear about.

As is becoming more and more evident, money given to elected officials (euphemistically called campaign contributions) gives those who donate the money an enormous unfair advantage in presenting their wishes for legislation to the wealthy. "The best Congress money can buy" is an ironic, unfortunately accurate, comment on the present political situation in this country.

The wealthy are doing their best to eliminate the federal estate tax. This tax not only provides funds for the government (and it is not a small amount), but it also helps prevent our country being ruled by people from families whose only claim to the power and prestige that great wealth confers is the accident of their birth.

The concept of the marketplace aggregating the decisions of all who come there—naturally sorting the useful from the not useful by virtue of the numbers of people who decide one way or another, thereby naturally and effortlessly creating "good" decisions—needs to be modified. It does speak a universal truth as far as it goes. But we need to reach back to the Greeks and remind everyone that enlightened self-interest is a standard that, for over more than two millennia, is unimpeached. Greed, after all, is designated as one of the seven deadly sins for a very good reason.

Milton Friedman might even agree, for the application of the mind to the problem is the mark of the intellectual, which he certainly was.

Good judgment comes from experience,

and a lot of that comes from bad judgment.

—Anon

#13 What Is It about Capitalism (that has gone so badly wrong)?

Young people tend to avoid politics, and I assume you all are not exceptions in that regard. So I offer this limited excursion into our country's taxing system, knowing it may turn you off. But keep this. It will be the same good argument in ten or thirty years, as I believe it is today.

In school, at home, in the newspapers, on TV, you have been told that the United States is the best country in the world. We have freedom to speak our minds, to associate with whomever we choose, to move about our country freely, and many more, guaranteed by our Constitution that people in many other countries do not have. It is a great country. It is based on a great concept of limiting government control of what we do. It is a model for many other governments worldwide.

But it is not perfect, and it would be foolish to not acknowledge there are aspects that could be changed to make our society a better environment in which to live.

It is important also to acknowledge a practical fact: we call our country a democracy. In fact, although we have aspects of democratic governance, the structure of government is not the rule of the demos, the whole of those who can vote, called upon to vote on everything; we rely on elected representatives to both make our laws and run our government. More importantly, our political system has developed over time so that it is now effectively based on capitalism. What that means, in practical terms, is that it is vital to our country that businesses and people with money who create and own businesses are of first importance to our way of life.

They are so important, our tax laws are organized to help them make and keep money. Our tax laws are continually changing, by increments usually, but occasionally in wide culture-changing sweeps. Tax reductions enacted during the 1980 Reagan administration, promoted by all except the most liberal legislators, greatly accelerated long-time trends in wealth accumulation and consolidation.

As long as taxes on income were high, it was not advantageous to have a high income. In 1980, CEOs of major US companies earned, on average, forty-two times the average wage of their employees. In 2000, under the Reagan tax laws, that had jumped to 532 times what an average employee earned.

Reduced estate taxes and special provisions of tax law allowed the richest to effectively avoid most estate taxes and permitted consolidated wealth to be passed on to future generations of the same families.

We have always had many poor and always had a few very rich. But the disparities in income and accumulated wealth are growing. The experience of other countries, expressed in health and longevity statistics as well as general contentment of the population, has been that the less income and wealth disparity, the healthier, the longer-lived, and the happier the people.

President Eisenhower knew what he was doing when, in 1952, he pushed through Congress and signed into law a tax bill that imposed a high tax on high incomes. High taxes on high income would be a deterrent to the obscene incomes that CEOs are demanding and getting from their compliant boards of directors.

High taxes on high incomes made from buying and selling money, the use of money, or the securities that represent money would take much of the fun out of controlling CEO decisions to make large employee layoffs just to please Wall Street and improve stock prices.

High taxes on high incomes would stop the rapid slide of this country toward oligarchy.

High taxes on high incomes would do much to prevent the current massive alteration in our class structure. It is presently moving rapidly toward a wealthy/poor class system and destroying the middle class of this country.

High taxes on high incomes would help pay down our national debt and help reestablish fiscal responsibility to our government.

High taxes on grossly large incomes paid to business managers would encourage redistribution of companies' earnings to an expanding percentage of workers and offer the potential for restoring to our country the existence of a large and largely economically secure middle class that could earn enough each year to be both consumers and savers.

Extraordinary income flows, based on unique talent or skill or innovative processes or inventions are not the causes of our problems. These could well be excluded from the imposition of what could fairly be termed confiscatory taxes on high incomes.

It is necessary to focus attention on why high taxes on some earnings are essential to our fiscal health. Our financial system has become trapped in a pattern that is not only unhealthy, but is also dramatically changing the way most of us live.

A large segment of the middle class of our country has been persuaded that taxes interfere with job creation and that accumulation of wealth over generations is both fair and good for the country. Neither is true. The evidence is clear and unmistakable. Tax cuts enacted during the thirty years starting with 1980 did not produce a thriving economy nor create jobs. Tax cuts have been the mantra of many conservative politicians, who tell untruths about tax cuts, asserting (against the evidence) that tax cuts are what create a vital growth economy and create jobs for those who need them.

Another untruth is that the estate tax is unfair and deprives families of wealth they have earned. The estate tax is important because it limits the accumulation of enormous wealth, something that happens over time to estates of great wealth, just because no one can spend money as fast as it accumulates simply by the passage of time. It also affects less than 2 percent of all estates yearly.

Our founding fathers had in mind a meritocracy, where each generation, by its own hard work and skills, created wealth for themselves. Handing down great wealth to unborn children skews that concept and allows those whose accident of birth puts them into families of enormous wealth the great advantage that great wealth brings, with no need to prove they are entitled to it by their own merit.

The bad tax laws of the United States are not a Republican-Democrat divide. As many Democrat as Republican Congressional types have been lured into passing bad tax laws and tax loopholes to existing laws by persuasive arguments about allowing people to keep their own money, about getting government of the backs of the people, about government interference in the fiscal affairs of the people, and about supporting and encouraging a strong banking system. It all sounds good, but it isn't.

Government needs to regulate the amount of money that people can keep from certain activities. It can and should encourage some activities, and it must discourage other activities. To fail to do this, through tax laws, is to encourage the country into an inevitable slide toward oligarchy.

Oligarchy is the control of government by wealthy individuals. They use their wealth, buying the votes of legislators and elected officials, to pass or kill legislation and policies in which the oligarchs have an interest.

There are always those who are smarter, cleverer, or more dishonest in their quest for money who will accumulate larger and larger sums. If there ever was any doubt, the recent past has shown us that money not only talks—money controls. It controls our government, and those with the most money can exercise the most control of our government. If they wish to subvert the processes of democracy to their own ends, their large amounts of money and the inherent cupidity and greed of humans allow them to do this.

Eliminating that trend is essential to preserving our democracy. If we do not tax away the potential for oligarchy now, we will have to control the power of the oligarchs themselves with stronger and more determined measures at a time when their wealth may well give them the political strength to prevent changes they disapprove. Oligarchs have the power through their wealth to destroy our form of government. We cannot allow that to happen.

As you grow into adulthood and begin to take part in the political debates, voting your preferences whenever a vote is called for, remember that the founders thought, rightly, that merit was important. Basic Calvinist doctrines, a part of the bedrock on which this country developed, is that we each should earn our own way and profit from our own skills and talent. Anything that dilutes or inhibits the expression of that concept in our society is probably detrimental and should not be allowed.

Without ambition one starts nothing.

Without work one finishes nothing.

The prize will not be sent to you.

You have to win it.

—Ralph Waldo Emerson

#14 Does It Matter?

Communicating clearly is something we often don't regard as having the great importance it does have. Too often we use words that don't express precisely what we intend. Too often we listen carelessly or incompletely to what others tell us. Much too often we allow things to stay unsaid that might be of critical importance to a relationship.

When people say to you, especially those whom you love and hope love you, "Oh, it doesn't matter," perk up your ears. Whatever "it" is may matter, and it may matter a lot.

The dismissive phrase can be a copout. It may mean, "I'm tired of talking about the subject." Or it may mean, "This is a sore subject, and I'm not willing to face the ramifications of discussion."

If it is a rejection of further discussion, the two alternative reasons are likely polar opposites. If the "it" is really inconsequential, then dropping the discussion portends no harm to the relationship.

But if the "it" is close to some fresh emotional wound or is painful to think and talk about, then it really may be important to find a way to gently probe the topic and make sure that one's own part in this transaction is not going to continue to be an irritant.

All of this involves several aspects of your close friendships but especially your intimate relationship with a partner, spouse, or child.

We tell each other how we are emotionally in many different ways. The direct way is to say what we feel in a clear, unmistakable expression. Not as easy as it sounds. But thoughts, and especially feelings, are not communicated only by words. Inflections, tone, and body language tell as much, often more, as the spoken words.

When you are listening, observe as well. Be like Sherlock Holmes was supposed to have been. Allow nothing to escape your keen perception. Do more than listen to the words themselves—listen to the tone of the voice, to the pauses between phrases or words, to the effort to find the right word, especially to inflections and emphases put on the words actually chosen and used. Observe as well: look at the posture, the facial expression, whether the speaker is coming closer, backing away, or staying in place. Are the arms folded? Is the attitude one of openness or protective? All this must be factored into the communication mix if there is to be no misunderstanding of what is being communicated.

When all the subtleties are understood the same way by all parties to that communication, something almost magical has happened. When those subtleties are missed or not understood the same way by all, that failure may lead to a ruptured relationship that should not have happened.

Understanding another promotes empathy. Empathy leads to tolerance and acceptance of another's right to be the way they are. For any relationship between two people to continue voluntarily there must be, first and foremost, acceptance by each of the other as they are.

So it is that the words "Oh, it doesn't matter" need to be explored to be sure that one side of the communication isn't suppressing something because they feel the other will not be tolerant and accepting of what is being discussed. If that is the reason that whatever it is doesn't matter, then the further inquiry would be more serious: "Is this relationship under stress? Is it deteriorating? What is really going on?"

The point is every communication matters, some more than others. Keeping alert to the emotions behind the words in every situation is important. Encouraging clarity and having an ongoing sensitivity to signals of discomfort, when and if they appear in communications with others, is vital to maintaining friendships, especially the close kind.

Words that soak into your ears are whispered . . . not yelled.

—Folk saying

#15 Changing Who You Are

In the context of habits and choices (#4 Habits/Choices), I have used the words "mind," "thought," "commitment," and "intention." But where is the mind, the thought? Who has made the commitment? Who has the intention?

These questions sometimes dominate late-night discussions of university students. They are what drive a few people to devote their lives to cosmology, religion, metaphysics, or searching for answers. I claim no answers but offer some food for thought that I hope may stimulate you to open yourselves to possibilities that are all around you but that you might not yet see.

When I made the choice to stop smoking, what part of myself was the choice maker? When I told myself that cigarettes were bad for my future health, what part of me was talking, what part listening? Importantly, what part of me became open to changing an established habit?

My search for answers to those questions led me to quantum mechanics. In the past ninety or so years since Niels Bohr developed his theories of quantum mechanics, the world as it had been thought to be since the days of Roger Bacon has changed dramatically.

The word "quantum" was coined for the purpose of describing what theretofore had been unthinkable; *something could be in one defined place in time and space and immediately after that be observed to be in an entirely new place in time and space without there having been any detectable movement between the two points: the quantum leap.*

The understanding of the universe changed even more dramatically as Bohr, Albert Einstein, and others expanded the theory with their own ideas of quantum mechanics (sometimes also called quantum physics).

Investigation into what constitutes matter has also dramatically changed accepted concepts that for over two thousand years were thought to be firm and immutable laws of the universe. Since the days of the early Greek philosophers, circa 500 BCE, all of the basic thinking in the field of physics has been founded on the idea that the whole universe is made up of tiny bits of matter, bits that were indivisible, and that each of those bits of matter could be identified as having a definite location in time and space.

Theoretical thinking, supported by experimental work, has now established that the tiniest bits of what the universe is made of are not physical matter at all but are simply bits of informed energy.

The smallest stuff is nonmaterial stuff. But it does contain information. However, neither this nonmaterial stuff, this energy, nor the information it carries with it can be said to have a definite place in time or space.

More than that, some experiments, intended to define how the smallest bits of energy act, confirmed that they appear to be in more than one place at the same time.

Distances between bits of energy, in what to our eyes appears to be solid matter, seem, in relative terms, comparable to distances we observe between stars in our galaxy.

Even more confounding to the physicists who have done experimental work in quantum mechanics, the very existence of these tiniest bits of energy seem to depend for their existence, in part at least, upon the intention of the observer to find them.

QM experimenters are of a group who could hardly be accused of making things up, yet their findings strain the credulity of the uninitiated. Because the current thinking is that these smallest fragments of what we ordinary folks think of as a real world, with real parts in it, these smallest fragments may not exist until we think they exist.

When the sages, seers, and *rishis* (exalted thinkers) of India, three and four thousand years ago, said that all is maya, or illusion, and the world is in our minds and not real at all, they were saying things that QM physicists are saying today.

What causes these smallest bits of energy to combine into things we can experience with our senses and deal with as reality, we do not yet know. That there is information with which these bits of energy are invested is deducible from the way they combine and the way the world around us works.

An example is the genetic information contained on each of the forty-six chromosomes in each of the 70 trillion (more or less) cells in our body, our DNA.

There both is and is not a typical human cell. All cells start their life as protocells, and then internal DNA instructions direct changes into one of the more than two hundred different types of cells in our bodies, each kind of cell performing a different function. Although the different functions cause some cells to be elongated and other cells to be fat and round, all cells contain basically the same parts.

To illustrate the concept of energy and information, it is only necessary to focus on the nucleus, the command center of the cell. Within this nucleus are chromosomes, each of which can be looked on as a library of blueprints for making specific kinds of protein. The name we have given to each blueprint is "gene." For each of the forty-six chromosomes, there is a library of about three thousand genes, each gene a blueprint encoding a formulation for creating a unique kind of protein.

Each chromosome is an elongated strand of DNA (deoxyribonucleic acid) molecules. The genetic encoding of each cell is contained on the DNA helix. Each DNA molecule itself has smaller parts, called nucleotides, which in their various combinations on the DNA helix contain instructions about which protein to make, when to start and when to stop, and perhaps other instructions as well. There are over a thousand nucleotides in each gene.

So forty-six chromosomes, on which we find about three thousand genes, each gene made up of over one thousand nucleotides, all exist along with other parts in the nucleus of a cell we cannot see without the help of an electron microscope.

And each cell contains all the information necessary to make a human body. When the cell is in place, performing a specific, limited function, all unnecessary programs to do and make and be, are turned off. Only the appropriate genes are active or can be made active.

Cells do specialize. As they replicate themselves into new baby cells, those baby cells continue the same specialization as their parent cell. All of this is due to the fact that at the beginning of each human life, once an individual cell has assumed its role as, for example, a skin cell on the right ear, the genetic code, the blueprint which could allow that cell in another part of the body to become a liver cell, are all turned off permanently. The cell's genetic encoding instructions will only be operable for the skin cell, the ear, and on the right side.

The purpose of this short summary of human cell biology is simply to illustrate that information is as critical to life as the energy you derive from food. How it affects you as a living creature is in the potential for controlling that information to influence your body for health.

Your body functions in ways you are likely not aware of until something starts malfunctioning. Cells divide, and the new cells take over the duties of the parent cells, which die and are carried off as culled waste; food is eaten, digested, and sorted for absorption as nourishment or discarded as waste; bacterial and viral invaders are identified and attacked.

All of these activities and more are carried on by your cellular structure (your body), automatically, without the need for any conscious direction.

We sometimes speak of these autonomic performance systems as being beyond our control, that the cells are simply programmed to perform in a predetermined way, and they do. But we can intervene with our thoughts and control many, if not all, of our autonomic systems.

Children at The Center for Attitudinal Healing (Austin, Texas) learn to visualize, and this seems to actually create, great numbers of macrophages, or warrior cells, to attack cancer cells and destroy them.

It seems, at the very least, that we can intervene in the automatic defense systems our bodies naturally have and cause them to amp up their activity in defending against tumors. Work is needed to establish if we can self-activate our defenses against viruses, such as the flu and common cold.

Among exhibitionists of the world, there are those who present their bodies to be pierced with needles, knives, and rapiers without bleeding or apparent harm to their bodies.

This shows a kind of cellular control so unusual as to be utterly unique to that person. But we all have some measure of that ability of the exhibitionist. If we decide to use it, we can by marshaling our intention, commitment, and practice.

What we can understand from this is that the body is much more subject to our control than we ordinarily think. Certainly it is much more subject to our control than the control we generally exercise, much more than the control we usually think we can impose on the autonomic system we each have.

It is not that we need to or want to take over the body's autonomic functions and direct them on a moment-to-moment basis. The programming built in is convenient for all the normal routine functions the body's cells need to keep all systems up and running properly.

Our bodies are like the jumbo jet that flies on automatic pilot for hours with no complications. However, when an emergency threatens, the pilot takes over and brings the aircraft safely through. So with humans, when an autonomic system is under threat and might be overwhelmed, the self can take over and control how the emergency is handled.

But like the pilot, these are not actions to take without training and practice. We need to know specifically what we want our cells to do and have some experience in being the pilot in control.

Feedback while learning tells us that what we are doing is having the effect we want. As with learning any new skill, you will spend more effort in accomplishing results during the learning process than when the skill is in place. Learning body control is not something that comes without effort. It may be that for you it will come as easily as walking. Still, watch a baby learn to walk, and realize that learning to walk takes effort, determination, and practice.

From bio feedback monitors, we know we can learn to control our blood pressure, temperature, heart rate, and many other bodily processes ordinarily on autonomic.

As humans, we share the trait of curiosity with almost all other warm-blooded creatures. But after being curious, humans have the unique ability to continue on, exploring and experimenting to see where that curiosity will lead them. This is particularly true with mental activities.

Curiosity will stimulate exploration just so far though. When effort of exploration is required, most people retire to their chairs and read about what others have done. That may be as much as you want at this time.

If you do want to go further and put some effort into experimenting and want to see what you can do to exercise control over parts of your body systems which you had never before thought possible, then start with bio feedback and begin your own control over your body.

That there is information which controls the energy of cell function is incontrovertible, even though we don't yet completely understand the how and why of it.

You and I, at the most basic level of existence, are made up of bits of energy and information. We can influence what we are and how we function by communicating with our own body cells on an information level. We can visualize the result we wish to have happen and then leave it up to our cells to manage the minutia of how to do it.

And if we can communicate with our own cells at the level of information, what would prevent us from communicating with the Universe at the information level?

Can we influence universal energy with our thoughts? Why not? How and what we think controls who and what we are. We learn that from seers, from sages, from quantum physicists, from the experience of doctors and healers. On a quantum level, information in the Universe and in our own bodies may be equally accessible.

Remember that we are not our bodies, that "we" are as evanescent as our thoughts. Using the pure energy of our thoughts, "we" should be able to access information wherever located, in our cells or in the larger universe.

All of this has been to offer proof that you have the ability to do much, much more than you think possible to influence the health of your body, how it functions, and what you experience because of how it functions.

To tie this back into changing habits, your cells accept a myriad of instructions from your mind, because the mind is the ultimate controller of how we function. The vast majority of information to the cells is through the autonomic nervous system.

But we can change the information the cells are given with the same mind that controls them autonomically. They will accept the communication of new information from the mind, and that is how ingrained habits can be modified or eliminated.

I have described in the sections on meditation (#25) and while explaining the meaning of "gap" (#26) that information is key to all of life. I hope this brief excursion into the way I see quantum mechanics confirming that principle has persuaded you that you have the power to send new information to your cells that can change your life.

The self is not something ready-made,

but something in continuous formation

through choice of action.

—John Dewey

#16 Sleep Needs

Our bodies are like machines in their need for constant maintenance and repair, yet unlike, in that the body cannot be shut down for this process. During maintenance and repair time, the body must continue to function so that the organism may continue to live.

When we sleep in response to tiredness (a sure sign of a need for body maintenance) or simply when we reach that time of day when the body customarily slows down, the body will not begin the process of cell repair unless we are in the nighttime stage of sleep. A nap during the day can be refreshing and energizing, but it is the dark time of the day when the real process of repair and maintenance of the body goes on.

Once we have gotten through the teen years, which psychologists now tell us should be recognized as often requiring different and greater amounts of sleep than older people (such as parents who rail at what is perceived as laziness), the adult body will respond most easily and comfortably to a schedule that will allow the usual, six to eight hours of sleep, awakening at or before dawn. Experience will tell us our body does not need an unvarying amount of sleep each night. Age has something to do with that. Recent studies also indicate that our genes have something to do with that too. Experiments with sleep involved studies of the natural circadian rhythms—biological responses to daily changes of light and dark.

There are some today whose sleep patterns do not fit the usual, who apparently get along well with less than six to eight hours sleep each night. Former President Bill Clinton is reported to do fine on five to six hours sleep a night. Comedian Jay Leno says he needs only four hours of sleep. Singer/actress Madonna says the same.

Thomas Edison and Nicola Tesla, inventors, both subscribed to a pattern of what has been termed polyphasic sleep—short periods of night time sleep supplemented by several naps during the day. Winston Churchill also said that he could not have directed the WWII effort of Great Britain if he had slept eight hours a night. He developed a wartime pattern of four hours sleep at night, plus daily naps. Albert Einstein, on the other hand, frequently slept ten hours at night.

Salvatore Dali napped with a silver spoon in his outstretched hand. When he drifted off to sleep, the spoon would fall and he would awaken, often, he said, with his next work of art visualized. He too reported doing well on four hours of sleep, plus naps during the day.

Others reported to need less sleep than most of us were John Kennedy, Leonardo Da Vinci, and Napoleon Bonaparte.

Our army has tested the effects of too little sleep on troop behavior on the battlefield and has found that sleep loss adversely affects stamina, cognition, and judgment.

In the hours before the Battle of Waterloo, after several nights with few hours of sleep, Napoleon was reported to have been distracted and slow in his responses to the exigencies of the battle.

Several years ago, Nori Nishigaya in Victoria, British Columbia, Canada, undertook a protracted period of polyphasic sleeping. He reduced his nighttime sleep to four hours with one or more half-hour naps during the day.

He kept a blog on this: polyphasic.blogspot.com. You can still visit this site (August 2009) and read about his experiences. He found the reduced schedule difficult.

Your cat will sleep thirteen to sixteen hours a day. Babies the same. Adults need six to eight hours; teenagers require nine or ten hours of sleep to stay healthy.

Staying healthy is the most important lesson to take away from this. Those who need less than what is considered the normal amount of nightly sleep are the exception. For the rest of us, the army studies that show loss of mental acuity and judgment are the most troubling.

A Swedish study also found that there was a statistically significant rise (5 percent) in fatal heart attacks in the days following the shift to daylight savings, something that caused a disruption of normal sleep routine. There was a lesser but measurable increase in fatal heart attacks in the days after return to regular solar time.

In my own experience, I worked during the daytime in TV and went to law school at the University of Houston at night. I studied both after class and, getting up early after a short night of sleep, studied before going to work.

One night, driving home from class, I was so stressed out by this schedule and lack of sleep that I apparently slept while driving. At a traffic light, only blocks from my home, I suddenly awakened to my surroundings. I had driven nearly fifteen miles across the city of Houston, Texas, with absolutely no memory of the route taken or of stops made at traffic signals or stop signs. I was on complete automatic. Fortunately, it was eleven o'clock at night so traffic was light. But lack of sleep zoned me out.

In Houston, Roy Hofheinz, the man who later developed the first completely enclosed sports arena, the Astrodome, was my boss at KTHT (radio) for a year, where I worked in his news department. He had a reputation for needing little sleep. In several projects where I worked closely with him, I watched as he used enormous energy to work long hours with occasional twenty-minute naps.

He had learned to allow his mind and body to completely relax and was able to fall asleep in seconds after lying down, making the absolute most of the time he would allot to keeping going on important projects. But when the project was through, he returned to a normal sleep schedule.

He unfortunately suffered a massive stroke at a young age and, though he lived several years after that, was never again able to use the immense talents he had. It seemed to me his stressful and short-on-sleep lifestyle imposed more stress than his body systems could manage.

Stress we carry to bed can interfere with sleep patterns. Stress triggers hormonal flows that keep the body ready for action. Stress can be caused by happy events as well; an expectation of more happy events to come is also a form of stress. That can keep the body too alert to sleep.

Eating too late can prevent sleep. The stomach generally needs about three hours to break down the food eaten into usable form and move it on to the small intestines. Going to sleep sooner than three hours after eating will put a burden on the digestive system and likely interfere with sleep.

Eating heavy foods during an evening meal, like beef, pork, or any food accompanied by heavy gravy, will extend the time food is in the stomach, increasing the likelihood of indigestion in the middle of the night.

When we put that extra burden on our digestive system, we increase the probability that there will be incomplete metabolism of food. Incomplete metabolism will create toxins that clog our tissues and interfere with good health.

Incomplete metabolism of food also results in fat molecules being taken up by the body as a potential nutrient and not treated as waste. These fat molecules are stored by the body for future use. Since most of us are not at this time troubled by fears of famine, excess fat storage is unsightly at best and a threat to good health at worst.

Two natural hormones can help restore natural sleep: HGH (human growth hormone) and melatonin. The natural stresses of life are handled more easily by the young. HGH has something to do with that. HGH declines as we age and drops off dramatically for many people over sixty-five. Getting HGH back into our systems in useful quantities is an important first step to restoring many aspects of older lives to a more comfortable younger biological age.

Stress is an inevitable aspect of current life in most aspects of US society. Managing stress well as it impacts us by diffusing it or accepting it and metabolizing it so that it doesn't come back later to bite us on the ankle is pretty important. Getting rid of or neutralizing stress before bedtime is important to our ability to have a deep restful sleep.

HGH also has a positive effect on general energy levels, sexual drive and performance, feelings of well-being, memory, and even neurodegenerative diseases like Parkinson's, AMLS, MLS, as well as autoimmune diseases and chronic fatigue syndromes.

HGH is normally released when we are fast asleep with an ebb and flow that follows sleep stages. The highest output occurs during the deepest stages of sleep and the lowest during REM (rapid eye movement) sleep, when we are dreaming. The cause and effect connection between HGH and sleep has been documented by studies of people with pituitary deficiencies, who also had abnormal sleep patterns. Giving human growth hormone to these folks restored normal sleep.

Studies establish that as we get older, it can be difficult to get to sleep. Sleep is lighter after about sixty and more wakeful. Getting back to sleep after waking can also be difficult. Injections of HGH have greatly improved all of those problems. In order to keep in harmony with nature, going to bed between ten and midnight is required. Being able to get to sleep is of equal or, perhaps, greater importance. Several amino acids stimulate the body to produce a higher level of HGH, as does DHEA, exercise, and supplemental doses of melatonin. HGH is helpful in producing the quiet state the body needs to do its heavy-duty cellular repair during sleep.

Melatonin has been touted for its recognized capacity to help quickly reset our internal clock when we jet across time zones. It also has the effect of stimulating growth hormone production. More important to this discussion, it can assist older people who have problems going to bed and sleeping quietly and deeply to regain that ability.

You can learn more about both HGH and melatonin at the marvelous Internet encyclopedia, wikipedia.com.

In the days of torches and candles as sources of light in the night, not that long ago in human time, it was common to speak of "first sleep" and "second sleep." First sleep lasted about four hours after retiring (usually about eight or nine in the evening, depending on the season of the year).

Then as the repair work the body had undertaken in those early stages of sleep quieted down, one would awaken, go to the bathroom, make love, or simply have a sip of water and, perhaps, talk with one's companions and then drift back to second sleep, ready to awaken at or before dawn's first light.

Morning and afternoon naps, even when one has had both first and second sleep, are mentioned in older documents and manuscripts that often ascribe naps to laziness. But the body has its needs. Naps relieved both physical and mental stress. Naps are often necessary to allow the cells to rest and keep the body/mind alert.

Studying, whether as a part of a school curriculum or simply when you have a need to know something and have undertaken an in-depth search can tire both the brain and your body generally. A short nap of fifteen or twenty minutes is both refreshing for the body and mind and essential for solidifying the content you have studied just before your nap.

When you cannot fall asleep, it is the mind that is not of your brain but that is all through and integral to your body, which cannot relax enough to sleep. Emotional stress affects the physical body, and the imbalance causes stress.

Meditation might seem like the answer to quiet the body and the mind and allow sleep to come if the body is tired. But meditation will usually cause the system to sink into deep relaxation and then, with the cells temporarily satisfied about their need for rest, the body comes out of the meditation even more alert than before. Meditating after about six in the evening will exacerbate and not help problems with sleeping.

Understanding that fear is at the basis of most, perhaps all, of the anxieties of life is a good first step in the direction of resolving stressful emotions. Stress involves and affects the whole body/mind. Stress must ultimately be metabolized and digested, saving whatever energy is useful for the body/mind and discarding the rest of the energy as waste. That process happens in a way that is comparable to the way we metabolize the foods we put into our stomachs.

We take emotions into our consciousness, think about what it is, evaluate what it portends for our well-being, and then we either find something that is worthwhile about it, that we can extract from the whole experience to use later and discard the rest as useless, or we pass the whole thing through as waste, not allowing it to poison our body/mind.

Anger is really nothing more than a form of fear, and fear is a potent stressor of the body. Letting go of anger, really forgiving, is a good move toward destressing your body/mind.

We don't usually think of it this way, but the opposite of fear is love. This has been told to us from the time humans first began to write down the words of avatars and sages. One can learn to defuse anger/fear with love with a very few pointers.

The first and most important is to replace fear with acceptance of life. Acceptance means being nonjudgmental about how and what other people happen to be, about the aspects of our own life over which we have no control, and about forgiving ourselves for any shortcomings we think we have.

When you turn fear into love, or at least acceptance, you have changed the hormonal dynamics throughout your body/mind and given yourself an emotion you can integrate and metabolize with life-extending results.

The second is to develop tolerance for the ways others are different from ourselves. What we are, how we are, and what we do and think are not role models for the rest of mankind. Each of us is entitled to be as different from others as our genes, our life experiences, and present life circumstances seem to require of us.

The third, and perhaps the most important quality to develop, is to banish fear from our anticipation of future events. Que sera, sera—whatever will be, will be—is a good motto to live by if one wants to rid one's life of fear. Acceptance of life as it is, at the moment and as it may be in the future, is important in all of our waking moments but especially the moments when we are trying to invite renewing sleep to come. Sleep cannot come easily and will not be renewing if your body enters sleep from a state of anxiety, even mild anxiety.

Finally, inviting love to come is different from the religious adjuration to love one another. It will take real effort from time to time to move beyond acceptance of life, as it is in order to replace anger with love. Yet it can be done and in a way that can be practiced, the same as you practice anything else.

First, determine if the fear is of infliction of a mortal wound or injury. If it is, then escape is your primary concern. But that will, hopefully, never occur to you while living in the United States. If there is no mortal danger involved, then find something about that person or situation that is ludicrous or contemptible or funny. Allow that new emotion to morph into pity. Once you have banished your fear/anger and your attitude is not one of revenge, then allow yourself to project a feeling of hope that the object of your attention will find peace and no longer act in such a way as to cause you fear.

Because we do not include this as a part of our education, either from parents or school, and church has become irrelevant in most secular lives, replacing fear/anger with love requires some self-training. But it is the best antidote you have to the stress of fear/anger that might at sometime dominate part of your life.

A warm shower or bath helps get the body ready for deep relaxation, as does a warm cup of milk. Bringing milk to a near boil increases the content of L-tryptophan. This natural amino acid stimulates production of melatonin from the body, which triggers an HGH release that further promotes a restful condition of both mind and body.

Even if you are usually intolerant of cow's milk, you should try this. Bringing milk to near boiling and drinking it warm increases the body's acceptance of it. If you really are intolerant of cow's milk, in many large groceries today you can find fresh Meyenberg Goat Milk. Goat milk is naturally homogenized, has a very pleasant taste, and is more easily metabolized than cow's milk.

Relaxing your body with a series of tension-release muscle exercises will both prepare your muscular structure for deep relaxation and take your mind away from any mental tensions that may linger from the day's activities. This will not bring you to an acceptance of life as it is, but it will put you to sleep when other body/mind tools have not worked.

Once you are in bed, take several deep clearing breaths through your nose. Starting with the right foot for men, the left foot for women, tense the muscles of the foot, increasing the tension over five seconds, then release the tension abruptly; let the foot sink down as though it was falling into the mattress. Do that with each muscle group up the leg and then the opposite leg, the buttocks, the back, the abdomen, the chest, hands, arms, until you have tensed and relaxed all of your muscle groups up to and including your forehead.

Controlled breathing will help focus the mind away from memories of stressful events. Breathe in deeply to a count of four and then breathe out fully to the same count. On the next breath, breathe in to a count of four and out to a count of six and then in to a count of four and out to a count of eight. Continue breathing in to a count of four and out to a count of eight. You will quickly fall asleep.

Another aid to refocusing the mind is to count backward from one hundred, but with this mind trick: count 100, 95, 99, 94, 98, 93, and so on. Having to keep the five number variant in mind will usually drive all other thoughts from your brain.

Reiki is a Japanese energy-healing discipline. The part of Reiki that is so marvelous is that it has focused our attention back to our hands as healing instruments. Your hands contain energy, energy you can feel. When any part of us is injured, we instinctively put our hands on that part and hold it. Reiki tells us that we let go too soon. Five minutes or more of holding the injured part of us will begin the healing process.

Using the energy you each have in your hands, you can calm the mind that is in your brain. Simply make each hand into a sort of paddle, fingers together and palms slightly cupped. Place each hand lightly over your left and right temple area, opposite each other. Empty your mind and allow the energy of your hands to flow through your brain to calm and pacify your brain waves into a sleep pattern.

It will take less than five minutes, and when you allow your hands to fall away, you will fall asleep effortlessly.

Affirmations are important. Saying them out loud will engage both sides of your brain. Do these at any time, before, during, or following the tension-relaxing sequences. Tell your body in your own words substantially this:

You are my body. I love you and love the way you are. I will take care of you and nourish every part of you. Now it is time for you to sleep and repair and renew all of your parts during sleep. You will wake up at _ o 'clock renewed, refreshed, and feeling absolutely great.

Talking to your body in the third person may seem strange at first, but it will help keep your body/mind reference clear, that you are not your body. It will help reinforce that your body and your mind are both separate and integral parts of the same unit. Though together, the body requires other and special care than the mind. Accept that your body truly needs love, care, and attention. It responds to love, care, and attention with amazing results.

Nearly one-third of your life is spent in essential renewing sleep. I hope that what I have suggested will let you choose ways to make that time most effective for your good health.

Dance like no one is watching.

Sing like no one is listening.

Love like you've never been hurt and

live like it's heaven on Earth.

—Mark Twain

#17 Pusillanimous

Pusillanimous.

I first heard the word in a Gilbert and Sullivan operetta long years ago. Since those two were noted for their deft ability to lampoon political types of their day, it may well be that that was their intended target. If so, it is sad that the world has not changed much. So many people, politicians leading the parade, deserve to be called pusillanimous.

But my missive to you today is not about politicians but about you. I offer you this advice: never act in such a way that you could fairly be called ... *pusillanimous*.

For "pusillanimous" means timid, fearful—even cowardly—small spirited, my dictionary adds.

In your life, in your choices, I urge you to put fear aside and act decisively, intending and expecting matters will turn out even better than you hoped. Of course, not every choice will turn out that way. Too many imponderables in every decision make some outcomes different than we intend. But of all the activities of your mind, your intentions are perhaps the most important. Intentions become the unspoken directions that will guide your actions to give the desired outcome the greatest chance of success.

But bear with me while I expand on "pusillanimous" first by reminding you of something I've said before: words are the building blocks our mind uses to think with. If your supply of building blocks is limited, so will be your thinking.

When you talk to yourself, you use words to express your thoughts the same way you would use words to talk to another person. Hopefully, talking to yourself will be a conversation that, looking back on it, you will think was both insightful and intelligent. The larger your vocabulary to take inchoate ideas and concepts and give them form, the wider the scope of the thoughts your mind will be able to think and then express either to yourself or as a part of an exchange of thoughts with another.

Again, words are the way we construct our communication to others, as well as to ourselves; and having a vocabulary that includes words like "pusillanimous" and other words that are not often used but have clear and concise meanings allows you to think your thoughts with greater precision and clarity.

A large vocabulary also means you do not have to fall back on the verbal crutches that we hear all too frequently from professionals, who earn their living talking, as well as from friends whose ability to express themselves is crippled by a deficient knowledge of words. Examples of verbal crutches, substituting for words that would have meaning if the speaker only knew them, are all the variations and conjugations of the F word that lets it serve as every form of speech from expletive to compliment.

Take, for example, one synonym of pusillanimous—cowardly. When would you want to use the word cowardly? Or cow-ard or cow-ardice or cow-er?

To make words come alive, it is often useful to take away any prefix or suffix and just examine the root of the word—in this case, "cow."

A century ago, when 90 percent of Americans either lived on a farm or had lived on a farm where they observed animal behavior daily, any sort of description that compared a person's behavior to cowlike behavior would have been immediately understood for the powerful image it would have invoked. Today, to cower is simply defined as "to crouch in fear or shame." But if you have lived where cows are a part of life, you understand what it is to cow-er.

When a single cow is confronted by a human, the cow will lower its head in an act of submission and its eyes will roll from side to side as it looks fearfully for some avenue of escape. Its head will then start weaving from side to side as it stands, perplexed and afraid, not knowing what to do. If the human spreads his/her arms, making themselves appear bigger, the cow will start to back away, head down and apprehensive. Simply by bluffing, a one-hundred-and-fifty-pound human can make a thousand-pound cow cow-er.

Recently, the Democratic majority leader of the US Senate accused the Republicans of cowering before the prospect of debating a bill. For those who know about cows, this would be a powerful, specific, contemptuous description of a political foe.

Your mate or partner will certainly be at least as intelligent as you are. To be able to have fun with ideas, to play with words, to express new ideas and variations of old ideas, the larger your vocabulary, the more pleasure you both will have from the simple act of living together and communicating about whatever comes into your lives.

So think about *pusillanimous* from time to time. The mere sound of it will make you smile. And it will remind you that owning a big supply of words is an inexpensive way to give your mind the ability to build more different and better ideas.

The policy of being too cautious is the greatest risk of all.

—Jawaharlal Nehru

#18 Raw Vegetable Salad

Most of you have no doubt heard that raw vegetables are good, better than cooked.

The value in raw is that the enzymes, abundant in all vegetables, are killed by a temperature higher than 115 degrees, a temperature that is hot to the skin but only warm to the tissues of the inside of the mouth. So eating raw gives your body access to a new supply of the very enzymes most needed to metabolize the foods you are eating.

Cooking, however, does do several good things, including starting the breakdown of cellulose and fiber so that plant material is more easily digested. Cooking, of course, can happen in many ways, including waterless cooking, which most nutritionists recommend for getting the fullest measure of nutrient value from your food.

Immersing vegetables in water soaks minerals and vitamins out of the vegetable being cooked, to be (usually) thrown away as waste. This is a great loss of nutritional value and requires you eat more to get the same amount of nutrients as with raw.

So raw may be harder to digest, but the bulk and fiber of raw are great additions to your diet, and the enzymes, minerals, and vitamins are mostly retained. There is some loss from peeling and coring, but that can be minimized by using a stiff brush to clean the vegetables, rather than peeling, which removes the flavorful and mineral-laden exterior.

Rinsing in a very mild solution of bleach or light soapy water will remove and neutralize most surface bacteria and wash away residues of pesticides and herbicides. The last one is a very good reason to always eat organic produce.

A word here about eating grapes—to minimize the risk of mold and airborne bacteria infecting vines, grape growers have learned to use drip irrigation, at great savings of water. The advantage to growers and the enormous disadvantage to the rest of us is that along with saving water by irrigation drip, growers can put herbicides and insecticides into the water, instead of spraying. The roots of the vines take up those poisons and deliver them to every part of the growing plant, including the grapes. The amounts are infinitesimal, and our FDA says it is okay for you and me to take these poisons into our systems. But I wonder?

Mary and I use organic, if at all possible, for all the reasons I mentioned. The nutrient supply of organically grown vegetables is more and better than that produced on agribusiness farms. The taste will tell you that organic is better. Carrots are sweet; eat only organic carrots and you will appreciate why Peter Rabbit always headed for Mr. McGregor's garden. Celery tastes like real celery. Too much of our food tastes like cardboard. Organic farming restores the taste that made humans want to eat vegetables in the first place.

A very good evening meal consists of a raw vegetable salad. Because it is so easy to make and so good in taste and so good for everyone, this simple and delicious change in your diet will take the pounds off like nothing else, especially when eaten at night. Here is a recipe I developed and recommend without reservation.

INGREDIENTS:

2 large carrots	1/2 medium zucchini squash
3 large stalks celery	1 medium yellow squash
1/2 red or orange bell pepper	1 small head broccoli (use florets only)
1 medium cucumber, seeds extracted	10 green beans
1 small section of cauliflower	½ cup chopped walnuts
4 spears asparagus (use about ½ stalk)	½ any firm tart apple
1 medium lemon	1 ripe avocado (garnish)

(I usually go down the produce section, picking what looks freshest and best. An onion will perk up the flavor. Other vegetables might tempt you. Use your imagination and delete or substitute at will. The mix will always be good if you use at least seven vegetables.)

Cut or break apart all the ingredients into cubes or pieces of about one-half inch or a little less in size into a large bowl. Add the juice of the lemon and mix well, making sure all ingredients are touched with the juice. This will insure a sweet taste, and if you and friends do not eat all of this at one sitting, lemon juice will prevent ingredients from browning or otherwise changing color.

Mix in extra virgin olive oil and a mild herbed vinegar, covering all ingredients. Place avocado strips atop each serving just before presentation. Crumble on a strong cheese and add croutons as desired. Serve with sesame crackers or a slice of rye or pumpernickel toast. A small glass of light white wine is a great addition to the meal.

This salad is not only very digestible but delicious and just right for your evening meal. From an ayurveda standpoint, it contains all the tastes (sweet, salt, sour, bitter, pungent, astringent) that we need in order for our systems to feel completely nourished and satisfied.

As I've mentioned before, with the evening meal, it is important not to eat anything that cannot be digested easily in order to allow your body the best opportunity to use its resources to do repair and maintenance of its cells and systems while you sleep. You don't want heavy protein hanging around in your stomach, only partially digested, to interfere with the body's essential rejuvenation processes.

Because of the satisfying nature of this salad, you will find it easy to follow Deepak Chopra's advice: push away from the table when your stomach is about three quarters full. That is particularly important in the case of the last meal of the day.

Seeing is deceiving. It's eating that's believing.

—James Thurber

#19 Feeling Tired?

When moving seems like an effort, your body's supply of something is diminished, and your cells are telling you to "slow down, conserve what is left, no telling when there may be more, so *conserve*." The most likely necessities of your body to be in temporary and easily increased short supply are water and oxygen.

We forget to drink water, not realizing that an adequate internal supply of water is essential for nearly everything our cells do. Cells require H_2O in adequate supply, instantly available, in order for the mitochondria, the energy central of all your cells, to do their work. Diminished hydration is experienced as slowly increasing lassitude. Your body requires a certain basic level of hydration in order to function at all, much less to function well. The common maxim of eight eight-ounce glasses of water per day sounds like a lot. It isn't and is probably about right for most people. More will be needed by those doing strenuous work, particularly if perspiration is more than just minimal.

Lack of an adequate supply of oxygen is also a likely cause of feeling as though you need to rest. Frequently we don't breathe often enough, deeply enough, to oxygenate our blood to the extent needed by our cells. Again the cellular response to not enough oxygen is to conserve energy, waiting for the level of supply to pick up. Yawning is a good indicator of a low supply of oxygen.

Our lungs are roughly comparable to sponges. Ambient air sucked into the lungs is about 16 percent oxygen. The structure of the lungs accommodates the constant flow of the some ten trillion red blood cells that make up the fluid content of the arterial and venous systems of the body. These red blood cells are sent to the lungs to make direct contact with the air we breathe and to, literally, leach oxygen from that air and change it into blood hemoglobin. The oxygenated blood then returns to the heart and is pumped abroad by the arterial system, carrying that hemoglobin to all cells throughout the body.

When you are feeling tired and not ready for the next task, resting is an excellent idea. But before you rest, give your body some help in replenishing supplies that may be low.

Drink at least one eight-ounce glass of water, always at or slightly above room temperature.

Why not drink cold liquids? The body must convert everything you give it into a substance it can use. That means, for one thing, that everything must be raised to body temperature before the body can allow it to move past the stomach. Starting with any cold intake requires the body to use energy to warm it in order to use it. Starting with a body that is in stress from lack of something and feeding it something that creates more stress in a demand for energy is just not very smart.

Do the *triple-five* breath routine: slowly take five breaths that are as deep and lung filling as you manage without strain. Hold each breath for a slow count of five. Then let it out through pursed lips for a slow count of five. Breathing deeply this way will involve all the areas of your lungs. Holding the breath will allow the maximum transfer of oxygen and breathing out slowly will exercise your lungs gently and expand the total surface area available for oxygen transfer to the most efficient extent possible for your lungs.

While you breathe, make the central portion of your body straight. In other words, don't slump. Allow your diaphragm to work easily and your stomach and rib cage to move in and out without restriction. A good way to tell if your lungs are functioning well is to place your hands, one on each side, just below the last rib, thumbs to the back, fingers spread around the front. If you are breathing correctly and to full capacity, you will feel that area between the bottom of your ribs and the top of your hipbone on each side, move in and out under your hands.

After drinking eight ounces of room temperature water and doing the five-breath routine rest for a while. Between ten and twenty minutes will usually do the trick. If your feelings of tiredness are caused by either lack of hydration or oxygen, you will feel dramatic effects from hydrating and oxygenating your system. The response of your body will be significant feelings of well-being.

It is hard to give practical advice about taking care of our bodies without seeming to be a medical authority, which I am not. But before the current industrialized medical care system was developed by the medical community in this country, there were countless books, pamphlets, and healers offering advice on keeping well and fighting disease.

Those who professed to have healing knowledge, less than a century ago, were split into several well-recognized groups, all of which survive to some extent today. The allopaths, who used drugs and potions to heal, have become the dominant medical concept of the world. In the United States, they formed and use the AMA to control how most medicine is practiced here. There were also homeopaths, chiropractors, naturopaths, and osteopaths, each of which groups now have licensing regulations in most US states. Other healing arts include Reiki, vibrational healing, herbal medicine, acupuncture, physiatry, psychic healing, and more.

None of these could exist without some positive response from those who go to them for healing or relief of one kind or another. What I suggest with my nonmedical advice has been derived from the advice of others, and it has worked for me. I hope it works for you too.

Courage is the power to let go of the familiar.

—Raymond Lindquist

#20 Where Have All the Songbirds Gone?

Mary and I have asked ourselves that question for several years. Only recently has one likely cause become known.

North American migratory songbirds have died by the millions on Central and South American farms in areas to which they have safely migrated for millennia

In some species, including the Bobolink, local spring bird counts have described population number reductions of as much as 80 percent.

Researchers in Argentina have found large numbers of dead birds in and around grain fields, apparent victims of rampant insecticide use, with concentrations as high as five times the recommended application rate.

Agribusiness greed and individual farmer ignorance are, of course, immediate causes of this tragedy. But looking further, it is possible to see that the burgeoning population of the world is the ultimate cause. Six billion hungry mouths has required that every arable tract be put to use to grow food crops, food for people and food for animals that will feed people.

Other factors are affecting our bird population.

The Canadian Red Knot, a bird that migrates biannually between the most northern arctic reaches on the North American continent to the most southern tip of Sierra del Fuego, a distance of 9,300 miles, is nearly extinct because of diminished food supplies along the shores of the Chesapeake Bay. Horseshoe crabs come onto the sandy beaches of the bay to lay their eggs at just about the time the Red Knot migration puts the birds down to rest on their northern migratory flight. Over eons, the supply of horseshoe crab eggs was so abundant that the birds could eat their fill and quickly bulk up the fat they needed and fly on to the arctic, where they would spend the summer breeding.

The demand for the horseshoe crabs' blood component for commercial use has made them so profitable that fishermen have decimated crab numbers, and Red Knots have been the victims. With diminished food supply on their migratory route, from about a hundred thousand strong just twenty years ago, the total Red Knot population is down to about five thousand birds.

As the world population moves up to the nine billion predicted, the demands for land to grow food will only increase. The demands for harvesting animals and fish and edible and commercially useful species of every kind has grown exponentially and will continue to grow until, even if we are careful, the extinction of most species is almost foreordained.

Population growth is, in part, the result of cleaner water and sanitation and more complete knowledge about treating diseases that used to result in short lives for millions of babies and their mothers and shortened lives of the elderly of every race and ethnic group. For a while, it was hoped that the increased likelihood of child survival into adulthood would cause families to limit their children to those they could support. Human nature and the innate drive to procreate have trumped that hope, and the much-desired reduction in live births per woman of childbearing years has not happened to the extent wished for by demographers.

Population growth has been accelerated by the policies of some religious groups that promote large families, teaching that each should have as many babies as the family can produce. Roman Catholicism used to be known as the religion that promoted large families. In fact, they merely disapproved of birth control. In the Western world today, many Muslim and Hassidic Jewish leaders are actively promoting large families to increase their religion's overall numbers.

The ultimate truth in politics is that numbers matter. The larger the group of those affected, the greater the potential for that group to influence the outcome. So the policy of Hassidic Jews and Muslims, both minorities in this country, is to increase their population to the point where they will have political influence merely by dint of numbers. It is unlikely the loss of songbirds or even many other species will affect the thinking of the leaders of these religious groups.

Our own government, by order of conservative President George W. Bush, refused to provide funds for NGOs in developing countries that promote family planning and the use of condoms for birth control. Some countries in Africa, in order to have politically large constituencies, promote large families to the extent that those countries are suffering from waves of famine from too many mouths to feed.

Large areas of Kenya, once quite fertile and prosperous, are now nearly barren, arid, and desolate because of the misuse of land in vain attempts to grow enough crops to feed the uncontrolled population growth in that country.

China, already greatly overpopulated by unmanaged population growth over the centuries and running out of arable land, has looked to Africa, not only for mineral and other raw materials for its factories, but also as a place to grow food crops for its people. With 1.3 billion mouths to feed, China has much less land than it needs to grow food crops. The Chinese attempts to limit population growth have been statistically successful. The rule of one child per family has resulted in China's population, according to their statistics, becoming more or less stable.

Surprisingly, the birthrate of the United States, having declined for nearly seventy years, is now (2010) climbing again, confounding demographers who had predicted a steady decline.

In Central and South America, large demographic groups are under the age of twenty, just coming into childbearing years themselves. Their babies will need to be fed.

In Mexico, however, the population information is slightly encouraging. In 2010 the population is about 110 million; the birthrate has declined to less than two live births per female of childbearing age, less than the statistical rate of births needed to maintain a level population number. In 1940, only seventy years ago, the population of Mexico was barely 20 million. The more than fivefold increase in people over just seventy years is a striking example of how quickly populations can explode.

As an aside, Mexican demographers predict that by 2040, their economy and their population will more or less come together, one supporting the other. Until then, they predict that between 350,000 and 500,000 Mexicans will immigrate to the United States annually.

The Silent Spring, of which Rachel Carson warned almost fifty years ago, is sneaking up on us. Our bird friends who survive give us moments of great joy with their songs and showy plumage. They provide the essential service to humans of protecting us from being overrun by insects. They earn their right to keep living by the simple fact of their presence in our lives. It is critical for our own well-being that we act now to protect these migratory birds from death by poisons in Middle American and South American lands.

Their deaths should also be a wakeup call that the foods we import from these countries may well be laced with poisons that our underfunded food inspection services allow to be imported and stocked on the shelves of neighborhood groceries. As we mourn the deaths of innocent birds, we must also act to protect ourselves and especially our children from foods that contain unseen poisons left by improper application of insecticides.

If we, the whole of the human race, do not act soon to find ways to reverse human population growth, we may well find that we have procreated our species to a point of unsustainability. In another million or so years, that may not make any difference to the earth. New species will evolve to fill the gaps that humans will leave behind. But for our children and grandchildren, the prospects are less than the bright future we had when we were young.

That bright, reasonably predictable future that we had is also threatened by climate change. Even more than climate change itself, the future of children born today will be more troubled and less predictable because of the unwillingness of many in this country to agree that a dramatic change in the earth's climate is occurring or that industry—and motor-vehicle-created pollution are the major causes.

So long as those with the power to change things refuse to acknowledge that modification of our way of living and reduction in our use of fossil fuels are critical if we (the people of the earth) are to ameliorate the effects of climate change, dramatic and extremely harmful changes in climatic patterns and in sea levels worldwide are inevitable. The only thing imponderable at this time is the speed with which changes will happen.

During all of the earth's history that scientists can be reasonably certain about, using tree rings from timbers found in ancient buildings, ice cores from glaciers in Greenland and Antarctica, and seabed cores from around the ocean's floor, the level of carbon dioxide in the atmosphere has varied in direct relationship with the earth's temperature. As the earth warmed, CO_2 levels rose. As the earth cooled, CO_2 levels fell.

The present levels of CO_2 in the atmosphere, having risen inexorably since the beginning of the Industrial Revolution, are higher than the highest levels of CO_2 that have ever been noted in the earth's climate history. Scientists around the world are more than concerned; they are alarmed and have been sounding warnings for the last ten years that civilization is facing catastrophic changes in sea levels within the lives of most people alive today.

A rise of three feet will put most of the wetlands of the world underwater at all tides. A rise of six feet will inundate large segments of coastline, including coastal cities, worldwide.

Doubters say there is not complete agreement among scientists about climate change or its causes. True. But the lack of 100 percent agreement is a canard. Over 95 percent of those studying climate change and the cause of climate change are agreed that there will likely be a three-foot rise in sea level within the next fifty years. How soon the sea level will rise to the extent that the rims of the continents will begin to be submerged at all tides is uncertain. What is certain is that such a change is underway. The only question is how fast the Greenland and Antarctic glaciers are melting to add their water volume to the world's oceans. To experience sea level increase that no one will be able to ignore, the earliest prediction is fifteen to twenty years. That is not long enough to make the changes needed, even if the doubters would agree.

The effect of these temperature and salinity changes upon fisheries and fish stock is becoming more certain: species are diminishing to alarming levels from climate change, not to mention human profligate and destructive behavior in overfishing that is depleting our oceans of edible fish.

The effect upon land is beginning to be acknowledged. Large areas of the earth that once were fertile and productive are becoming desertified. Wind and rain patterns are causing droughts in areas that always had abundant rain. Food supplies, not yet threatened, are in danger of declining to dangerous levels if the pattern of droughts continues.

I hate to close on a note of alarm, but it is called for. Those who understand must begin crying out for change until those in charge get the message. The future of civilization is at stake!

Nothing is easier than self-deceit. For what every man wishes,

that he also believes to be true.

—Demosthenes

#21 Organized Religion?

St. Gabriel's, a very small Episcopal Church in Hollis, Long Island, was less than 150 feet from my house. The minister's house was across the street from where we lived. Thomas J. Nagle and Elva, my grandpa and grandma (we lived next door to them), had been active in supporting that church from its founding. It was no wonder then that at age eight I was enrolled in the boys' choir. I have always loved singing, and being a part of organized group music making provides an experience like no other. The choir was an unexcelled experience for me in the power of music to cause joy in my life.

It was often suggested to me that perhaps I might want to become a minister. In spite of the example of two really superior men who became leaders of that church during my stay there, going into the church as a profession was absolutely unacceptable to me. As my voice changed and I started singing with the men, I joined the acolytes guild, assisting with the minister at the altar and also serving from time to time as a crucifer. Wearing the beautiful robes, the surplices, and white silk ropelike cinctures; performing the rituals; and helping to run the service brought with it a feeling of being a special person.

One Sunday, I was sixteen, sitting within the sanctuary, the space reserved for the minister and his helpers. I watched as Reverend W. delivered his weekly sermon. He was a very good speaker, animated in his delivery, his sermon full of pithy and relevant quotes. As I watched and listened, the realization came over me that we were putting on a really good show for the audience! I included myself in the cast. It was a performance. Quite good but a performance nonetheless.

From that moment on, organized religion and the experience of being at church became irrelevant to my life.

When our three children were young, in the Memorial Drive area of Houston, Texas, my wife, Joyce, thought that some religious training was important. So the whole family started attending Sunday school at the Memorial Drive Presbyterian Church, a dynamic church located less than a block away from our home. I could hardly stomach the pap that the volunteer teachers handed out as "gospel truth" but the kids got to draw, do puzzles, and mix with other bright children, so it was okay.

Charlie Shedd, the minister, organized a weekly series of self-help seminars and discussion groups for the young adults of the church, and I became a regular at those meetings. It was the time of bra burning for women. It was a time when the ideas that had formed the glue of society were being actively questioned and, often, rejected.

Do men have a feminine side? Should women be more assertive in a marriage? Was Jesus a man who was unafraid to show his feminine side? Can women balance the role of homemaker, child rearer, and industry worker? Can they survive, staying feminine, doing all that?

These and other questions for society are not yet answered in many cases. The very discussions were so threatening to Joyce that she stopped going. I continued, fascinated with the mundane and the metaphysical subjects being discussed. I found myself changing my basic ideas as a consequence of having to think about the topics chosen for groupthink.

I encouraged my girls to be more assertive, more independent, more a partner in any male relationship they established, and less accepting of the dominant male role often asserted by men. One evening at dinner, our usual time for the family to actively talk about whatever was going on, I suggested that the girls pay attention to women like Betty Friedan. I suggested the then-current protesting action of bra burning was a good sign of a womanly declaration of independence.

Joyce made a response that was later to be her mantra whenever I suggested something that was different from the world in which she had grown up. She said, "Oh, you don't *really* think that. That's not what you *really* think!"

In fact, that was what I did think. Her response was a troubling sign I didn't then see. The marriage was unraveling because one partner felt threatened that the other might have ideas that were changing and becoming different from what they had been. However we think and feel, if the ideas expressed represent basic aspects of ourselves too important to be denied and we see they are not accepted or at least tolerated by the other, a rupture of the relationship has started.

Charlie Shedd was too liberal and too aggressively ambitious to serve that congregation for a protracted period of time, even though he did guide the church through several years of spectacular growth. While tending his flock, he wrote several books and then took to the lecture circuit and was soon gone from Houston.

As radical Christian right groups have begun to show the power of their voting strength and to elect political types who will agree with or agree to follow the programs and policies of these churchy movements, I have begun to think about the place of organized religion in human society.

It has a place, and something like it would probably be invented if none existed. Being a member of a church offers many community advantages, not the least of which is a safety net of like-minded friends who will come to one's aid when times get rough. Churches, synagogues, and mosques also have a utility in providing a tested guide to youths developing their ethical principles about how to live in a complex society. The agreed set of rules for living that come from the Bible, the Koran, the Talmud, while not identical, each incorporate much of the same language in their rendition of the most basic rules of getting along. Infant, baby, young, and adult souls need this. Mature and old souls need it less or not at all. Transcendental souls have finished their experiences on earth as humans.

One of the prompts for this e-mail is an experience I recently had in the quite lovely town of Dublin, Georgia. Dublin is about two hours' drive from our home and a good place to stop for lunch when we travel by car to Atlanta. A very popular place to eat is the Old Time Buffet. Among the other diners there, a young man of about sixteen was wearing a shirt with the message "Darwin Lied" on the back. I asked him if he had studied biology in his high school, and he told me he had. I then asked if he had learned about evolution, and he nodded yes. So I asked him why he had those words on his shirt.

He said, "Evolution is a lie. Darwin was a liar. The schools are teaching things that are not true." I asked him how he learned that evolution was not true, and he said his pastor had told him so.

Readers who are members of authoritarian organized religions, like the Catholic Church, Pentecostal, and very conservative Christian right churches, such as the church this young man attended, may think what follows is nonsense. But read on if you are curious. You will likely find something to ponder.

The case for reincarnation I have offered elsewhere ("A Discovery Trip to Sweden," #30, and "Past Lives, Evidence For," #22). For now I am going to assume you have enough curiosity to continue and will either find the ideas intriguing or reject them, depending on the level of commitment to your own concept of how humans in this world are organized.

Briefly, there seems to be a general agreement that we exist as a combination of both the physical body and nonphysical energy (spirit or soul—I prefer the term soul). The soul is neither created nor destroyed; it simply is. The soul is like a spark of energy that exists with, though different and apart from, the physical body. We are not our body. We are our soul.

The soul is a creation of the Dao or some higher energy that, as humans, we do not know. "God" is the useful term that most acknowledge as the idea of the unknowable master energy of this life. The analogy of the trajectory of a human lifetime, from birth through old age, is a reasonable and reasonably accurate shorthand way to describe the transitions of the energy we call soul as it goes through many incarnations, using many physical bodies sequentially as it experiences life among other humans.

In my belief system, the soul starts its human experience in a physical body as an infant spirit. Souls choose the family into which they will be born and learn. Infant souls usually choose life near the equator, where the living experience is less stressful, where food is likely abundant and easily obtained, and where the soul can get used to being teamed up with a body for a lifetime. As the population of the earth has increased exponentially, it seems likely that there have been huge numbers of infant souls created by the Dao to meet the increased numbers of bodies needing souls.

Incarnations occur over millennia as physical bodies are available, and each soul sets out to have various learning experiences by choosing a human physical body to inhabit that will likely provide the environment for those experiences.

It is my belief that the soul pairs up with each new physical body it incarnates into at some time before or soon after birth, different times in each reincarnation experience as the soul evaluates whether the physical body and the environment in which the physical body is to live will provide the experience the soul wants to have in this lifetime. Life may well start with conception, but the soul in every body existed before the body started its life and will exist after that physical body dies.

Exactly when the soul and body unite to become one is not a matter of any real relevance. Except, there are some humans who do act as though they have no soul and, for all of us, when these apparently soulless bodies rip their way through society, the tragedies they cause among their fellow human beings are the grist for the tabloids we see at the checkout stands.

Observing humans in action, it is often quite apparent that a soul has chosen to experience a lifetime of service to others or of complete self-interest and self-absorption or of poverty or of opulence or of relaxation, etc. It does seem we chose and loosely follow a script for the pattern of each interval of human experience.

The understanding expressed here is an adaptation of the concept of soul development written about by Jose Stevens, a psychologist and psychic who channels spirit information from a group called Michael, also the name of the books he writes about the information they offer. The communications of Michael offered information about how spirits, or souls, join to be incarnate with physical human bodies and how spirits are created with basic personality traits which have overlays, permutations, and modifications in various lifetimes is compelling.

Personal observation confirms over and over that the structure Michael says is the basic framework for all spirits is all around us for anyone to see. Once I started looking with a hint of what to look for, the patterns are so obvious it is a wonder that it hasn't been recognized and written about before it was revealed to Jose Stevens from the spirit group Michael.

The United States in 2007 is showing itself to be a mix of predominantly young, adult, and mature souls, with few baby souls, fewer still infant souls and those last two groups mainly in the south. The ferment in the US political arena may well be due to an overbalance of young and young-adult souls that have a basic desire to experience power, money, and position.

Mature and old souls seem to be more prevalent on the upper east coast and along the western coastline up to the Canadian border. Their major learning concerns seem to be with creating a peaceful, stable world and with caring for all humanity. Ergo, we witness a marked and remarkable division between political philosophies dominant among the population on the US coasts as compared with those philosophies dominant in the interior and along the south rim of the country.

The Michael teaching are not all there is to know about humans on this planet, but from my own casual observation, much of the Michael explanations of why people are as they are and act as they do fit the actual human scene neatly and completely.

It is my experience that from about age sixteen to about age thirty, many of us frequently inquire into the whys and wherefores of human existence. As a part of your explorations of cosmology, when you wonder from time to time where you come from and where you go when this life is over, I recommend you seek out Jose's books and read more about Michael teachings. They will provoke some deep thoughts about life, whether you find the premise outlined there acceptable or not.

It seems likely that the United States will follow the path of Europe in gradually becoming more populated with old souls and more secular in terms of religiosity. Because old souls are less inclined toward competition and more inclined toward community and cooperation, the need for organized churches and a proscribed set of rules for living will diminish in this country, as has become the social pattern in most parts of Europe.

In the quest for the good life, the old teachings

are still relevant.

There is no question that, "to love thy

neighbor as thyself"

is the best way for humans to live together.

—GPD

#22 Past Lives, Evidence For

When you look in the mirror, who looks back at you?

The physical features tell us that it is us. We've seen that image before. When we brush our teeth, the person in the mirror and the person in front of the mirror are doing the same thing. It is easy to say "That's me." But who is me?

Is it the seventy or so trillion cells that have collected together in the form we call a body? Is that who is me?

When I look out at the mirror with eyes that see the shapes and colors of my body and when I hear my voice speaking, is that who is me?

Who is thinking the questions that I write? Who is directing my fingers to type on the keyboard all of the above? Do any of those actions, the first entirely cerebral, the second a combination of cerebral and physical, help me know who is me?

It is clear that the brain is the physical and the mind is the cerebral aspect of creating thoughts. But when the mind thinks thoughts, what is going on when those thoughts are shuffled and rearranged into multiple sequences that the mind then puzzles over, trying to arrive at a summary thought that something in me will accept as an answer or conclusion? And who is it that is doing all this thinking and working to find a conclusion?

Synapses in the brain that allow me to think are physical. The energy created by these synapses connecting, closing, and doing the physical part of thinking can be measured by sensitive devices invented to accomplish just such measuring. But after all the physical action of the brain, something else evaluates and decides if the conclusion arrived at is acceptable. Something evaluates and decides. Is that who is me?

Whatever, whoever is me, I am not the physical part of my body. I am not even the physical part of my brain, cells that somehow develop chemical-electrical energies that ebb and flow along the dendrites to create the synapses that form measurable amounts of activity in my brain. I might be the mind that thinks and questions and develops the answers of the questions pondered. But then again, I might not be that or not only that. I do seem to inhabit my body and there is no one else in here with me, but I am not my body.

I am, I think, simply an energy that temporarily uses my body to go places and do things. I am an energy that is neither created by birth nor destroyed by death. As an energy, if I behave as all other energies in this world, I can neither be created nor destroyed, only changed. I have no effective beginning and no end that I can know. I am the eternal part of life.

When I speak of the who that is me, that is the who I really am.

Reliving Past Lives: The Evidence under Hypnosis by Helen Wambach, PhD (Barnes & Noble 2000, a reprint of an earlier edition), is a book that first made me think about reincarnation in more than a desultory way. It ultimately persuaded me that the energy that inhabits each physical human body does so both temporarily and frequently. I have accepted and used the term "soul" to describe that energy because that is a common term and is generally accepted as a useful descriptive term for that energy.

That there are souls that do experience recurring cycles of human existence occupying a human body for a human lifetime and then exiting the body at the time of the death of the physical body, I accept as having a high probability of being the way thing really are.

Helen Wambach was a clinical psychologist doing work at UC Berkeley. Using a protocol she developed that followed scientific principles, using hypnosis on a broad collection of volunteers from the Berkeley area of California, she accumulated data on past lives that I'll describe in a moment.

The book is her collection of anecdotal and statistical evidence tending to establish the verity of past lives, that reincarnation is a fact, and that some information about one's past life could be accessed under hypnosis.

Hypnosis has been a trusted tool of psychiatry for decades. It can help access the roots of patient fears and anxieties. In many reported instances, hypnosis unlocked repressed early childhood memories allowing patient and healer to understand the thread of relationship between experienced youthful trauma and distress for which adult patients sought treatment.

The first published professional report of a past life unexpectedly popping up in such a treatment session, so far as I am aware, was by a psychiatrist in New York. He had no success in treating a patient with intractable alcoholism. Hypnosis was tried, bringing a totally unexpected result.

The patient, in a light trance, was asked to go back in memory to childhood. The doctor asked the patient to examine earlier and earlier life events. Nothing of any relevance to the alcoholism came forth.

The doctor focused on the birth process, which can be traumatic. The fetus, coming from a protected warm environment is (from the fetal point of view) rudely delivered into the world of bright lights and cold air. The process can be very traumatic for the baby. Again, however, no significant information was produced. He took the patient further back into fetal experience in the womb, still without anything useful related.

The psychiatrist reported he then decided to ask a question that opened up a whole new panorama of investigations into past lives. He asked, "Was there anything that happened before you were in the womb which now affects your craving for alcohol?"

There was. The patient offered a detailed description of being a soldier on a civil war battlefield, mortally wounded, companions plying him with whiskey to relieve the extreme pain. He died in an alcohol-induced haze.

The self-understanding that this account of how alcohol had provided ease from suffering in a prior life experience permitted the doctor and patient to successfully complete the treatment for alcoholism.

This small report, which must have taken a great deal of professional courage to make public, gave permission and encouragement to other psychiatrists to write of their own experiences exploring patients' past lives during therapy.

Several books by professionals in the United States and Canada have been published over the past two decades, recounting a multitude of clinical anecdotes of past life events being told by patients. Exploring past lives was beginning to be accepted as a useful, though unusual, tool of psychiatric therapy.

Reliving Past Lives is a persuasive treatment of the subject. Helen Wambach had the objective of using scientific methodology to verify (or not) that this phenomenon is real and that it is possible to bring forth accurate memories of actual past life events. Enlisting 1,088 volunteers in the San Francisco Bay area, she spent several years collecting and collating evidence of past lives her volunteers reported.

Using prepared scripts and controlled environments to move her own energies out of the way, with groups of twenty-five, she induced a light trance in her subjects and asked them to determine if they were alive at stated times. The time frames of her inquiries covered four thousand years.

Declaring a date, she asked her entranced subjects if they could "see" themselves as alive at that time. If they did, she asked them to look at their clothing and footwear, to go to the market, examine the shape of money being used, of things offered for sale, of structures and whatever else came into their "view." They were given suggestions that they were to remember what they had observed and recall that information after coming out of hypnosis. When the sessions were over, before any conversation or other distractions were allowed, the volunteers filled out long forms, reporting what they had visualized.

Not everyone reported being alive at each of the time periods she designated. None said they were anything but ordinary people, wearing ordinary clothes, doing ordinary things.

Wambach's interest was in statistics as well as psychotherapy. She applied statistical methods to analyze the accumulated data. In her book, she allowed the power of that data to argue the existence of past lives.

After translating into graphs the totals of those who reported being alive at various times over the years she explored, she took that information to UC Berkeley demographers. They compared her results to estimated world population numbers at those same times. There was a positive correlation between her graphs and the graphs of demographers of population totals over the four millennia explored. Descriptions by her volunteers of money, clothing, structures, and other things they observed while under hypnosis had similar positive correlations.

Dr. Ian Stephenson, (1919-2007), for many years chairman of the psychiatry department of the University of Virginia at Charlottesville, Virginia, became interested in past lives early in his career. Several studies he made have been published concerning children who reported recently lived past lives in the United States and India. His major work was *Reincarnation And Biology: A Contribution to the Etiology of Birthmarks and Birth Defects* (Prager, 1987).

The children investigated frequently told their new parents that they didn't belong where they were, describing other places where they said they should be in specific detail. Taken to those places, the children showed unexpected familiarity with these often distant and, to the parents, new locations. On more than one occasion, the children retrieved objects they had known about in their past lives, objects and locations that were unknown to the then-present occupants.

The whole idea of humans being able to access a detailed, specific, and correct memory of events occurring before their own conception strikes those who seek scientific certainty in such matters as ridiculous. Replication by others, the gold standard of proof in scientific inquiry, so far, has not occurred.

The experiences reported are all anecdotal. Yet the published evidence of past lives is compelling. Most of it strikes one as completely credible.

One anecdote of recent broad dissemination, I find particularly persuasive.

A young Australian woman, who at the time of first recounting to friends that she had lived a life before as a Scottish physician, had never been away from her home area in Australia. She offered detailed information about his life, including his name, office address, and particulars about his education, including attendance at a still-extant medical college in Scotland.

Investigators verified that a physician with such a name had indeed lived when she said he had lived and had indeed attended the school she described during the years she said he was a medical student there. Her statements about the location of his medical office, residence, and other details of the life of this mid-eighteenth-century doctor were similarly confirmed as factual and accurate.

The young woman's description of the layout of the medical college her past life person attended was quite detailed. Investigators thought they had her for fraud when they compared her description of student living quarters, teaching rooms, and other specifics of building design to what existed and found some glaring discrepancies.

It would have all been attributed to other than a true past life report except that the college librarian came forward with plans of the buildings, long in storage to which only he had access, which showed the student and classroom layout over two centuries before exactly as she had described them when the long-dead doctor had attended the school as a medical student. A video of this story has recently been available at bookstores around the country that specialize in things paranormal.

Christian churches talk about our having souls. Christianity, for a short time after its initial organization, agreed that reincarnation was a likely part of human life. That concept was discarded in favor of a more limited and controllable idea: that man did have a soul which, with close attention to church rules, could exist in a pleasant afterlife or with behavior that was otherwise consigned to eternal unpleasantness.

Since the church controlled knowledge and the propagation of information about such things, that was the concept that carried forward and the concept that is generally held today, except in Buddhism, Hinduism, Sikhism, and other Indian religions that do accept reincarnation as a fact of existence.

Our Western world is wrong.

The who that is me is an energy, subject to the laws of all energy. I am eternal. I cannot be created. I cannot be destroyed.

I am in my present body for an indeterminate (within physical limits) period of time, and when that body no longer functions and decays, the energy that is me will continue somewhere with the strong likelihood that it will return to this earth and take up another temporary residence in another body at some time in the future.

So are we all energies that have recycled before and will likely recycle to this physical world again and again?

If for no other reason, we should look out carefully for the health of the earth. We do not want to come back to an earth which is barren, polluted, and a difficult place for our new body to enjoy the lovely benefits of human existence.

[N]ow voyager, set thou forth to seek and find.

—Walt Whitman

SECTION 2:

LIVING MY WAY

#23 My Time with the Circus

When I showed up at the lot in Hartford, Connecticut, where the Ringling Bros., Barnum & Bailey Circus tent was set up, it was late Sunday afternoon. There was another show to do that evening, and then the circus would be packed up, loaded onto flat cars, and moved by train to the next stop—Albany, New York. I was sixteen years old.

I wandered around the area until I found the temporary corrals set up for the horses. Show horses and work horses were segregated into separate enclosures. Wranglers were doing what men who work around horses always do—carrying feed buckets, filling water troughs, wiping down horses that had been sweating in the July heat, and shoveling the manure into large metal trash cans. I had severed my ties with the Connecticut dairy farm, where I had worked for six weeks, and wanted a job. Confident of my ability to do whatever needed doing with horses, I asked for the man in charge.

He was gone but it didn't matter. The wranglers' response to my query about work was, "If you want to work here, you need a draft card."

Of course, at sixteen, in 1941, I did not have one.

What I hadn't known when I headed to Hartford to join the circus was that the circus insurance company did not allow anyone under the age of eighteen to work with the animals, and while I was big enough to pass for eighteen, without that draft card, I couldn't bluff my way into a job.

No worry! My guides sent a rough-mannered, good old boy to work things out. While I was being turned away from the horse corral, the circus health inspector and operator of the ice-based cool air machines that were used with the big top happened by. He heard the turndown and asked if I really wanted a job. He said he was an independent contractor and so could hire me to work as his employee on the air-cooling trailers. He didn't have to follow the circus corporate rules.

Effectively, I would be like one of the circus employees, sleeping in a circus bunk car, eating at the circus chow tent, and paid by the circus payroll clerk. But I would only do the work he assigned. Of course, I said yes, and so, that night, I was on the Ringling Circus train, in an upper bunk of a sleeping car, heading for Albany.

The circus at that time used four-wheeled wagons to carry and move just about everything they needed to create their show. Wild animals, show animals, sideshow exhibits, tent canvas, poles, ropes, chairs, and stands—everything moved to and from the circus train on or in these wagons.

They were nearly all a standard-size box of about eight feet wide, eight feet high (above the axles), and fourteen feet long. Each had two axles, and each axle had two automobile-type wheels with inflated rubber tires. A few had open-spoke thirty-six-inch wheels clad in steel dating from the early, early days of the circus, the war having interrupted the change to rubber tires. There was a drawbar long enough to accommodate a pair of draft horses and some still had harness ring hitches. A buckboard seat at the top front with a foot board and brake pedal identified the place from which, in earlier times, hostlers had controlled the teams of horses that moved the wagons.

From the beginning days of traveling circuses, horses were the main motive power. By the time I joined, wagons were pulled from the rail siding to the circus lot in caravans of up to four wagons, each drawbar attached to the wagon ahead and the front wagon pulled by a Mack truck we called a bobtail. It was hardly more than a cab over an engine—short, stubby, and powerful.

The Ringling Circus moved from venue to venue on railroad-type flat cars. Three old-time steam locomotives pulled three circus trains. When the trains reached the rail yard, portable bridges were put in position between the ends of the flat cars so that wagons could be rolled along the whole train to a ramp at the end, where they then descended to the ground and were assembled into wagon trains to be pulled to the circus lot.

Elephants were often used to move the wagons, one by one, along the flat cars; a long chain or rope was connected from a leatherwork harness that fitted around the huge beasts' shoulders to a pull ring on each wagon. Low sides on the flat cars kept the wagon wheels from wandering.

Mahouts using a stick with a metal prod on one end guiding and controlling the elephants usually rode up astride the elephant's neck, jabbing and hitting the big beasts about the head and ears to direct their movement.

One early morning, after traveling during the night to the next city, lying in my bunk and watching the unloading process through a small window in the sleeping car, I witnessed a mahout being particularly rough. The elephant trumpeted its objection and then, when it had enough rough handling, reached back with its trunk, grabbed the man, and threw him flying across the open area between the unloading trains. The mahout was immediately attended to by other workers, and the elephant was unhitched and led off to some other location. A tractor was brought over to continue the unloading. The mahout did get up, apparently not seriously injured, and the process of unloading never slowed down.

The assembled wagon trains had remarkable agility and were able to turn corners and maneuver through the streets of the towns and cities on the tour. Single wagons that held wild animals in cages and wagons that were part of circus acts were often hauled through the streets singly, with draft horses or elephants as the motive power, for the show of it.

The first wagons to move to the lot contained the huge mound of canvas that was the big top, covering as much as 180 by 75 feet. Laying out the canvas in its proper place, erecting the three tall center poles, and driving the stakes to which tent lashings attached was the job of the roustabouts. At that time, roustabouts were all very large powerfully built African American men.

Stakes to secure the tent were shafts of steel, about thirty inches long, pointed at one end, and splayed at the other from being pounded by ten-pound sledgehammers these roustabouts handled with such ease. After a stake was tapped into its place by the foreman, fixing both the location and angle needed to hold the strain of the tent ropes, four men would surround the stake, and one of them would call out a beginning short chant, setting the rhythm and his hammer would be the first to ring out, as it started the stake into the ground. Then each would swing his hammer in turn, striking the stake with a fast-paced rhythm and synchronicity that was astonishing to watch and hear. Each stake was fully positioned and secured in place in about fifteen seconds. The crew moved around the circumference of the spread-out canvas until all stakes were in place.

Before setting up the three center poles, the rigging crew threaded ropes through pulleys near the top of each pole and then attached the ends of the ropes to metal rings sewn into the canvas. A ring was positioned around the base of each pole during the layout of the tent on the ground. When the stakes were in place, elephants were the power that lifted the huge canvas into place. Fifty or so peripheral tent poles, each about four inches in diameter and twelve feet long, then had to be positioned to lift and support the outside perimeter of the tent. Ropes secured these poles to the stakes, and the roustabouts came in a team again, stretching each rope on each support pole, until the top of the tent was taught.

Raising the tent was a performance in itself. Each roustabout had several specific responsibilities, all of which required skill, strength, agility, and timing. The combined efforts of humans and animals performing this feat was in some ways as exciting as watching the show itself.

Once the big top was up, another crew positioned the show rings, sawdust and wood chips were scattered and raked, and the seats and the bandstand were all put into position for the first show.

While the top was going up, it was my job to duck underneath the ascending canvas and attach rings of colorful ribbons to each cool air outlet. These were designed to flutter when cool air came into the tent through canvas vent tubes sewn onto the tent top. All of this had the intention of persuading the public, sweltering below in the stands, that they were being cooled.

In fact, the system did drop the temperature in the big top several degrees. The six "cooler wagons" placed at intervals around the tent each held four 250-pound blocks of ice and a circulating pump to move water over the ice and then down a screen through which a forty-inch fan forced air into the canvas vent tubes. The added moisture from this design also made the interior of the big top, already steamy from the body heat of nearly twelve hundred excited people and the perspiration of a great many hardworking performers and animals, oppressively humid.

My work was not hard and quickly done. Ice was obtained from a local icehouse and transferred to the cooler wagons by noon. I turned on the circulating pumps and fans in the six wagons shortly before the matinee at two and off after the show at about four. I was free during the performance and until needed before the evening show that was usually at six thirty to about eight thirty.

In the early summer, the show let out in time for the crowds to have plenty of time to visit the carnival-like midway of freaks, clowns, the two-headed calf, the bearded woman, the tallest man, the shortest midget, the fattest person, and the like.

Right after the evening performance, the big top came down much faster than it went up. When the chairs and stands had been taken away, the ribboned rings around the cooler vents needed to be separated from the canvas before the tent hit the ground. It was a part of my job to detach the rings and secure them in an equipment chest.

I was provided an inverted Y step-ladder-straight-ladder combination for this work. The delta-shaped stepladder part was ten feet high with an eight-foot, round-rung, two-rail ladder for the upper part. This upper section rose straight up from between the two sections of the lower ladder. When the ladder was extended its full length, I could climb, straddling the upper ladder, one foot on each side, like climbing a flexible rope ladder, and get close enough to the canvas to reach and detach the rings, which were about fifteen feet above the ground.

I usually had someone to brace and steady the ladder and help move it. Occasionally though, after doing it several times, I learned how to balance my weight and do the whole thing myself. When I look back on it, I wonder at the confidence I had. But then, I was sixteen, and sixteen-year-olds can do anything.

One helper was a young member of the circus electrical crew, who became both a friend and protector, something I had no idea at that time I needed. Brad and five of his friends, all circus workers, all gay, were my first contact with a part of society about whom, at my then age, I had only the vaguest idea.

These were probably the most event-filled weeks of my life, as I traveled with the Ringling Bros., Barnum & Bailey Circus across New York State and into Pennsylvania, ending in Pittsburgh. From Pittsburgh, I traveled back to my family's home in Hollis, Long Island, by bus, just in time to enjoy an eventful sail-canoe trip with a friend on the Great South Bay of Long Island. And then it was back to Brooklyn Technical High School that fall.

While I never did work with horses for Ringling, I did have the chance to work spotlight for a trapeze act and during the opening lion and tiger act. But this is enough for now. Those stories and others will come later.

Live simply.   Love generously.   Care deeply.

—Anonymous

#24 Milk Run

My family believed that fresh air at night was vitally important for growing boys. In January 1936, that was Bruce, my four-year-old brother, and ten-year-old me.

My room was on the corner of the front of the house, with a single window looking out over the front porch roof. Across Hiawatha Avenue, a streetlight always shone welcome beams into my room. I knew that bears and other ugly things hid under the bed and lurked in the dark corners of the room and that they did not like beams of light. So I welcomed them.

The street then was lined on both sides with mature maples. The boughs arched across the narrow pavement, interlocking into a canopy of limbs. In the summer, the leaves were big and green, and there was an easy illusion that our street was really a green canyon.

The memories of early mornings during that winter are mixed and run together because there were so many alike. That year fills my mind as a time of heavy snows. On our driveway, many storms left undrifted snow as high as my skinny knees. Frequently the snow fell quietly and piled on the porch roof higher than the outside sill of my window. Snow would form a small white ridge on the inner sill while I slept. Many were the mornings that winter when I awakened, able to see my breath in the beam from the streetlight.

Sometimes it was vital for me to keep focused on getting up and getting to the bathroom (which felt like a haven of tropical warmth when the rest of the house was freezing). I had an embarrassing memory of the time that I woke up with a full bladder, resisted getting out of bed into the freezing air the open window allowed into my room and fell asleep again, only to awaken later to the warm, wet knowledge of having made a really bad decision. This memory was usually enough to force me up onto the icy floor, to close the window, and run to the bathroom.

But there were mornings when I was awakened by other than a full bladder.

Rankin Dairy was located at Jamaica Avenue and Francis Lewis Boulevard, not far from our house. Home delivery service was available for milk and other dairy products, as well as for vegetables and bakery goods. Mr. Bolton was our milkman, and in the dark hours of the early morning, with my window open on the street, I was often awakened by the friendly, comforting, unmistakable sounds of milk delivery.

The horses that pulled the Rankin wagons were beautiful. These were not the show Clydesdales we see pulling show beer wagons today but were work horses, marginally smaller than Clydesdales but still big. Mr. Bolton's horse was the color of cafe au lait with flax mane and tail. From my window over the porch roof, seeing that horse and wagon coming up the street, he was, I thought, beyond handsome. But those mornings when there had been an overnight quiet snowfall and the horse was breaking a trail through virgin snow, even at ten years old, I was able to recognize the beauty of the scene.

The first sound that usually brought me awake was the clink of the bottles. Mr. Bolton had a metal rack that held eight standard-size bottles. Full bottles and empties each had their own distinctive sound. With his carry rack full, he walked to the rear of each house on his route, opened the milk box at the edge of the back stoop, exchanged empties for full bottles, and filled any orders—left there by the housewives on scraps of paper—for extra milk, butter, or cream. He carried enough full bottles to service three or four houses without having to go back to the wagon.

When the air was really frigid, the wooden milk box was incapable of keeping the milk, already ice cold, from freezing.

This was before homogenization, and about two inches of heavy cream floated on top of the milk in each bottle. When the milk froze, as it frequently did that winter in the city, the cream expanded straight up out of the bottle, ready to be lifted off, put into a pitcher, and allowed to thaw for enjoyment in coffee or other uses that our family had for heavy cream.

While Mr. Bolton moved from house to house, the horse moved along too, positioning the wagon in front of the house where past experience told him there would be a need to refill the rack. The horse was very businesslike in this routine. He would occasionally snort, and when the air was particularly cold, clouds of vapor would condense in front of him. Two small harness bells were affixed to the top of his halter so that any head movement would cause a tinkling sound. The horse seemed to like this because often he would shake his head, causing the small bells to ring out as though saying, "here I am, look at me." I could see him paying attention to the process, keeping up with Mr. Bolton, doing his part of the job.

Rankin Dairy used rubber shoes on their horses, but that only made the sound of hooves striking the pavement more distinctive. Instead of the bright clip-clop of steel, the sound was softer, more mellow, and rounder. I loved it. In the snow, the sound of horse hooves was nearly completely lost, but there was the creak of the harness leather, the rattle of the harness chains, the clink of the bottles, and Mr. Bolton's occasional clucking and soft word signals to his coworker. In the dark early morning hours, through my open window, these were sounds that, for me, meant a little more time to stay under the covers.

One doesn't think of snow as having a smell, yet after a quiet snowfall, there is a distinctive, evanescent fragrance in the air. I learned to expect it when, leaning out my window, I curled a quilt around my shoulders and watched the horse move and wait, move and wait for Mr. Bolton. In the circle of light on the snow, exactly opposite my window, horse and wagon stopped, there was nothing but unbroken white ahead. Then he must have sensed that Mr. Bolton would need the wagon at a place further up the street. From behind a house, the man appeared just as the horse reached the new location and stopped. Deliveryman and delivery horse, both stolidly performing their duties, left a history of their morning's moves in new fallen snow. The scene was magical.

When the duo had passed out of hearing and out of sight, I brushed the snow from the inner sill, closed the window, and jumped back in bed to await the first of two possible events: either my father would get up, shake up the coal fire in the furnace, and the radiator would signal that the house was on its way to becoming warm and comfortable or my bladder would demand attention and, regardless of the cold, my feet would have to brave the icy floor.

That reminds me of another stark difference between the growing-up time of all of you grandchildren and my own young life.

Today there is hardly any aspect of home life that is not controlled by a switch or some electrical or electronic controller. Thermostats are a good example and lead into the story I want to tell you about growing up in the 1930s. With the thermostat, one cannot only control whether the heat or cooling equipment is on and operating, but also ambient household temperature.

In the New York City winter, our house, with wood flooring and rugs only in the major living area and hall, had cold floors, sometimes really cold floors. Getting out of bed in the morning, bare feet on icy floors, was a bit of a shock to my system. With the outside temperature in the twenties or below overnight, the inside of the house often became cold enough for me to see my breath, not only in my bedroom, where, as I mentioned, the window was at least cracked open, if not widely opened, but in every room but the bathroom, of which there was one in our three-bedroom home.

Heat in our home was a traditional setup in those days, consisting of a furnace in the basement that heated hot water distributed by a piping system to one or more radiators in each room. Each radiator had a valve by which one could vary or turn off the flow of hot water. In order to keep the bathroom relatively warm at night, whatever heating water there was went to that one radiator; all other radiators were turned to low.

When I was about twelve, my father developed tuberculosis, a not uncommon disease in those days and extremely debilitating. The cure was complete bed rest, and for this, hospital sanitariums were built across the country. In these, people with TB stayed for as long as it took for their lungs to push off the disease and return to some sort of functionality. Lungs seldom recovered completely, so TB was really a death sentence for most, although it usually took years for the final loss of lung function to occur.

Tending the coal furnace became my job when my father went to the sanitarium. The furnace was a coal-fired monster that heated not only the water needed for the house heating system, but also for bathing and cooking as well.

Coal was delivered, several tons at a time by the truckload, through a basement window, into a coal bin across from the furnace. A small opening at the bottom of the coal-bin wall allowed me to use a big flat shovel to scoop up several pounds of coal at a time to shovel into the furnace.

The objective was to never let the fire go out. The challenge was I couldn't put enough coal in the furnace the keep the fire going all night at the same intensity needed to keep the house warm in the daytime. Ingenuity solved that problem early in our human history: banking the fire.

Banking a fire has two parts: the first is to allow the fire to burn down to a bed of smoldering coal, the gases having all burned out and nothing left but glowing chunks of dense anthracite remaining. Then using ashes that have fallen into the ash pit at the bottom of the furnace, those glowing coals are covered with ash, the damper arranged so that just enough air is allowed through the grates under the coals to keep a small amount of oxygen available so the coals don't smother and not so much that they burn themselves up overnight. That allowed some heat to be generated, enough to keep one radiator hot if all the others were turned to low or off.

To say that my job was important would greatly understate the vital part the fire tender plays in a cold climate.

Of equal importance to properly banking the fire at night was the job of rousing the fire in the morning. Cold floors or not, icy air or not, I was first up in the morning, down to the basement to get the fire started, sending hot water to all the radiators, and making the house comfortable for my mother, brother, and me.

Then there was the chore of removing ashes (daily) from the bottom of the fire pit into an ash can and up the steps of the basement (once a week) to be set out for the New York City ash collection service. The basement steps to the outside were covered by what was called a cellar door, a five-foot wide, two-panel door that sloped at about a forty-five-degree angle from the side of the house down to where the steps to the basement began.

It was this common outside architectural contrivance that stimulated the childish activity to "slide down my cellar door," great fun almost any time of the day and a great place to position small cars to create races down the cellar door. When ice-covered, as it was after every snowstorm, that cellar door was terrific as a slide. It was a short but intensely enjoyable ride. Getting to the icy top of the door was a challenge that kept all of us ice sliders in stitches.

Maneuvering the ash can with one hundred pounds or more of weekly coal ash up eight relatively narrow steps took some time doing. I probably weighed less than that can full of ash most weeks. But taking it slowly and levering the bottom of the can up, step by step, I was able to do it. Only once did the can slip from my grasp and tumble down again to the basement floor, spilling ash and making a great mess. That one incident made all my future efforts up those steps so careful I did not repeat that disaster again.

When the fire went out, as it did when I forgot to feed it coal or didn't bank it properly, was a lesson in doing things when they need to be done that I never forgot.

Here is something my grandfather told me that has proved useful.

It is about accepting responsibility.

You can quickly take the heat out of a potential argument by saying,

"I'm responsible for that."

Even when you are not, or think you are not, responsible, saying that you are defuses potential anger and allows what could be an argument or confrontation to become something that can be rationally discussed. In most instances it is not who was responsible that is important so much as it is how are we going to resolve this.—GPD

#25 Two Continents-Three Centuries

A bit of history came to my mind during a tai chi class this morning. I have been fortunate during my life to have been connected, in one way or another, to two continents and three centuries. It involves my paternal and maternal families. Let me explain.

In the mid 1990s, I decided to try to find where my paternal great grandfather came from. The library in Austin, Texas, where I was then living, was able to get the microfiche records of census rolls from 1850 to 1920, except for 1890 census records lost to a fire. The first record of William Nagle was in the US Census rolls in 1870. He was listed as living in the Borough of Kings (Brooklyn), New York, as a jewelry salesman, age twenty-two, and listed Ireland as his country of origin.

My three-year-old perception of him was that he was tall, thin, and jolly and had a bristly mustache that smelled of tobacco, something that made me try to squirm away when I was placed on his lap. I remember being at Grandma's house when his funeral procession passed and being told that it was not something the family thought I should go to. It looked like a parade to me, and I really thought I was being punished by being excluded.

Those memories came back as I landed in Ireland and immediately set out for Cork, a city on the southeast coast of Ireland, from which great numbers of emigrants left. I had enough memory of family talk that I knew that was where William, my great-grandfather, had likely embarked from when he emigrated to the US.

I had landed in Dublin and explored that city for a couple of days, the light drizzle that continued for those two days in mid-April being a normal part of the Irish weather. The Dublin harbor is not much changed from a century and a half ago, according to the men I talked to there. It is edged and pierced with quays, where vessels once bound away from that ravaged island took on their ragged cargo.

There is a quay in Dublin called the death quay because so many people who passed along its tar-timbered pathways in the mid-eighteen hundreds died of hunger while waiting for ships to take them to a new land and a new life. The great Irish potato famine decimated the Irish population.

The ones who didn't die of hunger, migrated not only to America, Canada, and Australia but also to Mexico and Argentina as well. There are many towns and people in Mexico with Irish names. That surprised me until I researched the destinations of the Irish emigration during their hardest of hard times. Hungry they may have been, but they hadn't lost their Irish. They went to the places that offered the greatest hope for prosperity.

In the city of Cork, I walked around the square that forms the *centre ville*. Many of the buildings contained law offices, and the name Nagle appeared as solicitor and barrister so often I was certain this area was where my great grandfather, William, had originated. There is also a range of hills named Nagle Mountains that offered further proof of the likelihood our family progenitor came from that region.

And circumstantial proof was all I was able to find. In the city port records and church after church, the recorders and lay caretakers told me that the old records had been lost or consumed in a fire or eaten by rodents or otherwise had disappeared. It was not possible to find any list of those who had departed Cork sometime about 1865-1869, the period my great grandfather must have left Ireland in order to first appear in the US Census (1870) as a twenty-two-year-old living and working in Brooklyn.

The other vicarious connection with the European land mass was my mother. Born in 1899 on a small farm in the area of Enkoping (pronounced "en-chirping") about fifty miles west of Stockholm, Signe was twelve when war clouds started to gather. Her two older sisters had already emigrated to the United States (living in Brooklyn as it happened), and her parents, Karl and Ida Johanson, sent her to live safely with her sisters in America.

She and my father found each other at the New York State Institute for Applied Agriculture. Graduating in 1921, the giddy flapper stage of American society in its flamboyant beginnings both wanted the simple rural farm life as opposed to the grind of industry and commerce (early hippies maybe?). My contact with my mother was brief. I was born in March 1925 on the small egg farm they established in Plattekill, New York. Signe contracted tuberculosis a month after I was born, a near-certain death sentence in those days. In fact, she lived only another thirteen months in a sanitarium in Saranac Lake, New York.

I visited the farm where she had grown up. A neighbor lady, in her nineties, who had played with my mother, showed me where she and Signe used to play with dolls, on a natural shelf of a large rock outcropping near the still-standing farmhouse. She gave me a Husqvarna kerosene lamp from the home that Karl and Ida had given her when they moved away.

Her grandfather, Karl Johann Frojd (Freud), had been a soldier in the Swedish army. His family name was Gry but in a macabre sense of humor, the Swedes renamed all their soldiers with names that had the intent of influencing the attitudes of these mostly rural peasants. "Frojd" means "happy" in Swedish, and that was what he was called until discharged. Upon discharge, about 1876, he was given a plot of land along the north shore of Lake Malaren, where (1878) he built a mill driven by wind and became a miller to the area.

I visited that mill, no longer operating but still in excellent condition, now called Grysta Mill, and marveled at the sixteen-inch-square wooden beams that formed the frame and the even larger wooden beams that supported the second floor, where the milling machinery was connected to the four enormous vanes that caught the wind and powered the mill.

Connections to another century, another continent.

But there is more. My grandfather, T. J., owned a warehouse for his business; and on the property was a building that had formerly housed the local fire brigade wagon with adjacent stalls for two sturdy horses to pull it. A cupola topped the front of the building with a large alarm bell still in place to call volunteers to their duty. This all dated from about 1880, before the advent of municipal fire departments with trucks and pumpers and professional firemen.

The building was about thirty feet long and about fourteen feet wide. A large wagon, with firefighting equipment, was kept in the building and lined up with the tongue of the wagon nearly reaching the front doors. The equipment consisted of a big tank for water, a two-man hand pump and several hoses. Above the wagon tongue, a leather harness for each horse was suspended on ropes controlled by pulleys above where the horse would stand on either side of the tongue. The pulleys and old harnesses were still in place when I was a kid and interested in such things.

Cleverly designed, when the horses were brought from their stalls at the side of the building and backed into place, the two harnesses were lowered in place, and both horses could be fully attached to the wagon in less than a minute (according to my grandpa, who was on the volunteer fire brigade at that time).

Two large barnlike front doors opened onto the street. When thrown back, the whole front of the building opened wide. Horses and wagons could exit at a full gallop. The time it took to bring the horses from their stalls, place them in front of the wagon, drop the harness, complete the hook up to the wagon, and be out the door on the way to the fire was less than three minutes.

According to Grandpa, the horses knew their part. They would move quickly into place, one on either side of the tongue, and stand quivering expectantly until the harness was fastened and the driver on the wagon, and then all would burst out the door at a furious pace.

Hillside Avenue, the main east-west road of Long Island, paralleled a ridge of small hills that the Laurentian Glacier had left when it melted. Dug into the side of those hills, just off Hillside Avenue, near my home, were the ruins of an inn dating from colonial time and used until the latter part of the nineteenth century. Abandoned, not much was left when I was growing up, except a crumbled portion of the stone foundation of the main building and four adjoining stalls. But it was a great place for my imagination about how it all might have been and whether George Washington stayed there during his campaign on Long Island.

T. J., my grandfather, had grown up working in New York City. He related stories of early horse-drawn passenger trolley cars that operated on Broadway. When the cars were loaded and the tracks went up a small incline, the passengers would have to get off and help push the car up the hill. It was even more of a problem in the winter when snow and ice would complicate travel. The weight was just too much for the power of only two horses in good weather. In the winter, passengers often had to walk beside the trolley, even on the flat, because the horses couldn't get traction on the ice and snow.

The fire brigade building, the crumbled foundations of a colonial inn, the horse-drawn trolleys of New York City—each a part of my connection to another century each long gone.

Long gone too is the supply chain of food and other essentials to local households that was common in the early days of the twentieth century. Ubiquitous street vendors of many necessary products for the home were major suppliers to household larders when I was a boy.

Milk and dairy products came by horse-drawn wagons. The milkmen using their wagons as portable supply depots and, walking their predawn routes, delivered products to the back stoops of urban houses just before the time most families would be waking. The iceman was another who, before the invention of the Frigidaire, delivered ice to every house on the block every other day, filling the venerable ice boxes every home had with twenty-five-pound chunks of blue-white ice.

Bakery trucks had home delivery routes. Usually they operated during the daylight hours and often also hawked their wares in a gentile sort of way. The trucks had unique horns that the drivers would sound as they travelled along the streets, inviting housewives to come out and select breads and pastries for their families.

Produce vendors plied the streets, some in flatbed trucks, other with mule or donkey-powered wagons. Fresh vegetables and greens were displayed along the perimeter of these peripatetic vehicles, a large weighing scale swinging on a back corner. They would cry out their presence in a songlike call that told everyone they were near. Housewives would gather to buy fresh vegetables for dinner and share some neighborly gossip as they shopped.

In the summer, pedestrian vendors brought fresh-picked strawberries, peaches, other summer fruits, as well as large bundles of cut flowers, to the neighborhoods, often carrying them in baskets on their heads. In New Orleans, where I lived for a few months in the summer of 1947, the lyrical voices of those men and women echoed along St. Charles Street and the neighborhoods to the north of that lovely boulevard, crying out their wares of fruit, crawfish, and other edibles; they were the purveyors of (delicious) fast food of the time.

Who could forget the ice-cream wagons that played their tinkling melodies as they cruised the streets in the summer, luring children from often stifling houses, offering ice cream and flavored ices that tickled and delighted the tongue. Of all the street vendors of the past, the ice cream vendors have lasted.

The others are long gone and, by those under fifty, never even known.

And these are only some of the things that were common connections to life in the early—to mid-twentieth century that are mostly probably entirely gone and mostly forgotten. They have been replaced by a supply chain of large and well-stocked stores that offer more than fresh and preserved foods. They offer shopping for foods plus a broad variety of other household needs that is systematized, efficient, and probably much more sanitary than the process I have described; but the personal touch is no longer there. I knew the Rankin Dairy man who brought dairy products to our back door and the Duncan Bakery man who supplied our family with fresh bread, doughnuts, and cakes.

What can I say about the changes in transportation, communication, and entertainment that have come rushing in with the twenty-first century? For those of my age, the kaleidoscope of technological transformations is bewildering and a little frightening. How can we keep up? I don't know any friends my age who will not admit their trepidation at using the new phones that are more of a computer than a communication device. Yet here we are, not competing; we're mostly retired and out of the work force but engaged and trying to keep up nonetheless.

But it all has made me ponder the connections I have with the past. The few markers of forgotten aspects of society I related are but a few of the myriad of changes that have occurred in my lifetime. When you reach the age I am today, you will undoubtedly look back with some degree of melancholy at the many markers of your lives that have either been lost or have been modified to such an extent the essence you remember is gone.

How many time have I said nothing is permanent except change? It is true. It is the way of life.

The saying goes:

There are only two things certain in life,

death and taxes.

To truly understand life,

we must not omit the third certainty;

change!

—GPD

#26 City Kid on a Farm

In the spring and summer of 1941, our country was gearing up for war. In Europe, war had been raging since the spring of 1939. In this country, men were enlisting in the army in large numbers. Economic times here were still very bad, and work was not easy to find. Many simply wanted to earn the $30 a month, room, and board that the armed forces offered. Many, though, were really concerned about our friends in Great Britain, whose fate at the hands of the strong Nazi war machine was in grave doubt.

Although it would be several months until Pearl Harbor, the government was actively building our armed services with recruiting posters up everywhere and the need for a draft already decided. The problem was that men leaving the farms to enlist put that year's harvest in peril from lack of manpower.

But there was help for the country's needs. Boys fifteen to seventeen, too young to enlist but generally strong enough to do most farmwork, would be free during three months of the summer and could help do the work that men were not there to do. In towns and villages, young men were already often occupied doing work that would qualify as farmwork. But in the cities, a huge reservoir of boys was potentially available to help the country in its time of need.

I was sixteen years old and in my junior year at Brooklyn Technical High School. My extracurricular work was as an announcer at WNYC, the radio station for the schools of the city of New York. Brooklyn Tech was located in its own ten-story building. The studios and control room of WNYC were located in half of the top floor of school; our open, but completely fenced, play area occupied the other half of the tenth floor. One of the announcements I was assigned to read was about the summer farm program. The call was for volunteers to work on farms during the summer of 1941.

I volunteered. City boys would need some training. So in the early spring of 1941, there would be a week of learning farm skills during the Easter school recess for all accepted for this work. And then from June 1 to August 31, boys would be helping their country by performing farmwork instead of hanging around the streets of the city.

My week of introduction to farmwork was at the New York State Institute of Applied Agriculture in Farmingdale, Long Island. I had a connection to that school already, for that is where my mother and father met while they were both studying there in 1920.

The week I was there, snow was still on the ground, and in the mornings, an ice skim coated the puddles. Although I had been born on a small chicken/egg farm near Newberg, New York, that my father and mother were operating, from age three on, I had been a resident of the New York City suburban area of Queens. My father would talk longingly of farm life, and we would occasionally drive back to where he had his farm, giving me the chance to inhale the smells and hear the sounds of farm life. But I was really a city kid. The week of initiation into actual work in a real farm environment was an eye-opener.

Horses were then still a major source of farm power, and the horses at NYSIAA were huge Belgian Greys, standing more than six feet tall at the withers. Their ears were a foot or more above my own head, and I was then a skinny six foot two. Still, they were gentle geldings. They allowed me to curry their backs and necks where I could reach. If one decided to throw back his head, I had no way of reaching high enough to even put on a halter, much less curry all the mane or comb the forelock that came between the ears over on to the forehead.

They knew more about getting into the harness for work than I did and would stand patiently while I sorted through the straps and poles that connected them to the farm implements, sometimes glancing back to look at me as though concerned that this obviously unskilled kid might not know how to do what needed to be done. Often enough, I did not.

There were quick courses in feeding and care of poultry flocks, sheep, and dairy cows; in using milking machines; and in learning how to operate planting and harvesting machines. The courses were intensive and broad. By the time the week was over, I felt like a farm kid. What I didn't know was how brief and perfunctory this introduction had been and that there was still a lot to learn about bringing in the harvest or whatever I was going to be assigned to do.

On May 31, with the spring semester of high school just finished, my parents drove me to Grand Central Station in the heart of New York City, where I caught the train that would take me to Union, Connecticut, the town nearest the farm where I had signed on to work.

The farmer, Mr. Nelson, and his wife met me and drove me to their dairy farm, about ten miles south of town. I was given the attic room, with a nice view of the farmyard and the barns. It came equipped with a small dresser, the usual pitcher and basin for washing, and a chamber pot under the bed for nighttime relief. The bathroom was on the second floor below. With the farmer, his wife, a hired hand, and me all living in the rather small farmhouse, having my own washbasin and chamber pot facilities in my room was a real convenience.

Farmer Nelson had a herd of thirty milk cows, two draft horses, a relatively new Ford, a Farmall tractor, and a model T truck that was probably about my age. The work involved milking the cows (about eighteen head were being milked at that time), cutting and bringing in hay for the winter, and planting and cultivating a corn crop that would be cut for silage, again for winter feed for the animals.

The day started at 5:30 AM, when Mrs. Nelson rapped on my door. In five minutes, I was supposed to be at the barn, ready to start the morning milking. In early June, that part of Connecticut was cold at night, frequently dropping to freezing so that there was often ice on the puddles that collected in the ruts and gullies of the barnyard.

But the cow barn was always warm. We had eighteen animals to milk, twice each day. At that time of the year, the cows would stay out of the barn, except for milking, and would graze together in the pastures that surrounded the central area of the farm. By 5:00 AM and at 4:00 PM in the afternoon, they would all line up at the gate that controlled access from the farmyard to the pastures. Their udders would be heavy with milk. They wanted the relief they knew we would give them.

When we opened the gate to the barnyard, they rushed through the yard and into the barn. Each cow headed for its own assigned place (a place they each knew well and came back to without hesitation each time). There, they would put their head between the two stanchion posts that defined their place and begin to eat silage that had been laid out for them in the concrete trough. Cut corn silage was a staple in the winter, a treat in the summer. It was laced with molasses and salt, and by June, the previous year's silage was a little winey. They did love it.

Sitting on the three-legged milking stool, facing the right side of the cow to be milked, often crowded by the next cow over, was a comforting experience in the cold of the morning. There was a primitive milking machine, but it didn't always work well and was a nuisance to set up and clean. It would take about seven minutes to milk one cow by hand and another few minutes to wash the udder at the beginning and take the milk to the cooler when the bucket was getting too heavy to keep between my knees.

Milking six cows was about an hour's work if I kept steadily at the task. The hired man and I each milked six or seven, and Mr. Nelson milked the rest. Our job also included putting the silage into the trough before the cows came into the barn. Cleanup after milking, cows turned out again, consisted of shoveling and flushing out the manure from the channel that ran the length of the barn behind the line of cows being milked. Then we used the hose to wash down and clean everything and everyplace the cows had been.

Our cow barn had its supply of cats. They loved to sit on the walkway behind the cows and open their mouths to beg for a bit of warm milk. I soon learned to aim a squirt into an open cat mouth from about four feet away. They knew to disappear when the cows were coming or going, but during milking, they had no fear of walking around the barn.

There were two barns on the farm. One for the milk cows, with a shed stall on the south side for sheltering dry cows (cows not being milked) in the winter, and one for the two draft horses and various tools and implements needed for farmwork. Each barn had two levels with space for large amounts of hay storage above. The cow barn had a silo attached, where cut corn silage was stored.

A small shelter for a flock of some twenty chickens and a fenced kitchen garden near the farmhouse completed the formal, dedicated spaces and buildings.

Milking and caring for the milk herd was the primary focus of farm activity for my first few days, but then, haying began. A large hay field had been cut, and the windrows had dried enough to gather and bring in the hay a few days after I first arrived.

Horses are far better than a tractor pulling the hay wagon. Although different colors, the team on the Nelson farm was matched in size and strength. They had been on the farm long enough that they worked tolerably well together, with only occasional displays of distress with each other. Pulling the long flat hay wagon, they responded to verbal commands to start and stop, important when neither the hired man nor I, working in synchrony to lift and stack the hay on the wagon, wanted to stop to control the horses with reins. With one worker on the ground and the other on the hay, gathering, lifting, and stacking the hay became like a ballet.

Windrows of dry hay are light, but piles of hay can quickly become heavy. As the wagon went along the rows, the one on the ground gathered hay into a small pile, sank his three-tined fork into the pile, and with a sweeping motion, lifted it into the air beside the wagon. The one on the mounting pile of hay on the wagon reached down, transferred the hay to his own hay fork, and, with a continuous, sweeping upward-and-over motion, placed the hay where it would lock into and stack atop hay already onboard.

This process of lift and stack went on until the hay pile was so high the man on the ground could no longer reach high enough for the man on top to be able to reach down with his own fork and transfer the hay to the wagon.

At the barn, a cantilevered timber supported a pulley, which allowed a large heavy hay hook to drop onto the wagon load, pick up a large bundle of hay, and, through an ingenious trolley system of ropes and pulleys, moved the hook full of hay to wherever in the upper reaches of the barn the farmer wanted to drop it. Having the hay really dry before bringing it in was a function of field drying in the windrows. Stacking and storing the hay in the barn required that the pile not become too dense. There needed to be enough air space left in the stacking so that there could be a tiny amount of circulation. Any dampness risked an event of spontaneous combustion, with loss not only of the hay, but also of the barn and all in it. To store the maximum amount of hay properly and still have it readily available, easily separated and cast down for the animals below, took a good deal of skill.

More than skill, the job of haying took stamina and the ability to withstand the dust and pollens of the grasses. Hay fever is not an idle term. Bringing in hay from the field is a hot, nasty job that leaves one coated with hayseed mixed with dust and sweat in nearly equal portions. The one who stacks the hay in the barn does not have the advantage of the occasional breeze, offering lifesaving fresh air to breathe and to cool the often-intense heat of the upper reaches of a hay barn. It is a killer job. Hay fever in the summer will cause one to have chills and a fever and be cold and feverishly hot all at the same time. It isn't for sissies.

The ballet of lifting and stacking hay on the wagon, the satisfaction of controlling a team of intelligent horses with word commands, and the tired but good feeling of having really done a hard day's work all made haying worth the experience. I was lucky enough to not develop hay fever, although I breathed enough dust and pollen in my few days of haying to last a lifetime.

The Nelsons grew their own corn for silage, and one of my jobs was to take their relatively new Farmall tractor and cultivate the cornfield where the crop was about ten inches out of the ground. The Farmall was like a three-wheeler. The two front wheels were small and axled together so that they would roll along one space between planted rows of corn without harming the plants on either side. The two rear wheels were big, about four feet tall, and positioned so that they too would roll along the space between the planted rows without harming the crop.

A three-point hitch at the rear of the tractor was hydraulically controlled. The hitch lifted and adjusted the cultivator being drawn behind the tractor. The cultivator could be brought up for travel along the road or turn at the end of a field and then let down into place for cultivating between the rows of young corn plants.

At one end of a field I was cultivating one morning, there was a line of trees with branches that overhung the corn plants. I had to duck under these branches when I turned at the end of the rows and often had to fend off branches with one hand while steering the tractor with the other. I had been cultivating for a little while and was making a turn under the tree branches, when I suddenly felt one and then another and then a cluster of stings on the back of my neck. I had disturbed a wasp nest, and they were mad.

I had the cultivator already up for the turn, so I slammed the tractor into highway gear and took off across the field. Fortunately, the wasps did not follow. I was some minutes from the house and thought that I needed to do something quickly. So I went to the lowest end of the field, hoping there would be mud in a ditch I could put on the stings. The ground was uniformly dry everywhere. But there was exposed dirt that I had stirred up earlier with the cultivator, so I spit and spit onto a hand full of reddish dirt that had lots of clay in it and slapped it on the stings, which by that time had really begun to smart. In a few minutes, the stinging began to ease, and I decided I was going to be okay. So I lined the tractor up on cornrows that still needed cultivating and went back to work.

Both Mr. Nelson and the hired man were shorter than I was. I didn't realize that would make any particular difference, but it did in one aspect of farmwork. Mr. Nelson came to where I was working in the horse barn one day and asked me to come with him. He needed help with a cow, someone with a long arm.

I qualified. We went around to the front of the cow barn. On the grass, away from the hard dirt of the barnyard, the hired man stood holding a halter at the head of a cow that had just calved.

The calf was standing, wobbly legged, at the side of her momma. And the mother cow didn't look all that perky either. In fact, she wasn't. The afterbirth had not all come out, and for her and for Mr. Nelson, that was a problem. Afterbirth needs to follow the calf, or so he told me, or his cow would develop a fever and might even die. But his arms were not long enough to help his cow. Mine were.

What he presented to me was a bucket of clean, mildly soapy water and a large clean sponge. "Take off your shirt," he told me, and I did. "Now wash the arm you are going to use to help this mother cow," he continued, and I took the soap and sponge and washed both arms up to my torso. "Now," he said, "I'm going to hold her head while you swab out her birth canal."

So there in the bright sunlight of that June day, I stood behind this newly delivered cow. She allowed me to sponge off her hind quarters, and then, with the sponge full of warm soapy water, I slid my arm, hand holding the soaked sponge, into her birth canal, up to my armpit, and gently cleaned out the canal through which her calf had just been delivered.

At that time, I scarcely thought about anything more than this being an animal that needed help, and because of my long arm, I was better able to do the helping than the farmer. Later, I thought that this was likely a common experience for farm boys, but for this city kid, it was an early and, on the whole, very quotidian introduction into the events surrounding birth.

With the afterbirth removed and the cow able to walk to the clean paddock prepared for her, I asked the hired man about feeding the calf. He had already milked the colostrums from the mother into a rather small pail. He buried his hand in the milk in the pail and offered his milk-coated fingers up from the milk to the calf, which seemed puzzled at first but quickly started sucking at one of his fingers.

He did that several times over the next day until the calf got the idea that it didn't need a finger to suck on but could suck up the milk without help. At that time, the calf could be fed from a bucket and never be near its mother again until it became weaned and would meet her out in the fields. Milk that the calf would have otherwise sucked from its mother was the product and the primary reason for this farm's existence. The calf would get enough for good growth, with extra vitamins and nutrients added, but the major amount of milk the mother cow would produce was to be part of the farm's production.

When the buckets we held between our knees while milking became too heavy, we took the milk to the cooling room. Pouring the milk into storage cans through a cheesecloth filter over a large funnel cleared any specks of dust or flecks of feed that might have accidentally gotten into the milk. The barn was not exactly sanitary. But the pasteurizing process at the creamery would take care of any bacteria.

In the cooling room, the flow from a natural cold-water spring was fed into a narrow concrete tank. Our tank held eight ten-gallon milk storage cans lined up in pairs. At about forty-seven degrees, with spring water constantly flowing around the partially submerged cans, milk was rapidly cooled and kept at that temperature until we could take it to the creamery about ten miles away.

One pound of milk weighs about eight pounds, and together, the can and its contents topped out at just over ninety pounds. Usually, there were four to five cans to deliver. Those I loaded onto the bed of the ancient model T, three days a week, to drive to the creamery. At sixteen, I didn't have the right to have a driver's license in New York City, but that was not a problem in this rural community. Farm children all drove their family's vehicles. I knew the routines of clutching, shifting, and braking and had no fear of driving this neat, very small, and simple vehicle.

The truck was basic. It did have an electric starter, windshield wipers, and window cranks but no other amenities. The footpads on both brake and clutch pedals had both long since worn away, and what remained were two narrow flat metal strips that were slippery and shiny from wear. So was the metal floor of the cab. And the fabric on the bench seat was so thin from wear that I expected to be poked with a protruding spring every time I entered the cab. There were brakes, but I had to start braking well before the need to stop because they were as well worn as all the other parts of this truck.

My trips to the creamery were routinely after lunch. On one occasion, I had been driving along the hilly winding Connecticut road, just as happy as I could be. I loved the responsibility I had been given, and driving was the supreme manifestation that I was grown up. But I had little real experience, and my driving skills were put to an extreme test when, coming down a long hill, I saw a car stopped where there was no obvious reason to stop. The road I was on continued in a long sweeping curve to the left, and from the right, another main road merged with my road in a large Y intersection.

When the stopped car came into view, it was some five hundred or so feet ahead, at the point where the two roads came together. It was starting to turn right, back onto the merging road. Had it continued to do so, it would have left the road ahead clear for me to continue at the speed I had built up on this downhill run. So I continued to drive with undiminished speed downhill, expecting the road would be clear.

Unexpectedly, the car started to back up directly into my path. I simultaneously hit the horn and the brakes, but I was going too fast for the inadequate braking capacity of that little truck, carrying a load of five ninety-pound cans of milk right behind the cab. Fortunately, the area where the two roads came together had been cleared, and there was a large patch of gravel and dirt to my right that I was able to turn onto. The car stopped, and when my brakes finally took hold, I came skidding to a stop. As the dust blew away, I found myself slightly ahead of the car.

If there had been no place to turn, I would have plowed directly into the rear of that car.

It was a newish convertible holding two couples, and when I got out, swearing every word my Brooklyn Tech casual course in expletives had taught me, I got an astonished look from the driver who shrugged and said, "We were lost and didn't know which way to go. And besides, why were you driving so fast?"

Why indeed. It scared the dickens out of me. I had been very lucky, as had the occupants of that lost car. The Connecticut Highway Department's act of leaving a large clearing for me to turn onto had saved us all from a really serious collision. I have never forgotten that incident. I still watch carefully the actions of cars ahead to be sure I won't have to slam on the brakes and head for the side of the road to avoid a terrifying accident.

Food on the farm was simple, plentiful, and consisted of a mainly meat, potatoes, and vegetable diet, with a dessert always the finishing touch. Pies, cobblers, and bread puddings are my memories of the end of meals there with always lots of cold milk to drink.

I never had cause to complain about the food until one Saturday, when the Nelsons had gone to town and I came into the house, hot and sweaty from my labors, and found a note that read, "We've gone to town shopping. There is a three-bean salad in the ice box." "Three bean salad?" I asked myself. "What in the world is that? Where is the meat? Where are the potatoes? How am I supposed to do farmwork on a salad for lunch?"

I had never heard of having a salad for a noon meal. I HAD NEVER EVER HEARD OF OR HAD TO EAT A THREE-BEAN SALAD UNDER ANY CIRCUMSTANCES! It was the end of my stay at the farm. I couldn't work if they were not going to feed me.

I never touched that bowl of three-bean salad. It was many years before I deigned to try any three-bean salad. When I did, I was surprised and chagrined to find I liked it very much. But it was the offer of a three-bean salad after a morning of milking, cleaning the barn, cultivating the corn field, and sweating away as a hired hand doing farm chores that sent me out to find another way to spend the rest of my summer.

That evening, the last Saturday in July, walking along the road to a nearby dance hall, I happened upon a large broadside on the barn of a neighboring farmer advertising the Ringling Bros., Barnum & Bailey Circus then showing in Hartford through the next night. I came back to the farm, packed, and gave my notice. I figured I had done enough to help my country. Besides, conditions had changed.

Sunday morning found me on the Hartford road, suitcase in hand, flagging down an intercity bus. By that evening, I was approaching the Ringling Circus lot in Hartford. The circus had horses, workhorses, show horses, lots of horses. I was absolutely confident that I would get a job helping with their horses. I sent my parents a letter, saying I was leaving the farm, joining the circus, and I'd write more later. Some of my learning experiences, I describe in "My Time with the Circus" (# 23 in this series).

As children grow and move out into the world to claim their right to do what life puts in front of them, parents would do well to react as mine did in that situation. The woman I called mom and whom I loved as a son loves a mother was not my birth mother. I never knew my birth mother in the usual sense because she died when I was very young.

Mom almost always was in favor of letting me try whatever I wanted to do. Her philosophy was, "Let him do it; he'll know soon enough if he can or can't." All the while, I knew then and know now that she was careful to not let me get into a truly dangerous situation.

That being said, she allowed me to try and fail, to fall down and sometimes get hurt. She allowed me to learn from doing. As I moved into my teen years, she persuaded my father not to put many absolute restrictions on my requests. She did point out the dangers and the risks and talked with me about whether those were acceptable.

So when my letter arrived, she counseled him to relax and wait for my next communication to tell them what was going on. She trusted me. I have often thought that having a stepparent is not always as it is frequently portrayed. The typical portrait of the uncaring stepparent may too often be true, but in my case, as a child and later as an adoptive father of two young boys, I found that the role of a stepparent allowed a degree of equanimity about the child's process of learning to live that birth parents have trouble copying. Stepparents, in my experience, do not hover over those they have chosen to parent. They are protective but not smothering. Allowing a child the freedom to try and by trying find their strengths and their limits, makes a big difference in that child's learning process about how to manage their life.

Here's a laconic farmer expression that I like:

A bumblebee is considerably faster

than a John Deere tractor.

#27 A Christmas Story

Not all of my memories of Christmas past are of happy times and presents under the tree. One that bubbles up from time to time is about a certain Christmas tree itself.

On Christmas Eve, when I was nine, in 1934, my father and I started out at about eight o'clock on a mission to get a Christmas tree. Our house was only two blocks from the local shopping area that lined Jamaica Avenue, the nearby major thoroughfare. We lived in New York City, but our town of Hollis, Long Island, was what we now call suburban.

I had little appreciation for the actual temperature at that age. I judged how cold it was by the amount and density of my breath as each puffy cloud turned gauzy white in front of me. My breath was really dense that night.

Getting to our destination was a challenge. New snow had been cleared from most of the sidewalk, but tree roots had heaved concrete sections unevenly, and there were patches slippery with icy snowmelt under the new snow. In front of a large empty lot, we had to divert to the street and walk a single file in a rut made by the one car that had come along after the storm.

Our objective was the small store that, in those days, served neighborhood grocery needs. I walked by that store every day going to and from PS 35, my local NYC elementary school. For some time, fir trees had been on display, propped up against a supporting rope along the edge of a wide sidewalk.

Strings of colored lights draped in some store windows helped light our way. It was quiet, except for the squeak of our boots in the snow. We walked past Saint Gabriel's Episcopal Church, which our family had helped found. It was not a big church, twenty rows of pews could accept twelve adults each, with eighteen more places for the choir. Two weeks before, garlands of fir branches had been draped throughout the nave of the church. It smelled wonderful, the smell of Christmas.

I knew the big holiday was coming, but the lack of a tree in our house was not of any particular concern. My parents had things under control. I knew that. Whatever happened in my life was because they wanted it to happen. They loved my brother and me, of that I was sure.

When we reached Jamaica Avenue, the center part of the street snow had been packed by busy traffic. Along the curb, the snow had been rutted by cars parking. My dad stepped from track to track. I schussed along, making my own path.

That night, Jamaica Avenue was empty of all cars.

We could have walked in the travelled part of the roadway to Jamaica (two miles west) or to Queens Village (one and a half miles east) without fear of being hit. But all we had to do was cross to the store where Christmas trees were still out front. Some were leaning against the support rope; others were strewn on their sides along the sidewalk, left where they had fallen after the store closed that afternoon.

My father explained what we were doing. He said the grocer no longer needed the trees. Everyone who wanted a Christmas tree had already bought their tree and taken it home; the grocer would just throw the rest away the day after Christmas, when the store reopened. We needed a tree, and he just hadn't been able to get one until now.

We were taking a Christmas tree without paying for it. On Christmas Eve.

Sorting through the remaining scraggly trees we found the least barren tree, about as tall as my father, with few branches and those not rich with needles, a really skimpy tree, but the best of what remained. We took the tree and walked home.

As we retraced our journey, my father in the lead, me holding the tip of the fir tree that would soon be set up in our living room, I felt satisfied that the world would soon be as it should be and the crisp night air was sweet.

Only as I grew older and thought back on that little adventure did I understand some of the emotions my father must have felt that night before Christmas 1934. Times were tough. He had a job running my grandfather's paper business, Thomas J. Nagle, Paper and Twine. People weren't buying much meat or groceries or other products that required wrapping or carrying home in paper bags. Store owners didn't need to package what people weren't buying.

The United States hadn't quite come to a commercial standstill, but things really were bad. I learned later, when there was only enough money to pay the warehouse workers, that my dad and two of his brothers, the salesmen of the company, took less or no money in order to keep the one place they had a job from collapsing completely.

I never had a chance to ask him about that evening. He died in August 1943, just a couple of months after I enlisted in the navy. Now, having been a father and provider myself, I know the compulsion he must have felt that Christmas Eve.

What would you tell a nine-year-old and his three-year-old brother about why your house doesn't have a Christmas tree?

You just don't let that happen. You simply go out and find a way to make it as right as you can for them.

During the Great Depression, the gauge of poverty was much different than now. Now poverty is a statistically derived number, published by the Department of Health and Human Services of US government. These numbers show what it is in 2010.

Persons in family	Poverty guideline
1	$10,830
2	14,570
3	18,310

When I was young, men would come to our home, begging for food, asking for anything, even a dry crust of bread. Their clothes were ragged and threadbare. A few were dirty and smelly. But my mother always fixed something for them to eat. Even a small sandwich was welcomed by these men who stalked the streets, looking for work, but mostly just needing food to keep going. They literally had nothing. Poverty then was destitution.

We had a swing in our very small backyard, built by my dad from timbers he had been given by the power company. It was not very pretty, but it was sturdy. There was also a tree stump in the yard. These men would take whatever my mother fixed for them and sit on the stump to eat. I would join them, sitting on my swing, watching and sometimes talking to them.

A few had tears in their eyes while they ate, meanwhile telling me what a wonderful mother I had. One man, I remember, asked me if I would get another slice of bread for him that he could take with him to eat that night for his supper. I asked my mother and took the bread to him.

In the papers, there were pictures of men and women squatting next to buildings in New York City, holding out pencils or fruit to sell to passersby. As a child, I didn't really understand what was happening, but I was aware that things were not good.

My family was not wealthy. We did have a home and food, a car, and I occasionally had new clothes. Poverty was not in my neighborhood. My dad, when he came back from the TB sanitarium, had a job. My mother worked as a teacher for the New York City school system. The fathers of all my friends had jobs.

But poverty was not far away and came to call too often. Poverty then meant lack of any resources; men, and some women, wandered the country, riding the rails in boxcars, looking for work, having only the clothes on their backs.

It seems we have avoided a repeat of those hard times through prompt and aggressive management of the banking crisis by President Obama and just plain good luck. We are not quite out of the woods yet, but it appears we have avoided the terrible catastrophe of so many in abject poverty that I remember from my own childhood.

There was no law against children in bars in the 1930s. I went to one with my aunt one afternoon, where she was meeting a friend and was amazed by what was offered. At one end of the bar was a small counter on which were several loaves of bread and two very big haunches of meat; one was beef and the other a ham nearly as big as the beef. A large carving knife was there for customers to use to slice off whatever they wanted.

There was also a glass jar of olives, bigger than any I had ever seen and another, almost as large, full of pickles. As I sat with my aunt, people came in, ordered a drink, and proceeded to cut large slabs of meat and fix what we then called Dagwood sandwiches. That name came from a popular comic strip in which the main character was always fixing a multilevel sandwich of enormous proportions.

I asked my aunt if I could have a sandwich, and she told me that all the food I saw was for people who came to the bar to drink; it was there to lure customers. The bartender, hearing our discussion, asked me what I wanted and fixed me two sandwiches so big and full of meat I couldn't eat it all.

Another beer story. When I was fourteen, I worked in the summer at my grandfather's business, a paper supply company. It was hot and dusty dry with all those stacks of cardboard boxes of paper products in the warehouse. Beer to wash down lunch was the liquid of choice for three warehouse men. I was assigned to walk two blocks to the local tavern and bring back a bucket of beer for their lunch. The tin bucket they sent me with was about the size of a one-gallon pail. Half filled with tap beer, walking back two blocks without spilling any was a challenge. Today, no bar would sell two quarts of draft beer in an open bucket to anyone, much less to a fourteen-year-old boy. Things change!

What is past is prologue.

—William Shakespeare

#28 The Imperturbable Cat

Of the many places I have lived, three have had backyard pools. The appealing idea of having a backyard pool greatly outweighed its actual addition to my well-being. That sounds as though it could be true. Especially when, as has been the case for most of my life, the cost of having professional care for the pool meant that I did it all myself or, like an overseer with an emotional whip and harsh command, forced indentured laborers (read, children of the family) to do the many tasks required by the pool. In fact, a pool does require constant watchfulness over its condition. To keep it clean, sanitary, and ready for anytime use takes work, a lot of work. Some of it pleasurable, I must admit.

Many, many early mornings, I have been poolside in my bathing suit, barefooted on the cool concrete, watching the summer sun come up, listening to the awakening chatter of the local bird population, running the cleaning brush back and forth over the white plaster bottom of the pool, and finding the whole experience so delightful I can't imagine how it could be anything but satisfaction to the soul to have a pool of my own.

To skinny-dip at night, under a full moon or darkly shining stars, the pool water bathtub warm after a summer day in the Texas sun, has brought me to a state of undiluted joy more times than I can count. There was also the excited, delighted shouts and screams of children of family and friends as they played Marco Polo, scrambling to avoid being tagged in the ultimate frenzy of kid pool fun. Given the choice, I would never miss that.

Where I lived near Austin, Texas, our house was at the top of one of the hills that gave the area its name. Our pool was even further up the hill, in a corner of the backyard. A clearing had been made in a grove of young live oaks and the pool arranged, more or less, in the center of that clearing. The trees offered great shade around the pool during the day when the Texas sun can be blistering hot.

But that variety of tree also created greater-than-usual cleaning needs. Live oaks shed acorns, leaves, pollen, and twigs constantly. Although a concrete pool apron had been provided, as time passed, branches had spread; and those trees dropped a large share of their detritus onto the concrete. Because of the tannin in everything oak, it was important to clean the concrete of leaves, acorns, and twigs regularly. I found it useful to use a pressure nozzle on the hose and wash the concrete weekly.

I was in the middle of this task one Saturday morning when two visitors joined me. Our twelve-year-old cat, Fluffy, took up a position under a settee at the shallow end of the pool, out of the sun, and where she could oversee my efforts with no energy expenditure of her own. She often joined me, catlike, to watch and study the strange habits of her human staff, who worked when they could be sleeping or, as today, lounging with her and enjoying the morning poolside.

The other visitor was a squirrel, who had been nut gathering in the trees near where I was washing debris off the concrete. I worked backward, sweeping the area with the stream of water, moving away from where Fluffy had positioned herself, head on paws, watching.

The squirrel also watched. It cautiously came down the trunk of a tree at the edge of the concrete, pausing every few feet of descent to observe my reaction. When I kept to my task, he was emboldened. Once on the concrete, Mr. Squirrel took tentative steps away from the security of the tree and toward the open pool. He obviously wanted to cross the area at the shallow end of the pool to a small grove of oaks on the other side. With his eyes on me, he had not yet noticed Fluffy.

While watching me work, he advanced in several short spurts, keeping near the edge of the pool, his head turned in my direction. He never saw Fluffy until he was almost even with her position under the settee.

Something made him look to his left. All his attention then turned to this silent, still-as-a-statue cat. Without a thought of where he was, he turned right, and I could see and hear his little feet scratching hard on the concrete, trying to get traction to get away from that cat.

Trouble was, as he went hard right, feet scrambling, he quickly ran out of hard surface and his momentum propelled him right off the edge, into the pool water, landing about two feet from the side. I didn't know whether a squirrel could swim and prepared to get the leaf net to scoop him out if he seemed in trouble. But as I watched, waiting to go to his aid if needed, he furiously paddled back to the side of the pool, but the water level was many inches below the top, and he could see that was not his way out.

Flailing about, his efforts carried him to the corner, where there were concrete steps, the first one just below water level. He scrambled onto this half-submerged step, and then, with firm footing, he launched himself up onto the concrete surround of the pool. Out of the water and on solid footing, he never looked back but shot across the concrete to the nearest small tree. With a leap, he grabbed the trunk a couple of feet from the ground, swung around to the back of the tree, and kept going up to safety. I saw him pause just momentarily on an upper branch before he continued his travels, out of my sight in that grove of small oak trees.

This squirrel looked like a normal squirrel when dry, his fur providing some appearance of substance. Soaking wet, the poor creature looked positively miniature: he was skinny, bedraggled, and that usual fluffy tail was reduced to what looked like a long flexible straw.

Fluffy, meanwhile, kept her position, head on paws, quite obviously thinking the squirrel had acted like a complete fool. She never moved anything more than her head. From where I stood, if ever a cat had thought, "This is amazing," that thought showed in Fluffy's eyes. I'm sure there were about one hundred seconds of stark terror in that squirrel's life. But he survived. For me, the memory brings a smile every time I mentally picture that poor creature scrambling away from a completely imperturbable cat.

Believe in yourself!

Have faith in your abilities!

Without a humble but reasonable confidence in your own powers

you cannot be successful or happy

—Norman Vincent Peale

#29 Thanksgiving Years Ago (1937)

Living next to Grandpa (T. J.) and Grandma's (Elva) house meant that family gatherings, for Thanksgiving especially, were really easy for Bruce and me. We did have to get dressed in good knickers, shoes, and a white shirt and tie, but then, we could just go next door.

On Thanksgiving, particularly, the action in Grandma's kitchen was wonderful to be around. I'm not sure the date I have selected is really correct for all I'm about to tell you; after all, I was just twelve years old that year. But the family members, the layout of the kitchen, the table stretching from dining room to living room, and the variety of foods are all a true representation of what things were like for all the late 1930s that I do remember quite well.

Grandma's kitchen was a fairly large room, with a center island work area about three and a half feet square. The top was the same hard rock maple used to make butcher cutting blocks—impervious to liquid spills, easy to work on, and easily cleaned. Underneath were shelves and cabinets that held pots, pans, and baking equipment. Grandma was a great cook and baker. She was always busy baking some goody or other that she would put out for Bruce and me to sample. Those kitchen implements were well used.

A very large six-burner gas stove with two ovens was centered on one wall, a big two-door refrigerator was in an alcove on another wall, and a long porcelain-on-cast-iron sink with two large deep wells, flanked by two long work surfaces was on the outside wall underneath a big kitchen window. The whole sink and work space was about six feet long.

The fourth kitchen wall was short. It was where there was a mangle. This was a wide electric ironing device that could iron flat sheets and other linens. It was called a mangle because if one wasn't careful, a finger or hand could be drawn into the ironing portion with disastrous consequences. The finger or hand would be "mangled."

And then there was the butler's pantry—a galleylike passage between the kitchen and dining room with glass-fronted cabinets to the ceiling in which were stored china, silver, and serving platters. A long serving counter topped cabinets and drawers where Grandma stored the eating utensils, table linens, and so forth.

Grandpa was the seignior of the house. His domain was in the living room. I can see him still, reading the (very conservative) *New York Herald Tribune* while comfortably slouched in his favorite chair. A large ashtray was always on a stand nearby with his favorite brand of Cuban cigar quietly smoldering, perfuming the air with the fragrance that identified him.

Grandpa insisted on a kiss from all his grandchildren, both when we came into his presence and when we left. The distinctive smell of his cigars was about him always and very present with each kiss. It was strong but not unpleasant. It was Grandpa.

Gathering for Thanksgiving holidays during the mid 1930s were all the Nagle progeny; my dad (Jerry, the oldest); his brothers Bill, Fred, Tom, Martin, and Jim; and sister, Harriet. Jim was just nine years older than I and Martin just a year older than Jim. The last two were not married then, but the other uncles and Harriet were married. All told, they had produced (by then) five grandchildren, with ten more to come. Bruce was six. Uncle Bill's two boys were about seven and four years old. Harriet's first child was also about four.

To seat all these celebrants, Grandma would put in all available leaves to extend the large dining table to its longest reach and add card tables at the end to accommodate all at one table. The ensemble reached well into their living room. In later years, as the other uncles married and the grandchild brood increased, children's tables were established off to the side. Being the oldest, I was nominally in charge. No child wants to be in charge of his cousins, and I didn't like the job. So our child's table was pretty much a free-for-all, except when stern parental voices demanded order.

On Thanksgiving Day, starting early in the morning, Grandma's kitchen was a happening place. The daughters-in-law and Aunt Harriet congregated to help Grandma in preparing and cooking the variety of different foods that custom and a large family demanded. She had already done the pie baking, and those were in the pantry, ready to be brought out after the main meal for those who had just a little more room left for dessert.

A typical Thanksgiving dinner would start out with a round mold of tomato aspic on a piece of lettuce for all, with three shrimp carefully spaced around the aspic for the adults. Then, of course, there was turkey and a ham, two kinds of dressing, gravy boats filled to the brim, mashed potato, mashed turnip, mashed sweet potato, string beans, pearl onions in a cream sauce, little peas in butter sauce, cranberry sauce and cranberry jelly, rolls and butter, and, for Grandpa, a special glass of beer to help his digestion. Milk was on the table for us children. The adults mostly drank apple cider. Grandma would put two—or three-gallon jugs of cider on the outside steps to the back porch the night before, letting the night time chill get the cider the right temperature for the turkey-day dinner.

Dessert was at least two kinds of pie ("small slices, please," said all the women). Delicious apple, mincemeat, and pumpkin pies were brought out, homemade vanilla ice cream was dipped from the hand-cranked ice-cream maker, and I can remember the smell of coffee as the adults pushed back to enjoy the feeling of being really stuffed with terrific food.

While busy passing bowls of vegetables and concentrating on food consumption, not much was said. I wasn't a part of the conversation anyway. Children were then "to be seen but not heard." As the adults finished the main course, loud and animated talk rapidly filled the room. With new energy from all that good food, it seemed everyone had something to say, and all were saying it at the same time. At least, that was my twelve-year-old perception.

A piano in an alcove at one end of the living room had been tuned, ready for the holiday. Martin played well, and a couple of others could noodle around, not bothering with the written notes. A group of self-styled Irish tenors competed to see who knew the most lyrics of the popular songs of the day without having to look over Martin's shoulder to read the words. Our dad played the banjo, someone else played a bulbous mandolin, and I remember a violin being tried at one time. The afternoon went quickly and, I thought it was great fun.

Then it was time for turkey and cranberry sandwiches. To my taste, those sandwiches were every bit as good as the big meal itself and a lot more fun. We could take them outside or anywhere and didn't have to eat at a table. The old ways have changed, and in a way, I miss them. But you will all be with your families and, soon, with partners or spouses, creating your own traditions. That's as it should be.

This isn't good or bad. It is just the way of things.

—Anonymous

#30 A Discovery Trip to Sweden

Memories of past lives are often considered merely a product of a very active imagination. The "debunking" community of professional debunkers has a sarcastic reaction to most stories of past lives. I am open to most new ideas, and the concept of having lived before, while not exactly new—the Hindu religion, for example, believes in reincarnation—it was not something I had ever explored. But the experience I had with Peggy really opened my thinking about this.

I went with Peggy to her appointment with M, a psychotherapist who had experience helping people access memories of past lives. We both trusted him in his professional life and as a friend. It was he who had suggested a process that might bring understanding of something that was blocking a planned trip to Sweden.

M had a broad interest in and knowledge about the paranormal. He had been to our home to lead discussions with friends about out-of-the-ordinary experiences. He was also skilled in hypnosis and other techniques used to induce the brain to access what might be called "its outer limits." Our reasons for seeking his help in this instance seemed mundane, but it was a problem we had been unable to solve by ourselves.

Peggy had always been an enthusiastic traveler. Now she was uncharacteristically hesitant about a trip I was planning for us to fly to Sweden. The chance to renew contacts with distant cousins and an opportunity to visit the small farm near Stockholm, where my mother had grown up, called to me. I really wanted to go.

In the past, when I would suggest any trip, Peggy was quick to start packing. Her anxiety about going to Sweden just wasn't in character. It was in direct conflict with what I knew to be her love of travel.

Our own attempts to dispel the fears she felt had not worked. Unable to bring to light anything specific with our own efforts, we decided professional help was needed. In a phone conversation with M about what could be causing the discomfort, he suggested it might be interesting to determine if some event in one of Peggy's past lives might be the trigger. He was willing to use his skills to help us find out. We decided to do it.

Going under hypnosis to explore her past lives, though safely in the hands of a trusted friend, was exciting. And we both rationalized that the experience would at least expand our understanding of reincarnation, whether something specific to our concern was learned or not.

Past lives had been a subject of occasional discussion, but neither Peggy nor I had ever seriously considered exploring our own before this opportunity presented. She had, however, shared with me a book on the subject, *Reliving Past Lives: The Evidence under Hypnosis* by Helen Wambach, PhD (Barnes & Noble, 2000). That book had opened for me the understanding that not only had we all experienced past lives as a part of humanity's recurring cycles of reincarnation but that, with skilled help, it is possible to find out some things about those past lives.

The session with M was scheduled for late in the afternoon, when his practice offered time with no structured ending. Peggy wanted me present in order to have our own record of what happened. She feared her recall of what she might say during hypnosis would be problematic. With our purpose for trying this procedure, we didn't want to lose anything she might say. M would be attending to the professional part of making it happen. I was to be the recorder.

M's office was on a quiet street. The small chamber he chose for this session had no windows. The light level was low; all external sound was insulated out. Furnishings were simple—three chairs with a low table between. I sat to Peggy's side. M was across from her.

Peggy went from being present and conscious to a hypnotic state very quickly. She was ready for the session, and it took only moments for her breathing to become shallow, her affect to show her submission to the process.

When M asked if she was comfortable and able to clearly hear him, her response was so soft I found myself leaning toward her, straining to hear.

After a couple of questions about her present life to see if she understood him, he quickly moved to the issue. Have you ever been to Sweden?

In this lifetime, she certainly had not. Yet she answered tentatively, as though puzzled by the question. Her head nodded slowly no, and I wondered what she was sorting out before answering.

Professionals who do hypnosis therapy tell us those under hypnosis have a scrupulous regard for the truth. Answers are frequently delayed when the subject has to take time to establish the precisely correct answer. The next question made clear her earlier answer.

Have you ever *lived in* Sweden? She nodded yes.

Now we were on track. Is your having lived in Sweden connected to your fear of traveling there? Again she nodded yes.

Her movements in this were positive but subtle. M gently asked her to speak her answers, and like a child having been prompted, she softly said yes.

Keeping her engaged in the process, he then asked if she was willing to answer questions about her life in Sweden, and she nodded affirmatively. Again he asked her to speak her answers, and again she quietly agreed to do so.

The questioning went on. Were you a man or woman in this lifetime? Boy, she answered.

Can you tell me what year it was when you lived there? She both nodded and said no.

Do you understand that we are trying to find out if something happened while you lived in Sweden that causes you to be afraid now? Yes. Are you willing to keep on answering my questions about that? Yes.

How old were you when something happened that made you very afraid? I was young.

Where did you live? In a small house.

Where was the small house? In the forest.

Did you live there alone? No. Who lived there with you? My mother, my father, my baby sister.

Did you go to school? They tried to make me. Who tried to make you go to school? The men. Did they make you go to school? I ran away.

Where was the school? At the convent. Where was the convent? Across the river.

Can you describe the convent? It was very cold. What was near the convent? The river. Anything else? The church.

Time did not exist for us in that room. The slow and methodical questioning M used was answered by Peggy just as slowly and methodically, frequently in monosyllables. I strained to hear, not wanting to miss a word. With the absolute absence of outside sounds, I didn't miss a thing. I was enthralled.

The story that emerged was of a young boy, who had a remarkable ability to be at one with wild creatures. His father made a living from the forest, but the boy had a withered arm and was allowed the life of a free spirit. He loved his baby sister and told her stories of the lives of the birds and animals he visited in the forest.

One day, away from home until past dark, he returned to find the house burned to the ground with both parents and baby sister lost to the flames.

The people of the village took the boy into their community and placed him with a family in the village. That family sent him to the convent school. The nuns asked about his life before coming to the school. He told them of his family, of his freedom to come and go as he liked, of his wildlife friends, and that he often just roamed around all day, talking with the creatures of the forest. The stories the young boy told, with innocent lack of sophistication, began a tragic cascade of events.

Communicating with birds and animals was not an approved activity in Sweden at that time. Testing him to determine if the stories were mere fanciful imaginings, the nuns found that birds came to him to be fed. Animals accepted his presence without fear.

The nuns told him he was possessed, and he was beaten to drive out the evil spirits.

He ran away to his forest, but the men of the village always found him and brought him back. Shortly, the village patience was empty. He was possessed without possibility of redemption; such was the declaration of the convent authorities.

A trial was held in the square. No one spoke for the boy. The nuns witnessed that wildlife responded to him without the usual fear of humans—proof enough that he was possessed. It was decided. He must die to prevent harm to the village.

When asked to describe the area of the trial, Peggy slowly spoke of the river, a bridge to the convent, school, and church on the other side. Very tall trees on both sides of the river figured prominently in the description.

The whole proceeding, trial, verdict, and execution occurred summarily at the edge of the village common in front of a building she described as an eating place. When M asked, if the building had a name, she was quiet for a moment and then said, "Kogen."

The word was spoken so softly and the sound of it so indistinct that both M and I asked her to say it again. "Kogen," she repeated. What does "Kogen" mean? Where they hung me.

M immediately gave her a series of posthypnotic instructions designed to keep her from carrying her recollection of this death into the present when she came out of hypnosis. He told Peggy to know that she was completely safe and secure, that the events happened a long time ago, and that she would not remember them in detail when she awakened.

With that, the session quickly came to an end. Information that she had been hung as a boy after a trial at which it was decided he was possessed of the devil was enough. If true, it certainly was sufficient reason to not want to be in the area again.

Peggy remembered few of her answers to M's questions. She had been very deep into her trance. It had been well over an hour. She was exhausted.

When the three of us spent time going over the information that had developed, M and I asked again if she recognized the word "Kogen," and Peggy was genuinely perplexed. "Is that what I said?" she asked. She had no understanding of the word, declaring she had no conscious knowledge of it and could offer no help in adding any context to determine what, if anything, it meant.

One result of having this tale of religious justice related back to her was that a tolerance for the trip settled in. She agreed to put aside her past anxiety and go. In fact, her curiosity surged to a high level. Part of the purpose of the trip, now, was to search to find where all this had happened. Peggy had no hesitation about accepting as true all that had come out of the session with M.

Christian, my cousin's husband, was then a professor of dramatic literature at Arhus University in Denmark. Like many academics, he had a curious mind about everything and anything. We told him about past-life regression and the word "Kogen." A native Dane, he was literate in many languages. He had no knowledge of the word but enthusiastically helped with our investigation to find any Swedish location with "Kogen" as a part of its name.

He produced a very detailed map of Sweden that we all examined intently. Among other points of interest, it showed historic church sites which were designated national landmarks. Finding no word on the map even close to "Kogen," Peggy and I narrowed our search to any site that included an old church by a river.

There was one site by an old canal, with a footbridge shown as a crossing, at the site of an abbey and church that the map noted as a historic ruin. All of this was just north of Norkoping, a city about three hours' drive away. It was not an exact match, but there were no other sites that even slightly hinted of the landmarks we searched for.

We rented a car and headed for Norkoping. As we approached the city, Peggy said she felt uncomfortable in a vague, undifferentiated sort of way. It was just before noon when I turned the car north, away from the city proper. We made our plans to visit the historic church site and then have lunch.

As we approached the area shown on the map, her discomfort increased.

This was a marked change. After the past-life session, Peggy had become quite sanguine about the whole affair. With no towns named Kogen having been found on the very detailed maps Christian had produced, she showed an attitude that declared it was all probably imagined, and the story which had come from her hypnosis was put into the category of maybe and maybe not. She was merely curious to see the countryside when we started on our travel to Norkoping.

I was intrigued then, as we drove closer to the place marked as the historic site, when she became quiet and said, "This all is beginning to feel uncomfortably familiar."

The abbey was at the side of a very large church close to the area designated for parking. It was the first building we encountered. Though the abbey was in ruins, the nearby church was still intact and functioning. Both church and abbey were made of brick.

The park handout, in several languages for tourists, including English, described the ruins as having been a nunnery. Some still-standing walls were above my head level, others had been reduced by time to mere outlines of what had once been an imposing structure. The roof had long ago decayed and been removed.

A school had been a part of the Abbey, supervised by an order of nuns. Enormous trees, the first branches towering nearly fifty feet above us, were scattered on both sides of the nearby canal.

We strolled in the late morning sunshine of a lovely day. As we moved through the maze of fallen brick walls that outlined rooms, corridors, walkways, and plazas that were the remains of the abbey and school, Peggy's sense of dread increased. Her request was, "Let's take a quick look at the church and then get some lunch. This place is chilling!"

We were in and out of the church in short order, Peggy complaining of a gut sense of foreboding. She could not identify any specific area as remembered nor could she put the emotions she felt into words. She just felt apprehensive. It was all very nonspecific.

Something there seemed to connect to her past-life memories, particularly the ruins of the school.

We left the historic site and headed across the canal for lunch. A tourist sign at the bridge said the canal had been created about a century before to move commercial boat traffic between two fairly large lakes, a small river having been deepened and extended for the purpose.

We crossed the footbridge to a group of modest buildings near a turning basin, where several midsized power and sailboats were tied up. The midsummer temperature was pleasant enough to think about eating out at the edge of the water. More tall trees shaded our walk to a structure which offered promise of food and tables on a patio by the canal.

I remarked to Peggy that the area had a sense to me of the description she had given of the place where the trial and hanging had occurred. By then, the prospect of having a pleasant lunch on a terrace adjacent to the canal had banished most of the edginess she had felt in the ruins and the church. She was easy with my comment. We went along with other tourists ready to relax and have lunch.

The young man who attended our table was bright and gregarious. Speaking English, as all young Swedes do, he engaged us about who we were, where we were from, and generally did his best to make us comfortable with the menu, which was only in Swedish, and explained the offerings of food shown there.

As he reviewed our order to be sure it was what we really wanted and started to leave, I asked, "By the way, do you happen to know the word 'Kogen'? Is it Swedish?"

"Sure," he answered. "That's not a word that's used very much around here anymore. This is a Kogen. It refers to a small tavern or eating place. Why do you ask?"

A phrase from Hamlet is worth repeating here:

There are more things in heaven and earth, Horatio, than are dreamt of in your philosophy.

—Shakespeare

#31 To Make a Grown Man Cry

After my birth mother died, I lived with my grandparents for the next two years. Grandma Nagle had a saying that she faced me with every time something happened that started tears into my eyes. "Big boys don't cry," she would tell me. Of course, I wanted to be a big boy. What little boy doesn't?

So I would sniffle and finally stop.

I carried that injunction with me into manhood. I never cried. Even when my dad died when I was eighteen and I had just joined the navy in WWII and felt like I would burst if I didn't let some tears roll, I accepted and followed those words of my grandma and held them back.

Actually, she was wrong about that. Big boys do cry. Grown men too, for that matter. It is healthy to cry and let emotions out instead of bottling them up where they can fester and come up later, often in completely inappropriate ways. But that is knowledge that came much later in her life and mine.

I thought of that when I decided to tell you about a civil rights trial I had in Houston. Civil rights for all citizens are critically important for any country to survive and prosper. The color of skin should not matter, but it does. Particularly in the courts, where I spent many years representing people of all colors and economic conditions, everyone's rights should be treated equally by the laws under which we live and by the judges and juries that uphold and sometimes enforce the laws by their verdicts.

Brown—and black-skinned citizens are still, in 2010, at a great disadvantage in our country; their rights are held in low regard by many white folks. The situation is worse in the South, particularly Georgia, where I am presently living.

In Houston, where I lived and practiced law in the 1960s and '70s, the civil rights issue was actively debated, and by some, President Lyndon Johnson was roundly condemned for pushing through Congress the civil rights legislation that has done so much to change the political face of our country.

I never represented businesses or practiced any corporate law. All my clients were individuals. I never knew what sort of person would walk into my office and bring to me what sort of problem they need help on.

One day in late 1968, a young black man came to see me about a beating he had received at the hands of the Houston police, a beating he said he had not brought about by any conduct of his own. I'm going to call him John.

John's story, as he told it and my investigation later confirmed, started when his wife, having a cold, asked him to go to the nearby 7-Eleven to get an over-the-counter cold remedy.

It was about 7:30, a warm summer evening, and he walked the five blocks rather than take his car. As he was walking, he had no knowledge that a robbery was taking place at the 7-Eleven that he was going to. Even as he approached the corner where the store was located, he didn't see much out of place, except that a police car was parked in front of the building with its front door open and no one inside.

What was blocked from his view was a Houston police officer on the ground, a short way from the police car in the other direction and a gathering crowd of mostly African American folks standing nearby, watching.

The officer had been shot, fortunately not fatally. On the ground and still conscious, he had used his shoulder radio to send out a call, "Officer down! Assist the officer!" It was only minutes before sirens could be heard and several police cars converged on the scene.

John was standing outside the 7-Eleven, puzzling over what he saw taking place, when someone pointed to him and announced, "There's the man. There's the guy that shot the officer!"

John was quickly slammed onto the sidewalk, handcuffed, and beaten. When two ambulances showed up in response to the call to assist the downed officer, John, obviously also needing medical treatment, was picked up and thrown into the back of one of them. Two officers climbed in with him and, on the way to the hospital, questioned him about where his gun was and why he had shot the officer and, when he protested his innocence, beat him with their fists.

He arrived at the hospital bloody and bruised and was admitted for four days of treatment.

It was only after he had been in the hospital for perhaps an hour that the true facts came out—John was an innocent bystander, unjustly and erroneously accused; the police had had been entirely too ready to respond with their own kind of justice before they knew what had really happened. The one who gave the true story was the injured officer.

The arrest had been justified based on a statement of a self-described eyewitness. But the manhandling, the beating, was a violation of John's civil rights. Under the new civil rights law recently passed, he had the right to sue for compensation.

I represented John in a trial before a federal judge, before whom I had tried many cases in Galveston. A very conservative Republican, he had been appointed by President Eisenhower, with the blessing of the local conservative bar.

From his rulings in past trials, I knew him to be prejudiced against African American plaintiffs, whom he seemed to regard as inferior citizens. I could win a favorable ruling on evidence only if I showed him that some appellate court had already ruled my way on the point in the evidence I was offering.

In this civil rights trial, the city attorney's office represented the two policemen and the city of Houston, whom I had sued jointly. A six-person jury elected an associate editor of the *Houston Chronicle*, the very conservative local newspaper, as their foreman, but I thought he could be fair. I was wrong.

During the trial, all the evidence went as I had expected. Rulings were generally against me, but I got the story before the jury just as my client had told me. The two officers absolutely denied they had laid a finger on John. They lamely explained his severe injuries by saying he had fallen when he was handcuffed and later hit his head when he climbed into the ambulance. They simply made up facts to explain away any responsibility they had for his injuries.

My client's story held up beautifully. The officers' story had many obvious inconsistencies.

During the trial, a lawyer I knew from the local bar came in to watch and, when the day's proceedings were over, came up to me and asked if he could speak to me confidentially.

I said sure, and we went to the empty jury room, where we could be absolutely alone and nothing could be heard outside its closed door. He said, "Dave, I just wanted to tell you I represent those two officers you have on trial in some other matters. They asked me to tell you that your client has told the truth. They are really sorry about what happened, but they were so incensed that John had apparently shot one of their fellow officers they just lost it. They are just glad that he wasn't injured permanently."

I told him that was good to hear, and I would take him before our judge and let him tell the judge what he had just told me. His response left me open mouthed. He said, "Dave, I can't do that. This is something my clients told me in confidence, and I cannot reveal it without their approval. If they reverse their testimony now, they will never be able to go back to the department and work as police officers. They will be ostracized or worse. Their fellow officers would tear them apart."

So we tried this to a conclusion with the jury finding that the officers told the truth, that there was no violation of rights, and the foreman led the jury through all the technical parts of the verdict, making sure the officers and the city were exonerated.

The jury brought their verdict in at about 7:30 in the evening, and by the time the end of trial activities were over and I reached my car in the federal court parking garage, at about 8:00, I couldn't hold back any longer. I threw my briefcase on the trunk of my car, laid my head next to it, and cried like a baby.

The damage to the body of my client from the beating had been terrible, but he had thankfully recovered well. The damage to the spirit, his and mine, from being rejected by the court, by the jury, and, really, by society, had been just too much. I couldn't hold back.

Regardless of Grandma's injunction, I cried for the first time in forty years.

There's an old folk saying that comes to mind about this.

Forgive your enemies. It messes up their heads

SECTION 3:

LIVING WELL

#32 Good Health Is Not a Right

What do you think you will be like at age seventy-five or eighty-five or older? You are all young now, and fifty years from now seems a very long way off. But it will come quicker than you can imagine. Taking care of yourself now is important for now. But it is also very important for how you will be when you are my age.

To say the obvious, good health is the end result of taking care of yourselves, your bodies. As a general rule, we talk about and usually treat our body as though it was a single unit, whole unto itself.

When asked how we are, we usually respond with a global statement about what's going on within our body. When we feel good, we feel good all over, and we say, "I'm okay," or words to that effect. When we feel a lack of energy or out of sorts, the feeling is one we experience in our whole being. It is the whole body that feels rotten.

Most of us pay little attention to any of the internal organs or systems that make up our body until one or more of those organs or systems attract attention by failing to function efficiently, causing us to feel a discomfort to some degree.

What we seldom, maybe never, think of is that the human body is basically a highly organized and integrated collection of cells.

All of the organs, all of the systems, from the largest to the smallest, from the most complex to the simplest, are composed of cells. There are a little over two hundred different types of cells in the human body, varying widely in both description and function. Each type of cell has developed to serve a particular essential part of the function of the body as a unity.

It is one of the wonders of our world that this highly organized collection of so many disparate cells all cooperate together to, first, create a body and all its highly specialized parts and then work together in symbiotic harmony to maintain the healthy condition for which they are genetically programmed. I'm leaving out the part about human stem cells being capable of migrating to particular parts of the body and then adapting themselves to become one with other cells already there and to perfectly perform the functions of those cells. That's more than we need to talk about for this brief review of your responsibility to keep well.

The most marvelous ancillary effect for your body when your cells are all in tip-top condition is that there is a glow of physical well-being which comes, literally, from deep within. To keep in healthy, fully functioning condition, your cells and cellular structures have as a common need good nutrition on a continuing and full spectrum basis.

Ultimately, you will be healthy or not at a cellular level.

That is where you must focus to maintain good health, to regain lost good health, and where you must start if your goal, when you are older, is to restructure your body to a biological age that is independent of your chronological age.

Cells have their own needs. Fail to pay attention to and satisfy those needs and your cells not only will fail to function at an optimum level but several consequences can also happen, any of which may have long-lasting effects.

Malnourishment, in addition to causing cell function to slow, cell walls to thicken and stiffen, and energy levels to drop dramatically, also throws the process of metabolism off. Naturally occurring waste products, like free radicals, are not quickly neutralized. While these hang around, they can damage the DNA molecule of nearby cells as well as other parts of the cell structure.

Malnutrition also can cause cell damage. The results of continuing malnutrition are essentially the same to cells as to the whole organism. The leathery-skinned, gaunt, hollow-eyed starving people we observe in pictures are merely outward manifestations of the process occurring to cells within from persistent malnutrition. Insufficient nourishment will cause cells to age swiftly and then will ultimately cease functioning and die.

When cells are damaged, a repair sequence begins that first determines if the cell can be repaired. If it can be, repair molecules swing into action and start the process. If the damage is too severe and it cannot be repaired, the cell dies and the waste managers of the body, the macrophage and neutrophil cells, come and carry it away as waste.

In between repair and death of the cell, there are other consequences which are bad for the body. It is possible for the cell DNA to be damaged so that it cannot be repaired by the usual cellular repair program but not enough for the cell to decide to destroy itself. It can't replicate and it won't die. It just hangs on. One theory includes this kind of cell damage that does not result in cell death as a major cause of physical body aging.

One purpose of meditation is to put the body into a deeply relaxed state, where the cell's healing mechanism, always at work, is encouraged to heal the DNA back into its original pristine condition in cells where it might have become damaged.

Malnutrition is different from reduced intake of calories. Our cells do need energy (measured in units of body heat called calories), but they need other vital nutrients even more. With reduced caloric supply, weight will go down, reproduction will falter, and hormone output will plummet, but longevity (in experiments) effectively nearly doubles. While it was learned that caloric content can be reduced by as much as 50 percent with life-extending results, at 60 percent reduction, the laboratory animals perished.

More than calories are needed. Your body is the result of an evolutionary response to nutrients generally available to our ancestors over the millennia that *Homo sapiens* have been roaming this earth. Cells are not picky about where nutrients come from. Animal protein contains a wealth of enzymes and minerals, as does vegetation that people can digest. Nutritionists all agree that a well balanced intake of both animal and vegetable products, grown on and in soils that have an abundant supply of minerals, will allow your body to extract what is needed from what is ingested.

But back to cellular life; cells also die because they age naturally. The aging of cells is a process that happens even to the healthiest cells. Although we have not yet established how many times the event happens in the human body, laboratory experiments have established that healthy cells from the human body (skin, endothelial, and other tissues) divide and replicate a finite number of times.

The mean number of fetal endothelial cell divisions (fetal endothelial cells are those cells that will create the essential internal organs of the body) is generally accepted as about fifty times. The time of division of any given cell is not a predictable event. About thirty-five of these divisions are thought to occur in the normal, healthy human body until the chronological age of about eighty-five. Cell division continues with the continued healthy life of the organism, and there are theories that this could be as much as 150 years.

That brings back the question I asked at the beginning: what do you think you will be like at seventy-five, eighty-five, or older?

To maintain a healthy body, good nutrition needs to be available everywhere, twenty-four hours a day. Digestive cells and enzymes extract whatever nutrition is available from things you take in. Stomach and intestines are where nutrients transfer into the bloodstream. Floating chemical and mineral molecules, extracted from food, water, and air, are carried along for distribution to your cells by blood fluids.

Specialized molecules, created and released into the blood by various vital organs, also nourish and stimulate a variety of different cells. But at the very basis of all life is what you take into your body. If what goes into your stomach has a sufficient quantity of what the body needs, your cells respond, and you feel energetic and healthy. If what you put into your stomach, no matter how great it may taste, does not have the nutritional components your cells need, then they are deprived of their energy source and can't function as intended; you feel dragged down and out of energy.

What is available from the food supply system of our society is usually commercially grown produce from soil, noted in the 1920s, to be terribly short of natural minerals. The situation has not gotten better. Farming corporations have learned how to stimulate production with just three chemicals: nitrogen, phosphorus, and potassium, and these show up in commercially grown food, but those three are not nearly nutritionally enough for your body.

Your body requires a mix of about seventy trace minerals—called trace because such tiny amounts are needed. They all used to be in the varied foods we have eaten since our beginnings as mammals. Yet those tiny amounts provided nutritional molecules that were and are essential to cell functioning.

There is, in the United States, plenty of food. But the mass-produced agricultural crops are mostly not nutritionally fulfilling to our bodies. Those three elements that stimulate growth of crops do not provide the nutritional mix of molecules our bodies need. It is why vegetables don't taste as good as they could and should. It is why animals raised on grains and grass that are nutritionally deficient taste like nothing or even, sometimes, just taste like the cardboard they were packed in. All of us, from children to centenarians, need supplements to our daily diet to provide to our cells the nutritional spectrum of minerals and other substances essential to keep us healthy.

Because we have all, since birth, been living in a food world that has been more and more nutritionally depleted, some of your cells have been stressed and need special help. The cells of your heart, cells lining the arterial system, cells which have been abused by smoke and other airborne irritants, and cells of many of our primary organs all require enzymes, coenzymes, and many of the phytochemicals found in various plant leaves and fibers. Your young cells need this. Aging cells that have been nutritionally deprived really need help from a variety of plant-derived sources to get healthy again.

Women have special needs for hormones that can be met using natural plant-derived substances. During and after menopause, progesterone extracted from plants has aspects that make it superior to the synthetic variety provided by patent pharmaceuticals. Substances made from wild yams, rubbed on the skin, are now known to stimulate natural estrogen production by the female body. That natural estrogen is in amounts the body apparently needs, not too much, and without apparent side effects.

Any man over forty-five has the potential for benign prostatic hyperplasia, a noncancerous condition that causes the prostate cells to swell. This, in turn, reduces stream flow, often requires frequent trips to the bathroom at night, and creates a sense of urgency in needing to empty the bladder. This can be helped and frequently controlled completely by taking a concentrate of Saw Palmetto Berries, a natural plant substance that has no known detrimental aspects. Transdermal vitamin B12, applied to the scrotum and carried to the prostate with seminal fluid offers beneficial easing of a BPH problem.

The current popular way to describe natural, plant-derived supplements is to speak of them as phytoproducts or phytonutrients. Essential elements that are effective chemicals and minerals helpful to humans are phytochemicals. And you need them, not every day while you are younger, for the body does store up a lot of what it needs, but trace element supplements are very important to your continued good health.

Each of us has travelled a different nutritional road. Each of us, at whatever time we decide to make changes and find our biological age, has a different list of changes to make to do that. Necessarily, different nutrients and supplements will be on your kitchen counter than on mine.

That means you have to do your own research into what specific help your cells need when you begin to take control of your body. But there are some general things we know that are helpful to all people at nearly every age, especially after the age of about sixty.

Sesame seed oil is as useful and important to good health as any product you can buy. It should be used regularly on your body. It absorbs through the skin quickly, and the body uses it to help with continuous cleansing.

Sesame seed oil molecules, as they move into the tissue beneath the skin, attract and neutralize oxygen radicals and other toxins, acting as a carrier to move those toxins to the waste removal system of the body. There is no better detoxifier. Be sure to get organic, cold-pressed oil you intend to use on your body.

To be sure impurities are removed or made harmless, carefully pasteurize all commercial oil you bring home to use on your skin. Do this by heating the oil to 212 degrees. You can know when the oil has reached 212 degrees by placing two small drops (*no more*) of water in the bottom of the pan into which you then pour the oil. As the oil heats (and do this on moderate, not high, heat), the water will snap and crackle as it turns to steam but cannot escape until the oil above it reaches the 212 mark. At that point, the water will evaporate through the oil, and you must turn off the heat and allow it to cool naturally. *Never put water into heating or heated oil.* It will cause an explosion of the hot oil.

Coenzyme Q10 is a specific for cardiac cell and arterial wall cell repair. It is a must to keep the arteries flexible, healthy, and free of petechial (microscopic) inner arterial wall injuries or bleeds that are likely the start of cholesterol accumulation the body uses to repair such injuries.

MSM guarantees that your cells have a plentiful supply of sulfur, essential for cell wall flexibility and permeability. All of the messenger molecules of your body require that cell walls be permeable so they can either pass into the interior of the cell directly or pass their information through cell walls without hindrances or obstructions.

Meditation is your connection with the universe. Meditation is both quick and effective in helping the body, both physical and emotional, manage stress and keep blood pressure down. Meditation is the communication channel between your essence and your body. Meditation is your tool to connect with the higher energies of your world.

Massage stimulates the immune system and is an essential ingredient of good health. Massage stimulates the skin, the largest organ of your body, to produce potent immunomodulators, interleukin, interleukin-2, and interferon—which help boost your ability to fend off bacterial and viral invaders.

Yoga *asanas*, or positional yoga exercises, are gentle, effective, and sufficient exercises to keep bodies healthy and flexible at all ages, even into your eighties and beyond.

Good health is not yours as a matter of right. But you can choose to have it.

As your body changes, which it is constantly doing, choosing good nutrition, clean water and air, emotional stabilizers, and a satisfying and health-bringing lifestyle for yourself will direct those changes toward good health. And you will likely coast into your advanced years feeling great about your body's ability to keep you happy to be alive.

To live is the rarest thing in the world.

Most people exist, that is all.

—Oscar Wilde

#33 Your Biological Age

You, my grandchildren, are all in your twenties as I write this. Thoughts of middle or old age are not likely ever in your mind. So some of this may seem inapplicable to you. It isn't. I started at age sixty-nine to find out if it was my time to die. After all, most of your (and my) ancestors, both paternal and maternal, died at about age seventy-two. There was no reason for me to think I would be an exception. But I have been.

Because all of you are young and concerned with career and relationships and finding a comfortable niche in which to move your lives forward, the things I am going to tell you in this e-mail are likely not of much interest to you at this time.

But keep this. It will help you focus on a couple of things that are important no matter what your age. When those first wrinkles appear, the first gray hairs, the first little paunch that upsets your idea of how you want to look, recall this: aging is a choice. You can choose to have a biological age that is considerably younger than the chronological age you state when asked, "How old are you?" There is more than vanity involved in this. What I am about to tell you involves your very existence—who, what, and how you are.

Nutrition that supports your body is something that should concern you as soon as you have the good sense to think about it. When we take in food that has little nutritional value or, worse, is tainted with toxins, such as industrial agricultural chemicals, even in amounts our government says is safe, our bodies will tell us that we have failed in our duty of good care. Excess salt, sugar, and ubiquitous preservative chemicals can be as deadly as agricultural poisons.

It is worth remembering that everything you take into your body that is not beneficial or useful to your cells has to be removed or neutralized in one way or another. Your body's waste system takes care of most of this, but there are some toxins that the body neither eliminates nor detoxifies, and these generally are stored in fat.

Habits can be toxic. Smoking is probably worst for the human cellular co-op. Tars and other trace elements in tobacco smoke are deleterious. Natural tobacco plant fiber is adulterated by cigarette manufacturers with a multitude of substances intended to please smokers' palettes and, incidentally, quicken the addiction process. The circulatory system is subject to real damage from tobacco smoke, even so-called second-hand smoke that may be in your atmosphere.

Alcohol also presents your body's system with a toxic substance that must be promptly detoxified by the liver. Eating sugary products, smoking cigarettes, and drinking alcohol are habits that don't add to your well-being. Changing habits is a choice that must be made to keep true to the more important choice to care for your cells, to care for yourselves. It is more than a matter of looking good, although that will be the result of taking good care of your cells.

With knowledge, you can make the choices to change . . . or not. It is your choice. You can choose to be a healthier you. In my case, I wanted to be a younger me, and I think I have succeeded. In large measure it was because I searched and found ways to help my cells in their natural inclination to keep young and keep healthy.

Once you decide to be healthy and to hold on to your youth, the work is not hard. It will take persuading yourself *that it is what you really want to do*. Once your choice is made to drop toxic habits and adopt new and healthful habits of living, life becomes quite easy.

I have had to research this for myself because there are precious few authorities in the health field who offer any hope that this can be done. But that is not discouraging when my own experience tells me that I have done this, and inferentially, it is an ubiquitous human ability. It is not magic. It is simply decisional.

I've told you this before, but it is so important that a quick review is in order. Your body is composed of colonies of cells. Each human has over two hundred different kinds of cells. From the time a single male sperm attaches to a single female ovum, stimulating the creation of a small mass of just a few cells, beginning the process of making a body, cells constantly divide, create new cells, and differentiate into specialized cells to perform all the functions a human body requires for existence.

Cell biologists have been able to isolate a particular chromosomal attribute (the telomeres), a string of disposable fragments of DNA, designed to protect the end of the DNA molecule. These shorten each time a cell divides, making the life of any normal cell and its descendants finite.

Even without trauma, disease, and the normal wear and tear of life upon the cellular structure of the body, all cells and, therefore, all human bodies have a finite, terminable existence measured by the number of potential cell divisions.

Other researchers have shown us how to extend the lives of cells, while they search for a way to activate the substance that all cells have within their DNA molecule that would cause the telomeres to not shorten at the time of cell division. This is probably the wrong approach, for no one wants to live forever. But along the way, information about cell life and longevity is being accumulated, and that's worthwhile.

Studies have shown that while we live and for as long as we live, even past one hundred years, our cells will respond favorably to good nutrition. Asked to grow to provide muscle mass to strengthen an arm or leg or any part of the body, we know the cells will do that, even at eighty and ninety chronological years.

It appears that our cells will do that for us until we die. The reported centenarians of the Caucasus Mountains are said to work in the fields and dance at festivals at advanced chronological ages of 110 and more. Reportedly on the Greek island of *Ikaria*, men are sexually active into their 90s.

Studies of fetal endothelial cells, those cells that become vital organs in the individual, established the number of those cell doublings at an average of fifty. The same studies also showed that the cells taken from a forty-year-old doubled forty times. Even more interesting, cells taken from an eighty-year-old doubled thirty times. How frequently these cells, critical for continued life, replicate in the body is not known for certain but thought to be about every two to three years.

Enzymes, coenzymes, hormones, and other substances in human systems have been identified, their roles ascertained, and the information published to help us supplement our diets, adding those essentials which become in short supply as the chronological years go on.

For those over fifty, there is almost certainly a need to supplement the diet to fill in those things which the body no longer makes in the quantity needed to stay healthy and energetic. For those over sixty chronological years, supplements are absolutely essential to good health and critical to maintaining a biological age less than one's chronological age.

The time to start establishing a biological age different from (and younger than) your chronological age is whenever you are ready to do it—the younger, the better. Even if one or more of the body's systems has been damaged, the cellular structure of your body has a built-in repair program that you can activate to return your body to a condition of good health and good energy. There are flexibility exercises you can easily do, no matter how stiff you are when you start. Herbs and minerals and other aids to nutrition and to metabolic efficiency are available.

A different approach to living is required, but it will not change your routine much. Mostly you will need to develop an awareness of what foods and other nutritional substances are useful for your system. We are each unique. Our nutritional needs are unique, something the world of industrialized food production has not yet recognized.

In other e-mails, I have explored *kinesiology* with you, a simple, effective way to communicate with your cells. Since we are each unique, what your cells believe is in their (thus your) best interest is vital information for you. Kinesiology is the easiest way to find out how your cells react to any food, action, relationship, or whatever. Kinesiology is really quite remarkable.

You probably cannot find this information at your favorite doctor's office. Nor from your health-care insurance provider. The US health system just does not offer information about ways you can reverse or maintain your true biological age, except through products that the pharmaceutical industry and the medical establishment want to sell you for a temporary fix of, at the most, a few of the body's aging signs and problems.

The development of a US for-profit medical care system, including investor-owned (and doctor-owned) hospitals and clinics, imaging centers, and doc-in-a-box corner health stations means that decisions about what a patient needs are skewed by the desire of investors to maximize profits.

Viagra and HGH (human growth hormone) come to mind as recent quite-expensive pills and injections offered to reverse a couple of the aging conditions our bodies normally experience as the years add to our chronological age. I have elected to go my own way, drawing from both recent research and ancient wisdom to experience what has been a reversal of my chronological age and a substitution of a new and more energetic me that I like a lot.

Basically, the physical body we each occupy while we experience the human condition is simply a collection of cells. Seventy trillion or more is the generally accepted number.

These cells are organized into systems and subsystems, all interacting without ceasing, from before birth until the time of death, with the primary goal of keeping themselves, each other, and their host (you) alive, healthy, and happy. Health defense mechanisms are built into each cell and into the systems that the collection of cells we call our body have developed. Internal repair mechanisms are built into the cells, and we can tap into and enhance those with our thoughts.

Using thought to enhance life and increase the health of the body is a subject I have addressed in other e-mails. But it is worth noting more than once that we do have the power to influence, not only our own cells, but also our environment and our future by our thoughts.

Cells are in many ways like individual cities. They have their own energy systems (the mitochondria), their own central library of plans which contain the formulas of what they can and cannot do (the DNA), their own manufacturing systems (to make proteins according to the DNA plans), their own garbage system (to carry toxins and waste out of the cell into the blood stream), and their own repair system (for repairing the DNA when free radicals or other toxins cause injury).

Cells take in from the arterial blood stream oxygen, minerals, and other substances and energy molecules they need. Some cells export products that other cells need. Cells respond to information messenger molecules sent out from the brain, the skin, from the immune system, and from one of the various vital organs of the body, glands, and nerve centers, providing supplies or engaging in actions initiated by those messages.

The external envelope, which surrounds each cell, must be flexible and permeable in order for it to perform efficiently. This envelope has places on it, frequently described as docking sites, where only certain information messenger molecules with the proper configuration can attach. Once attached, these information messenger molecules then either transmit their message through the external envelope to the interior of the cell or may be taken into the cell itself in order to achieve whatever its intended purpose may be.

Keeping all of our cells healthy so that they can, individually and in conjunction with all the other cells in our bodies, perform their functions is a matter of our paying attention to several things: nutrition is probably first in importance.

Not only should we know what our bodies can metabolize and convert into useful energy for the rest of the body to use, but we should also be aware that, to some of us, many substances commonly accepted and used as food are really toxic. Foods to which we may have an allergic reaction we identify quickly. Other foods, which simply drain our energies or have the potential for causing more subtle damage than an allergic reaction, we also need to know about. Kinesiology will help you find out what your cells like and don't like and what will likely produce unpleasant reactions if you persist against their preferences.

The information I have passed along came to me from many sources and at many different times. My life over the past sixteen years has been like a sampler, searching for, finding, trying, and adopting various ways of accomplishing my goal of "youthing" back to a biological age I found comfortable. At some time, if you are like most other humans, you will ponder about doing that too. I hope you will find this a useful reference when that day comes.

In the long run,

we all die.

But we all want to have

a long run.

—GPD

#34 Ayurveda Healing

When I closed my law practice, I was pretty burned out. To try and regain my health and my energy, I went to see Deepak Chopra, who had recently written a book called *Quantum Healing*. The ideas about well-being and health he outlined in that book were quite different from the Western medicine I had been dealing with as an attorney. I know you all are rebels at heart and would be interested in his different approach to keeping well. So let me tell you a little about that experience.

Western medicine is quite effective in many ways. But with cancers and many other conditions that threaten life, Western medicine is no more effective than any of the more ancient healing arts. Particularly, *ayurveda* is a venerable healing art that many turn to when the allopathic doctors offer a death sentence of having done all they can do.

The difference in their approach to health is stark. Western medicine is very parental in its approach. Though unspoken, the message we get from Western medicine doctors is usually, "Sit down and let me tell you what is wrong and what I am going to do to cure you."

Ayurveda, on the other hand, is more "Your body will heal itself if we can cleanse your body of accumulated poisons. Then *you* need to help yourself by changing what you put into your body and also change the conditions under which you require your body to function."

Ayurveda healing is ancient. It comes to us from the Vedic people who invaded and settled northern India sometime in the third millennium BCE. Brought to this country by Maharishi Mahesh Yogi nearly sixty years ago, there are presently two major ayurveda healing centers that his organization established—in Lancaster, Massachusetts, and The Raj in Fairfield, Iowa.

In the township of Lancaster, Massachusetts, about sixty miles northwest of Boston, is a 208-acre tract on which is the Maharishi Ayurveda Health Center. It is next to the Lancaster township forest of about six hundred acres and a Massachusetts state forest of comparable size.

This healing center is the former Bayard Thayer Estate, the main house built around 1910. At that time, the whole area was meadowland. Now it is completely grown over with forest. Much of the existing township forest was at one time a part of the Thayer Estate and was planted by estate foresters with white and red oak and white pine trees, which now have grown to great heights. Rhododendrons from Korea and China planted in groves now form a canopy under which one can walk as though in a natural cathedral.

The main building is the former Thayer mansion, about sixteen thousand square feet, with sixteen guest rooms. Many other bedrooms and suites house the staff ayurveda healer and his family, the *Jyotish* (see note below) when there, and various other staff members.

The common areas for guests are elegant, with dark wood-paneled walls, ornate sconces on the twelve-foot ceilings, sunrooms, reading rooms, large entry halls and stairways, and both a large dining room and an intimate sunroom/breakfast room.

The treatment area is a six thousand-square-foot wing, annexed and attached to the main building. Its origin derives from when the place had been operated as a Catholic convent, used then to house nuns and novitiates.

There are five treatment rooms on the men's floor and the same number on the women's floor, with two tiled bathrooms with showers on each floor. In the 1990s when I was there, yoga and other teaching classes were held in a large basement activity room. In 2009, that activity had been discontinued.

The compound is isolated from the community by fences, gates, and distance, with walking paths into the woods and around the property, which allows plenty of room for walking without getting into civilization to break the spell of the quiet isolation.

At its peak, in 1995-1996, the staff numbered around forty, including housekeeping, kitchen, serving, and office staff. By far the most contact I had was with the staff of male massage technicians, their numbers varying from time to time with the numbers of guests.

These technicians were then and, from the experience my wife, Mary, and I had in October 2009, are still, without exception, gentle, proficient, knowledgeable about the treatments, and very skilled in the performance of every aspect of their work. Many have worked in their craft for years at Lancaster and other centers. Some, in the past, have worked at the center of the Maharishi Medical Treatment program at Vlodrow, Netherlands.

At that center, Ashtavaidya Moos, an ayurveda healer who is from one of eight families in India who have the responsibility of maintaining the purity and continuity of the ayurveda tradition in health care, directs the establishment of ayurvedic treatment programs worldwide. He also consults by phone with other ashtavaidyas, ayurveda physicians at the various centers in the United States established to treat and to promote the ayurveda path to good health.

The treatment center in Lancaster has evolved from providing only Panchakarma treatment to being a center for treatment of both acute and chronic health problems.

"Panchakarma" is a term that, literally means "five actions." "Pancha" means "five" and "karma," no matter what you might have heard about that word, merely means "action," nothing more.

The common use of karma in the parlance of the 1960s is taken to mean that one gets what one deserves. And in the cosmic sense, that is true. Each action we take has ramifications which do come back to affect us. But for the purposes of these pages, *karma* merely means action.

The recommendation is to have Panchakarma three times a year: at the change of winter to spring, at the beginning of summer, and again, at the beginning of fall/winter. The intent is to cleanse the system of the buildup of toxins in one's physical and emotional body since the last PK session.

In the case of one who has never had this sort of cleansing process, the accumulation of toxins is usually a serious matter, and the first time one has a week of PK is an experience to celebrate.

In traditional PK cleansing, the preceding week involves slowing down the tempo of life, allowing the body to get ready for the serious business of moving toxins out. There is a preparatory cleansing of the colon through oleation and purgatives. The body also is oriented during this prep week to a totally vegetarian diet.

Oleation consists of taking increasing amounts of ghee (clarified butter) each morning over four days, mixed with hot water. This loosens the contents of the bowel, which, for most in our Western world of daily workday tensions and not very digestible foods, is a necessary prelude to really getting rid of toxins we unknowingly carry around with us.

These toxins are attached to the wall of the large intestine, encased in old undischarged fecal matter. A purgative of castor oil or other herbal potions was added to the routine along with a hot soaking bath on the day before starting PK to assist the elimination process.

The five actions (Panchakarma) in traditional ayurveda include cleansing the body with purges (emptying the stomach through vomiting), purgatives (cleansing the bowels with *bastis*, small and large), bloodletting, vapors and nose drops to cleanse and empty the nasal passages and sinuses, and massages to cleanse the external tissues and circulatory system.

Only three actions are used in the United States. Bloodletting and purging are not a part of the usual treatment here. An interesting side note: because of diet and the processes of aging, red blood cells tend to become not as flexible as we pass over the chronological age of fifty; they tend to clump or aggregate, rather than stay singular, inhibiting their ability to pass through the capillaries and nourish all the cells of the body. The process of bloodletting, stimulates the creation of new, young, and healthy red blood cells.

The first two or three days of the PK treatments are always a time of major detoxifying. The body naturally requires rest and quiet to assimilate and integrate the good effects of the treatments.

In 1995-1996, during my first three PK weeks, each about four months apart, I slept eight to ten hours at night and then napped for a couple of hours during the day. Particularly during and after treatments, which provide both a blissful experience and one in which my body was being asked to work to rid itself of toxins, I found that both my mind and body were in a state of quietness which demanded my body be horizontal.

In addition to Lancaster, the Maharishi's organization provides another place where various ayurveda and PK treatments are provided, with overnight facilities for guests. Having one's own room in the same facility where treatment is being received is by far the most satisfactory.

The Maharishi University of Management in Fairfield, Iowa, has near it, on the rolling plains of the southeastern part of that state, a place called the Raj that offers Panchakarma as well as other ayurveda treatments.

The guest facilities accommodate ten in the main lodge and another ten in cottages, scattered campus style, over several acres. The Raj boasts a world-class gourmet vegetarian kitchen to provide meals for all guests. The facility is quite isolated, and the loudest thing I heard while visiting there was the wind across the prairie.

Deepak Chopra, a Western-medicine-trained physician, well known and highly respected as a writer, lecturer, and healing process teacher, successfully created Lancaster-like arrangements for ayurveda healing and PK in a small hotel, the Auberge, in Del Mar, California.

To his great misfortune, the hotel changed hands, and the new owners wanted Deepak and his guests gone. He moved his clinic, first to La Jolla, California, and later to Rancho Santa Fe, California. His operation separates sleeping accommodations and clinic areas. The whole is just not as warm, cozy, quiet, and comforting as at Lancaster or the Raj.

Visiting La Jolla, I found that having to leave the treatment facility to go to a hotel, with quiet time and sleeping arrangements isolated and widely separated from the healing facilities, breaks the spell of good energy the treatments create.

During the first few sessions of PK, there absolutely needs to be someplace to go for rest and quiet after each daily treatment. After having had PK many times, I now find that three consecutive days of PK are enough and that separation of massage areas from sleeping and even eating locations is not as objectionable.

In Lancaster, the treatments are intense. Scheduled for two to three hours, they frequently take a full four hours. The male techs I encountered there were all marvelously competent. Although I have had contact with only the male techs working on me (and the women have only women working on them), the women guests with whom I've talked have had unstinting praise for the women techs.

To have a PK massage by two experienced techs simultaneously is a marvelous experience. The first massage of any PK treatment is usually an Abhyanga, a full-body massage that takes two techs about forty minutes to accomplish.

The consequence of total involvement with the experience is that at the end, one is blissed out. The technicians finish by draping a light cover over the patient, turning out the lights, and leaving the room for fifteen to twenty minutes to allow the experience to be fully integrated before the next procedure is begun. Usually, I do not stir. If I don't slip into outright sleep, the massage has put me in a state of feeling so good that I lie completely motionless, letting the joy of the moment fill me.

In PK, Abhyanga massage is generally a prelude to other cleansing actions. The warmth of the oil itself, combined with the response of skin to the friction of the massage, opens the pores, allowing the oil to penetrate into the tissues to begin cleansing the body of toxins.

Sesame oil is one of those marvels of nature which man has discovered to his great benefit. It is such a wonderful, useful product that I have devoted a whole e-mail to you to sing the praises of sesame oil. But some of it is worth repeating here, from information provided in a personal interview with Dr. D. Edwards Smith, who, in 1996, was a member of the Maharishi North American organization and author of two studies on sesame oil.

I remind you about this oil, because it is so beneficial to your overall health. Sesame oil is bacteriostatic—that is, it will not support the growth of bacteria. It will not turn rancid, even though left unrefrigerated. When applied warm to the skin, it absorbs through the skin into the tissue of the body, all the way to the marrow of the bone. On the way, this oil picks up toxins and *ama*, the sludge that accumulates in body tissues from fats and other nonmetabolized portions of foods we eat, toxins we accumulate from the environment we live in, and from unmetabolized emotional traumas we suffer in the ordinary course of living.

For toxins and *ama*, this oil becomes a carrier. At the cellular level, the oil transports nasties into the capillaries of our circulatory system, thence into the veins, on to the kidneys, liver, and waste system, and on to be eliminated from the body.

Warm oil massages not only help put the carrier oil into the body, but the massage pressures and manipulation of body tissues also loosens the bad stuff and helps the oil do its job as a transporter.

When the time for the next part of the treatment arrives, the techs return silently. Ayurvedic techs do not speak together in the treatment room nor do they talk to me, other than to inform me quietly about what they intend to do next or ask me to change positions.

They wear hospital-operating-room type booties so in walking about the room, they make no sound. Their preparations are always outside the treatment rooms so no sound of that intrudes on the soft silence of the experience either.

The last part of every treatment, every day except the going-home day, is a *basti*, an herbalized oil or warm water enema (some small, some larger) administered by the same techs that do the treatments. The herbs are intended to be absorbed by the lower colon as treatment or simply to assist in elimination.

Once *ama* and other toxins have been moved into the intestinal tract by the various treatments, the objective is to move these out of the body quickly before they can be reabsorbed. *Bastis* are really effective for that.

The types and sequences of massage, the herbs and the oils used, and the variations of procedures are all under the direction of an ayurveda physician. The techs that I have had work on me have been, without exception, totally professional in their approach to their tasks and knowledgeable and skilled in their presentation of various PK treatments. Nonetheless, the purpose of PK is to create good health in the patient, and that's always under the direction of a physician-healer.

Choosing from many variations of PK massage and treatment, the Ashtavaidya at both The Maharishi Center and the Chopra Center always outline the PK schedule after an initial examination and conference.

The exam includes a pulse evaluation (and diagnosis) and (sometimes) a tongue evaluation, unique to both ayurvedic and traditional Chinese health professionals. If any Western doctor has ever looked at my tongue, it has been as a consequence of looking in my mouth to examine a sore throat. The tongue, I have found out, has many clues in its overall color, shape, spotting, and other qualities, which give information to an informed healer about one's overall health. Not only does the upper surface of the tongue offer quite specific information about the health condition of various body systems, but the under part of the tongue also contains a wealth of indicators about the body's level of toxins.

As might be suspected, the length, intensity, and variety of treatment vary considerably. The repertoire of standard treatments is long and ayurvedic physicians prescribe many specialized treatments for particular problems that are unique to the patient.

In India, it has been reported that partially blocked coronary arteries were unblocked by using sesame oil. The treatment process was to use a paste of cooked and mashed mung bean to build a raised donut-shaped dam on the chest of the patient, directly over the heart. Then with the patient lying on his back, warm oil was poured into the center of this donut and allowed to remain there against the skin for half an hour. After several of these treatments, it was reported, the arterial blockages disappeared.

When I complained of memory problems, a similar treatment was prescribed for me, except that in my case the dam of mashed mung bean was created around the crown of my head and the warm oil poured into the crater it made. I kept my head still for thirty minute each time, allowing the warm herbalized oil to penetrate into my scalp and head. There were ten days of those unusual treatments.

For a short while after coming home following those treatments, from time to time, I felt a little spacey, not quite my usual charge-ahead self. But gradually my memory improved, and I credit that treatment as one of the reasons. I suspect that the arteries in my head are in much better condition now for having had that treatment.

Standard treatments that are popular with the guests at both the Chopra Center and the Maharishi Center are Swedena (a sweat tent), Pizzichilli (warm sesame oil is poured over your body from head to toes for about forty minutes), and Shirodhara (with the head tilted back at the end of a massage table, warm oil in a pencil-thin stream is swept slowly back and forth across the forehead). There are also rubdowns with silk gloves, rubdowns with milk and cooked rice, herbal packs, herbalized mud rubs, and a wide variety of other massages.

Food served at both centers is all vegetarian and very tasty. Innovative ways to fix and serve a wide variety of vegetables, grains, and fruits are a part of the skills of the cooks at both centers, and the amount of food served is ample. No one would ever go hungry during treatment.

Light fare is intended to complement and assist the program of ridding the body of toxins by providing only foods that are easily digested and with lots of bulk to aid in elimination.

I have been to Chopra's center on six occasions, most recently in 2003, and Lancaster seven times, the most recent in October 2009. The visits have been as short as four days and as long as two weeks. Each visit has offered a different package of massages and treatments, and all of them have been among the most satisfying experiences of my life.

At my last visit to Lancaster, there were prominently displayed models and plans for the creation of an ayurveda college adjacent to the Lancaster Ayurveda Health Center, intended to provide housing and training facilities for two hundred doctors, fifty architects, and fifty teachers. The timing couldn't be better. The need for more doctors will only grow. Financial help from both the state of Massachusetts and the US federal government is expected to give a big push to these ambitious plans. One can only wish for Lancaster and its new prospects a most glorious future.

*Jyotish*es have been short-term residents of the Lancaster Center. These are men of family lineages who have studied ayurvedic astrology for generations. *Jyotish* traditions reach back millennia. They offer consultations about the effect of the planets upon one's life, past and future, much as other astrologers do.

An interesting note about the readings of the *Jyotish*es is that they calculate the effect upon one's life of an astrological object that is not present visually in the skies. They describe it as merely a reference point in our solar system.

Zechariah Sitchin, In his book *The Twelfth Planet* describes a planet, Niburu, a member of our solar system but whose elongated orbital path around our sun is at about a fifteen-degree inclination to the plane of our present solar system and whose orbit is so large that it takes 3,600 years to make one revolution out and back around our sun. According to Sitchin, Niburu was last in the neighborhood perhaps twenty-five hundred years ago.

Sumerian clay tablets have been translated, which describe this planet, its action, and the beings (aliens?) that came from it to earth. To humans in the ancient valleys of the Tigris and Euphrates rivers, these beings were regarded as gods.

Sitchin makes an interesting case that representations of these nonhuman people, depicted on ancient clay tablets, show them wearing headgear much like our present astronauts. He also has a strong argument for drawings on clay stele that show cylindrical objects he identifies as spaceships.

Vedic written history is several thousand years old, and it seems more than coincidence that their astrological tables should mention a now unseen object in our solar system which affected the earth in those ancient times. Sumerian clay tablets from the third and fourth millennia BC also describe a now-unseen object, a twelfth planetary member of our solar system.

Each time our earth observatories announce that they think they have spotted another planetlike object in our galaxy, I listen, wondering if I will hear some confirmation of the existence of the planet that Sitchin named Niburu.

When you are tempted to assume that we are now at the pinnacle of human thought, that we are so much more advanced than our ancestors, ponder this:

The sages of India, circa three thousand years BCE, just sitting and thinking, reached an understanding about the physical world that is confirmed today by our present leading cosmological thinkers.

#35 Sesame Seed Oil

When I was a youthful reader of the Bible, the several descriptions of feet being washed with oil set me wondering: why didn't they use water? I didn't find the answer until I discovered sesame seed oil as a massage oil in Panchakarma treatments and, following my first PK, used sesame seed oil every morning for my own self-massage. From here on, I will call it sesame oil.

What I know about sesame oil and its marvelous attributes, I learned from massage technicians both at Deepak Chopra's clinics (in Del mar and La Jolla, California) and at the Maharishi Vedic Health Center in Lancaster, Massachusetts, from Deepak Chopra himself and most especially from Dr. D. Edwards Smith in 1996, the to-be-dean of a proposed Maharishi College of ayurvedic medicine in Albuquerque, New Mexico. That project ultimately failed to thrive, to the world's detriment.

Dr. Smith brings special expertise to the information I pass on here about sesame oil, having done several studies to determine beneficial properties of that oil and having coauthored articles in professional journals concerning the effect of sesame oil on "Selective Growth Inhibition of Human Malignant Melanoma in Vitro" and also "The Use of Sesame Oil and Other Vegetable Oils in Inhibition of Human Colon Cancer Growth."

Dr. Smith told me he was first attracted to sesame oil when he observed its use in Panchakarma, the term for the ayurvedic procedures intended to rid the body of toxins. PK involves many different treatments, nearly all of which involve technicians using sesame oil as an integral part of their work with PK patients/ clients.

Even though the sheets and towels used are all fresh and clean for each different patient and the technicians are meticulous about cleanliness themselves, with no prescreening of patients for fungus or skin disease, the surroundings and the process seemed to Dr. Smith to present a troubling potential for spreading skin disorders. However, what he found not only relieved his concerns about that but also persuaded him to do the research mentioned above.

Sesame oil is quite inexpensive and nonpatentable and so the pharmaceutical industry is predictably uninterested in sponsoring either experimentation into the beneficial properties of sesame oil or promoting the spread of information about the therapeutic uses of this oil. The information about how it can be used, both in ordinary life and in medicinal applications, starts with the Vedic literature from India and the oral traditions of its use as a part of the practice of healing.

Sesame oil has long been known to have antifungal and antibacterial properties. It is bacteriostatic—that is, bacteria will not grow in sesame oil. Curing this oil for massage purposes is described below, but that does not alter the natural bacteriostatic properties of this oil.

It is useful for control of common skin pathogens such as staphylococcus and streptococcus and will inhibit the growth of common skin fungi. Studies involving periodontal disease revealed that sesame oil kills most of the bacteria that causes gingivitis and other gum problems. Sesame oil, sometimes with herbs (such as ginger juice) added, is very effective for control of common sinus bacteria and has been used to cure chronic sinusitis.

Sesame oil rubbed on the skin will penetrate into the tissue to the very marrow of the bone. It is a potent antioxidant. On its way through the skin and into the tissue of the body, it will neutralize any free radicals it encounters. It will attract to itself fat-soluble toxins. Some will rise to the level of the oil film on the skin, to be washed away with soap in shower or bath.

For other fat-soluble toxins, sesame oil acts as a carrier. Toxin molecules attach to sesame oil molecules and are carried through the circulatory system to the kidneys or liver, neutralized, and simply moved out of the body as waste.

Sesame oil has anti-inflammatory properties and, applied liberally to injured tissue or joints, have hastened the healing process at an injury site and added flexibility to stiffened joints. It has been successfully used to treat and cure anal fissures.

During the time when bathing was thought to be bad for the health of humans, at least in some areas of the world, the problem of lice was a serious one. Even today, we hear of outbreaks of head lice among children in the schools of some parts of our country. Sesame oil, used liberally in the hair of the head (and on all the hirsute areas of the body where lice commonly hide and multiply), will protect against the infestation of lice. It kills the lice by clogging the insect's breathing apparatus. Sesame oil would be a very cost effective and nontoxic (to the children) way of controlling such a health threat.

Orchardists have seen its usefulness as a mite-controlling substance, which is environmentally safe and harmless to beneficial insects and harmless to the trees and the fruit itself. Mixed with soap and sprayed on the tree and especially the bark, the mixture seeps into all the crevices where mites hide, coating their bodies and filling their pores, causing their demise.

So when the ancients told tales about the magical properties of sesame (remember the tale of the cave filled with chests of coins and jewels and one had to say the magic words "open sesame" to gain access to the cave?), they were drawing on information everyone then had that has been lost in the general trashing of the accumulated healing wisdom of the ages by our modern medical establishment.

Washing the feet of a traveler with oil is reported more than once in the Bible. I always wondered why they would use oil. But is seems reasonable to me that those same healing properties we know today about sesame oil were as well known in India more than four thousand years ago.

Most probably, sesame oil was known in all the areas of the world where it was, and remains, a serious seed crop, including the areas where the writers of the scrolls that became our Bible lived. It would have offered many benefits to the feet of the pedestrian traveler; the antibacterial qualities, the anti-inflammatory properties and interestingly, from an ayurvedic healing perspective, sesame oil helps balance the metabolism of many people.

Feet that have been on an ancient road for any length of time, in sandals or bare, would have been more than ordinarily active and would necessarily have accumulated excess energy as well as nicks and bruises. It is highly probable they walked through dust composed in some measure of the excrement of animals with which people shared those ancient roads.

Sesame oil has one other quality that is of interest, though there have not been any human cell experiments to show how this attribute might affect humans.

A major component of sesame oil is linoleic acid, nearly 50 percent by volume. In experiments with baby mice, it has been observed that as the mice reach maturity, linoleic acid is detected in increasing amounts in their bodies, leading to the conclusion that linoleic acid is one factor inhibiting the rapid cell growth which is essential to growing juvenile mice but which would be destructive to the organism once maturity is reached.

That observation along with the studies done by Dr. Smith establishing that, in vitro, human skin cancer cell growth was inhibited by sesame oil could easily lead one to conclude that sesame oil might also affect the rate of duplication of normal human cells. (I have searched but found no other studies examining the effect of sesame oil on cancer cell growth besides the study done by Dr. Smith.)

That is important information. We know that all cells contain two chains of chromosomes, the DNA molecule, and that each chromosomal chain has at one terminal end a tail-like component—a telomere. As the cells divide, producing new baby cells with new and identical sets of chromosomes, the new telomere shortens by one unit. This process is called replication.

It is important, when discussing anything so intensively studied as cancer, to be sure that you do not take away from this the idea that sesame oil will inhibit all cancer cell growth. Even so, the Dr. Smith study and conclusions are cause for questioning why the establishment in "the war on cancer" has not initiated some comparable studies using sesame and other seed oils since the study using human colon cancer cells proved so heartening. All physicians have access to all the medical literature and certainly could have read about Dr. Smith's work had they been inclined.

Cancer cells are called by cellular biologists "immortal cells" because their telomeres do not diminish with each cell division. In the laboratory and, presumably, in the body, cancerous cells keep on dividing and dividing, seemingly eternally, so long as they have the requisite nutrient broth in which to live. Studies still need to be done to establish what is really going on when sesame seed oil (or perhaps simply the linoleic acid which is its main component) inhibits the growth of cancer cells.

The aging process is more complicated than simply speeding or slowing cell division. Studies by Dr. Leonard Hayflick at Stanford University that showed an average of fifty cell divisions of endothelial cells before replication stopped, the Hayflick number, needs to be considered.

So also does the fact that more young cells, in the aggregate, might make the body feel and actually be younger. That the elemental components of our cells, continuously being replaced, have not been in place for more than about twenty-four months, also may need to be considered. But substances like linoleic acid that limit cell division could potentially have enormously positive effects on the human aging process.

Using sesame oil as a part of a daily routine has done several things for my skin. It is tighter and not saggy, and the pores, particularly around the nose, have not enlarged with the years; there is resiliency of the skin around the eyes and on the backs of the hands, areas which are very prone to becoming toughened and less elastic, less flexible, because of cellular damage and cross-linking, a natural aging process in the body I have told you about in other e-mails.

A note about the use of sesame oil on the face: I have seen advice to women address what is called the delicate skin on the face, around the eyes, and on the neck. The advice is usually to treat such areas very gently.

Skin is tough. It is very difficult to hurt skin by rubbing. When sesame oil is used around the eyes, the face, and the throat areas, the oil penetrates and helps make the skin more flexible and resilient almost immediately.

When I started using sesame oil and wanted the skin cells of my face to respond to massage and be healthy and youthful as baby skin cells were being continuously born and rising to the surface, I used (and still use) vigorous circular motions all around my face and neck. For me, the results have been very gratifying. My facial skin still looks as it did twenty years ago.

Sesame oil is not just for external use. Some manufacturers make what have been named sesame pearls to take as a nutritional supplement.

When I started Youthing Strategies, a small company that made only sesame oil products for personal use, I had several clients receiving chemotherapy who took sesame oil pearls that I offered, made from ayurveda cured oil I supplied as the ingredient. They told me that the sesame oil helped their nausea and calmed their digestive system. Raw sesame oil (organic and cold-pressed, of course) that one might use as a morning mouth rinse can also be taken by the spoonful for the linoleic acid it provides.

Remembering Dr. Smith's work, if human colon cancer cells could not live in sesame oil in a petri dish, taken as a prophylactic, sesame oil may deter the development of cancer cell proliferation in the colon of one who takes a couple of spoonfuls of the raw oil before breakfast. At the least, it will help lubricate the colon and aid elimination.

In times of dry weather, when I am about to take a plane trip or go to a very dry climate (like Las Vegas), I use sesame oil to coat the inside of my nose. I find that it prevents the drying and bleeding in my nasal passages that frequently result from very dry conditions.

Opportunistic bacteria, often prevalent in the concentrations of people at airports and in the planes themselves (which have very poor provisions for fresh air, circulating over 75 percent of the air in the plane again and again) are effectively barred from causing a focus of infection by the presence of sesame oil as a coating in the nasal passages.

In response to a skier who had found that using sesame oil to coat the inside of his nose prevented nose bleeds from the high altitude and exceedingly dry air of the Rockies, I developed *Nose Oil*, ayurveda-cured sesame oil blended with a hint of peppermint essential oil.

When a friend, whose immune system had been terribly compromised by chemotherapy, intended a trip by plane to Australia, he used Nose Oil as protection against all the potential bad things he could breathe in on the trip. The very long trip over and back was made without the illness he usually developed on such adventures.

Sesame oil for massage should be organic and cold-pressed. It will say on the label "expeller extracted." That means "cold-pressed." This will insure that no solvents were used in the extraction process (molecules of which might remain in the oil you use, not a good thing). "Organic" means no agrichemicals and poisons were used to grow the crop. These are taken up by the plants and are found in the seeds (and oil). Agrichemicals are used to kill something. They are poisonous. You don't want them in your oil.

Ayurveda has found that sesame oil works best if cured. Curing is simply heating the oil to 212 degrees. This drives off any water molecules that might remain from the extraction process or introduced during bottling. Though the potential is remote, water molecules could harbor toxins or viruses and so need to be driven off as steam.

An added reason to cure the sesame oil before using it is that the heat changes oil components sesamin and sesamolin into sesamol, a powerful antioxidant. Curing the oil also creates smaller molecules of oil for better absorption by the body.

To determine when the oil has reached 212 degrees, put one or two small drops of water (no more) into the bottom of the pan before putting in the oil. Put the burner on moderate heat. *Always* stay with the oil during this process. You do not want to overheat the oil.

As the oil approaches boiling water temperature, you will hear popping and crackling as the tiny water droplets you put into the pan turn to steam and try to escape but cannot rise through oil which is still below 212 degrees. When the popping and crackling stops, you know all the oil is now at 212 degrees and the pan of oil should be removed from the stove to cool before putting it back into the bottle it came from. As I've told you before, *do not put water into oil when the oil is hot! That can cause a very big explosion.*

Organically produced sesame oil can be obtained from Maharishi Ayurvedic Products Inc. (MAPI) in Colorado Springs, Colorado, from Whole Foods natural food stores, from youthing strategies.com, my former company that is still operating using the processes and formulae I created, and from skindharma.com, which also uses processes I developed that lightens and purifies raw sesame oil. Disclosure: Skindharma is a company created and operated by my daughter Jill Kirscher.

Spectrum Naturals of Petaluma, California, sells an excellent organic, cold-pressed sesame oil. Though there are always a variety of Spectrum products on the shelves in food chains, organic, cold-pressed sesame oil is not always available and must be ordered. I have found all stores to be very helpful in ordering sesame oil when I have asked.

Be sure to get cold-pressed oil that has no additives. Raw, natural, organic, cold-pressed sesame oil has a nutty fragrance which can be easily modified with a very tiny amount of fragrant oil (essential oils) from one of the massage oils put out by both the Maharishi's organization (available through MAPI) and by Deepak Chopra's organization (Infinite Possibilities). Both have a listed 800 number for ordering as well as a website.

I find that five to eight drops of prepared Vata or Pitta balancing massage oil, each of which has a light, delightful fragrance, will dominate the fragrance of eight ounces of pure sesame oil. You should choose an essential oil not for the scent, but for the properties it can bring to your search for good health.

If you know what your dominant ayurvedic *dosha* is, order the massage oil that has the recommended essential oil for your *dosha*. Then add a few drops of that to the sesame oil. Or use the prepared massage oil itself as it comes from MAPI. They are all sesame oil based or have substantial amounts of sesame oil in them.

I use Vata or Pitta balancing oils for massage because my *dosha* profile is Pitta-Vata. Vata is the *dosha* that is most frequently out of balance for everyone. The Kapha balancing oil has a slightly sharper fragrance to help nudge the Kapha personality into action in the morning.

The bacteriostatic properties of sesame oil is particularly useful when combating allergies or the beginnings of a head cold. Use a cotton tip soaked in sesame oil to coat the nasal and sinus passages. Or just put some on the tip of your little finger and swab the inside of your nose. Not only will it soothe the tissues which become swollen and fluid filled with the effects of the body responding to allergens or viruses but sesame oil will also separate the mucus buildup from the underlying tissues, allowing you to easily expel that waste product, thus depriving the allergens or the viral invaders of the protective covering the body has inadvertently provided for them as a part of attempting to protect itself.

And since tissues which are swollen and indurated are a likely fertile breeding ground for any opportunistic bacteria which happens by (from the sneezes of local airborne bacteria contributors or from any of the pieces of paper which we freely pass around, not realizing what viral and bacteria carriers they are) the coating of sesame oil is a powerful preventive of that sort of cold complication.

Ayurveda-cured oil on a cotton tip, swabbed into a baby's nose and ears, with drops into the ears if an infection develops there, is a lovely way to help the baby's own immune system fight colds and ear infections. Sesame oil used on the diaper area will nearly always prevent diaper rash. If the baby's waste products are too acid for sesame oil, a small amount of organic almond oil mixed with sesame oil will absolutely protect that tender part of baby.

What I have thought of for nearly all my life as a cold really started off as an allergic reaction to some weather event or airborne pollen or chemicals. The allergic reaction of my nasal passages set up the condition for an invasion of viruses and bacteria.

I am particularly sensitive to molds, and a recent trip to Ireland put me in two-hundred-year-old B&Bs as well as in the presence of and handling old papers and books, where I searched for information about our Irish forebears. The smell of mold was strong everywhere. Rain and cold and blowy conditions further sensitized my nasal passages, and within four days of arrival, I had a full-blown head cold.

Sesame oil put into the nose and sniffed back into the sinuses and used as a throat wash every couple of hours kept the cold from developing, as it predictably would have, into a serious head, throat, ear, and chest infection. I confess to using the whole homeopathic armamentarium against head colds though, including ester C, echinacea, and extra doses of MSM to create a nutritional broth for my cells, which would make them strong fighters of the invaders, whatever they might be.

I also had absent healing from a very powerful Reiki master. My body had as much help as was possible. A usual ten-day cold was reduced to three days.

The sesame oil provided an external barrier to viruses and bacteria with which my body's defenses were unfamiliar, giving them time to mobilize and take care of any invaders. A syringe or dropper absent, a small pool of oil in one hand and the little finger of the other hand dripping with oil and used to coat the inside of the nose and then sniffed back into the sinuses worked very well.

Of all the helpful ideas and products I have found in my search for good health, sesame oil has had the greatest beneficial effect on my body. If you accept nothing else I have written to you as a basic truth, accept that sesame oil is very good for life.

Your cells depend on you to make good choices;

nutrient-full food, pure water and unpolluted air

are what they need for their good health and yours.

—GPD

#36 Morning Routine

Mornings are difficult for many, particularly for young people starting in their jobs or professions. Evenings are a time for fun and courting and often it just isn't possible to get to bed with any hope of getting eight hours sleep before the urgency of the morning is here.

Still, morning is when the body is most apt to benefit from just a very few minutes of extra care. This is about how to use those precious few minutes to your best advantage.

In 1994, a major change happened in my life. I went to see Deepak Chopra and learned about traditional ayurveda healing, which Vedantic culture developed in ancient India between four and five thousand years ago. You may have heard of the Bhagavad Gita. It is a text in which the teacher is Lord Krishna, the Hindu representation of God. These holy writings are from the Vedantic civilization. Other traditions from that civilization have come down to us in the form of ayurveda (Ayur = body + Veda = wisdom) health principles.

Ayurveda teaches that toxins accumulate in our bodies in the form of a sludge that remains in the body from unmetabolized food or emotions that the body has been unable expel as waste. As *ama* accumulates, it slows everything down and must be removed if the body is to stay healthy.

Keeping the energy pathways open and helping your body to get rid of *ama* are two of the purposes of the morning routine. What I learned from Deepak Chopra and here pass on to you is that the two most potent and, therefore, useful ayurveda tools to control *ama* are sesame oil and Yoga *asanas*. But there are other things, simple things, you can do for yourself to start the day, taking care of the body part of yourself.

The healthful effects of drinking hot water first thing in the morning should not be overlooked. An eight-ounce glass of hot water in the morning will help keep the lower intestinal tract, the colon, cleaned out. Hot water during the day helps the body keep *ama* moving out of the body as waste on a continuing basis.

Sesame oil is one of the world's most useful oils for humans. I think this particular oil is responsible for both my good health and my ability to live considerably longer than anyone else in my family. You will get a lot of information about this oil from me.

When cured by the process described on other pages, the natural antioxidant in this oil, *sesimol*, is increased. It is a seed oil, produced from the abundant seeds of the sesamin plant. Molecular components of the oil are also reduced in size by curing, permitting greater penetration of the tissues.

Sesame oil is quite inexpensive. Keep a small (4-8 oz) bottle of this oil handy in your bathroom medicine cabinet ready for use every morning. Although the fragrance of the oil naturally has a pleasant nutty quality, it takes only a few drops of any other fragrance oil or essential oil to dominate the natural aroma of sesame seed oil.

Essential oils are not used with the primary purpose of providing a fragrance but for the basic effects such powerful oils have upon the physical and emotional body. Essential oil fragrances, when such oils are used on the skin with sesame oil as the carrier oil, evaporate within about half an hour, as does the natural fragrance of sesame oil itself.

Four to eight drops of an essential oil added to six ounces of ayurveda-cured sesame oil are sufficient to provide a delicate aroma to the oil. Essential oils are available from most health food stores. *Whole Foods Market* has excellent essential oils.

Oil absorbs heat very quickly. Placing a small bottle of the oil into a cup or glass of very hot water for a few minutes while shaving, brushing one's teeth, etc., will bring the oil to about body temperature, just right for quickly spreading on and penetrating into the skin.

When doing my morning massage, I pour a tiny amount of oil into the palm of my hand, I put the other hand into a very small stream of hot water, allowing the water to coat my hand, and rub my two hands together. Oil and water are not supposed to mix, but this procedure will coat my hands with moisturized oil, and that is what I transfer to my skin.

I start with my face, throat, neck, and ears. Ears, palms of the hand, and soles of the feet all have many nerve endings, terminals of energy pathways that lead to major organs of the body. They should get special massage attention from you every morning.

The skin reacts over time to the oil, becoming smoother and more flexible. Wrinkles really do lessen and, in some cases, disappear. Pores tighten, and skin texture also becomes finer with continued use of the oil. Since it is naturally antibacterial, regular use on the face helps control blemishes.

It works for teens particularly well. Girls should know that after rubbing sesame oil into the skin and then washing it off with mild soap in the shower or bath leaves the skin glowing and not oily.

Teenagers have heard that oil on the skin is a cause of blemishes and usually recoil when I tell them that sesame oil is really different. It is. The process to get those zits off is quite simple and very effective. Start by cleansing the area on and around eruptions with a clean washcloth and mild soap. Using a clean washcloth every time sounds extravagant, but reusing the same wash cloth for more than one washing guarantees that poisons causing the blemishes will be spread to other parts of the body. After cleansing, gently massage tiny amounts of the oil into the skin. Then blot that area with the clean washcloth wrung nearly dry, as hot as your hands can stand. In three or four days, blemishes will disappear.

Because some blemishes are hormonally caused, some caused by diet, not all will respond to this treatment as well as those that are bacterially caused. But I have had teenagers, my own children included, when they were that age, tell me they couldn't believe how quickly blemishes resolved without scarring by using the oil as I recommended.

Contrary to what might be expected, putting this oil on does not increase the oiliness of the skin. Sesame oil is unique in the manner in which it penetrates into the skin, into the tissue beneath, binds to toxins, and carries them to the bloodstream, on to the elimination processes of liver and kidneys, and then out of the body. Those toxins nearest the surface that are oil soluble are dissolved in the sesame oil, brought to the surface, and then washed off with the later soapy rinse.

When massaging the ears, take the time to firmly press on the webbing of the ears. Take the fleshy part of the upper curve of the ears and the ear lobes between the thumb and forefinger and make sure those parts get a robust pressure rubbing.

The same with the hands. Using the thumb of the opposite hand, give the palm and fleshy mound of the thumb a good rubbing on each hand. Then with the thumb and forefinger, firmly massage the web between thumb and forefinger. That's also a good place to rub if a headache is starting. For an existing headache, press firmly for fifteen seconds to induce the nerves causing the headache to loosen and relax.

Massaging the web between the thumb and the hand each morning will almost guarantee a headache-free day. Keeping the headache energy points well massaged and unblocked is simple, effective, and carries no cost to your health or pocketbook.

The massage technique described above for getting oil onto the body should be done while standing on a large towel or washable rug. No matter how careful one may be, some tiny spots of oil may fall to the floor in the process of rubbing the body down while standing. Sesame oil easily washes out in soapy water or with a product such as Pinesol though, so there should be no concern for permanently staining any towels or rugs.

The term "chakra" (shock-ra) deserves attention here. Chakras are energy centers that require special massage actions. Across the shoulders and down the arms, ayurveda advises using long strokes; over each joint, the strokes should be circular.

The body has seven major chakra centers. The base of the spine is generally spoken of as the first chakra; genitals the second; solar plexus, the third; heart, fourth; base of the throat, fifth; the point between the eyebrows (the third eye), sixth; and the crown of the head, the seventh chakra.

In Sanskrit, "chakra" means wheel. There are those sensitive enough and whose vision so well tuned they can see energy at these centers. Their description of the energy at each chakra is that it spins like a wheel.

In addition to the major chakras, there are other energy points called *marma* points in ayurvedic teaching. Generally, these are at the joints. The recommendation for massage over all chakras and *marma* points is that the hands should apply the oil and rub with a circular motion, to be in harmony with the spinning of the energy that emanates from these centers.

Since there may not be a spouse or partner to oil the middle of the back, that part of the body can be reached by putting oil onto the backs of the hands and fingers and reaching up the back as far as possible. Then with oil on the fronts of the fingers, reaching over the shoulders and under the armpits, rub your back and sides as far as you can reach. This will get 90 percent of the back for most people.

Do not be concerned about missing one part or another of your body on any given morning or of not putting enough oil on. By the time a week has gone by, every part will have been touched with oil many times. Always massage your body with the maxim that *less is better.*

If you take a bath or shower at night and do your oil self-massage in the morning, you will quickly find the right quantity to use effectively but leave your skin non-oily. For face, neck, and wrists, where you want to be sure that you have not overapplied the oil, use a damp, hot washcloth over those areas as the final step of the morning massage. You will love the results.

Use a loofah or rough washcloth to scrub down your whole body, removing dead skin cells that are continually being pushed to the surface by new cells being constantly created underneath. Your skin will consider it good maintenance if you keep a moderately rough loofah handy and help the removal process along every day or two.

One medical writer estimated that we shed about 1 1/2 grams of dead skin cells every day, a volume equivalent to the contents of three 500 mg capsules. If you visualize that amount of dead skin cells coming from your body every day, it makes clear why clothes worn next to the skin need to be washed to be fresh and why clothes worn just once and hung back up in the closet do not smell fresh. Those dead skin cells start to decay after a while, and an unpleasant smell is inevitable. In his book, *Clock of Ages,* Dr. John J. Medina comments that about 75 percent of house dust is composed of dead skin cells shed from the inhabitants.

Those who shave underarm hair will find that sesame oil is very effective in keeping that part of their body fresh and odor free. Natural smells of the body emanate from fluids produced by glands in, among other places, the armpit. Although we tend to want to mask these odors, they carry pheromones, both male and female, that send messages to the opposite sex.

Odors from all our body areas that stay warm, moist, and dark are partly caused by bacteria that thrive there. When these bacteria die (they have a cycle of life too), that event creates the offensive smells we associate with people who don't bathe frequently.

Sesame oil alone is not fully effective as a deodorant, except in limited climatic conditions. Where the climate is cold and dry, it will work for most people. Keeping the underarms shaved, men as well as women, is a further aid to keeping bacteria colonies at a minimum. The oil works as a deodorant only for a short while in any climate where one is likely to sweat. The body can produce copious quantities of sweat fluids in warm moist climates while regulating its temperature. Bacteria from many sources colonize in those fluids. The combination of sesame oil and aloe vera, juice or gel, that also has antibacterial qualities, is very effective as an underarm deodorant when used daily.

It makes sense to avoid using any underarm deodorant that contains aluminum oxide or any other mineral-based product. Even though any connection between aluminum and Alzheimer's disease is not established, the history of humanity's use of lead and tin for cooking and cosmetics is conclusive proof that heavy metals can be absorbed through the stomach and through the skin with disastrous consequences to the brain and the body. Aloe vera-based deodorants are quite effective and safe for humans.

Most grocery and all health food stores carry sesame seed oil. Organic is important because there are no agrichemicals in the oil. "Cold-pressed" means the oil has not been abused with harsh solvents or excessive heat. The best is Spectrum (Petaluma, California) organic, cold-pressed oil.

Ayurveda-cured organic sesame oil can be obtained from youthingstrategies.com, maharishi.com, and from skindharma. com

We live in a world of allergens. Pine, oak, cedar, and other trees broadcast their pollen for several weeks each year. Grasses, animal dander, dust swept off fallow fields by strong winds, all are allergenic to some folks. For all of us, allergens in the air mean being alert to the dangers they pose and using a regular schedule of caring for the nasal passages. Waiting until a head cold develops is a little late. In ayurveda, the nose is considered to be the pathway to the brain, and care is taken to see that pathway is kept open and cleared of obstructive mucus.

If you notice blood from your nose when you blow it, that's a sign that tissues have been irritated, perhaps torn, by the effects of an allergen, or perhaps it is the beginning of the invasion of a virus or bacteria. Sneezing twice or more in succession is another sign of a beginning invasion. Using the *neti* pot then will often stop the virus with only one flushing.

It is common knowledge now that antibacterial pills and shots of traditional allopathic medical practice have no effect upon viruses. But salt water does. If used regularly and especially if warned of a nasal viral invasion by blood or sneezing, flushing nasal passages with dilute salt water can help your body fight invaders and also help to keep allergy attacks to a minimum.

A *neti* bowl used every morning will go a long way to protecting you from opportunistic bacteria, viruses, and allergens. A *neti* bowl has about a three-ounce chamber, a handle, and an elongated spout. It looks like a small stretched-out teapot. The chamber is filled with warm salty water. With the head titled to the side, the spout, which is tapered to fit into the nostril and prevent fluid from running any way but up into the nasal passages, is gently put into one nostril; and the whole assembly, *neti* pot and nose, are tilted until about half the salt water runs into one nostril and out the other. Then the sides are reversed and the process repeated.

Salt water is cleansing and, to some extent, purifying. It is very effective in loosening mucus that may have accumulated overnight. What doesn't flush out with the water will come out when you blow your nose.

Using sea salt instead of iodized salt is recommended. You'll find the right proportion that feels (and tastes) good to you. Sea salt in dilute concentrations has an almost sweet taste. It is every bit as effective as table salt, which is quite harsh on delicate tissues of the nose and sinuses.

A word about the need for iodine: the thyroid gland needs iodine to function. Iodine prevents the development of goiters. Iodine is a critical trace element that we need to take in frequently, if not daily. That's why the government ordered salt makers to iodize their common table salt.

If you use sea salt on your table and in cooking and do not also eat shrimp or shellfish or other ocean foods regularly, take iodine as a part of the trace minerals in your daily intake of nutrients.

Breathing through the nose is recommended over mouth breathing for all the reasons you learned in school. The nose naturally brings the air to body temperature, and the cilia (tiny hairs in the nose) filter out dust and pollens before they reach the lungs

Neti pots can be found at most health food stores and are not expensive. Everybody in the family really should have his or her own. School-aged children, who live in a sea of bacteria, viruses, and allergens, would benefit from knowing how to use a *neti* pot and having their own to use every morning. Kids think using a *neti* pot is fun, and it is another means of protecting those we love from potential harm.

Your morning routine will either start your day with a body smoothed out and energized, functioning at high efficiency, or one that slowly gets up to speed. Your body is the vehicle in which you get around and live your life. Your body is worth much more than your steel and plastic automobile. It deserves the attention necessary to keep it functioning well. Simple prophylactic body maintenance takes time but is well worth the attention you put on it.

Your body is composed of about 75 trillion cells. Each cell is constantly changing; nutrients in, waste out, proteins and other products distributed.

Your cells depend on you to make good choices of nutrients, water and air, the materials they need, for their good health and yours.

—GPD

#37 Exercise

What do you think about exercise? If you are like most of us, and I include myself in this group, we don't much like to exercise just for the sake of strengthening our muscles. But it is hard to argue with what happens to the body and your supply of good feelings when you do exercise. All of it is good. The body does respond happily to a twenty-minute run, a half an hour of fast walking, and fifteen or so minutes of work with weights. Even for those over seventy who, like me, do mostly stretching and easy walking on a treadmill, the feel-good day that follows is well worth the time and energy spent.

The tenets of ayurveda health that I subscribe to say that exercise designed to strengthen the muscles is for those who are training for athletics and that the ordinary person not only doesn't need that sort of stress but should avoid it. I embrace that concept with all my heart.

I confess, I really don't like to exercise simply for the sake of exercise, so I don't. Pain takes away all the gain for me. But I do want to stay flexible, be able to move about with confidence and enjoy my daily activities, be able to go up and down stairs, do moderate work in the garden, and not be limited by stiff and aching joints and muscles. So I do what is called Hatha yoga. The positions are called *asanas* (ass'-un-uz).

Hatha yoga is simply position yoga, stretching and holding that stretch for a count of about fifteen to allow the body to get used to challenging extensions of long muscles and extra torsion of joint ligaments.

Stretching, keeping limber and flexible, making sure the joints work as they need to, and maintaining strength in legs, ankles, and feet for good balance—that's what exercise at my age is all about.

In October 1994, when I went to Deepak Chopra's center in Del Mar, California, the then-director, Brent BecVar, held classes in Hatha yoga, designed to loosen the stiffening bodies of people like me. One of the stretching exercises was to sit spread legged on the floor, keeping both knees extended. Then we were to bend the left leg at the knee, tuck the left foot into the groin, bend at the waist, and stretch and touch both hands to the toes of the opposite outstretched leg, placing the forehead on the knee of that outstretched leg.

You've probably seen ballerinas do this exercise with smoothness and grace, bending like so many rag dolls so that their foreheads comfortably touch the knee of the outstretched leg. In fact, one of the center staff, a woman of about forty-five who joined the class, was able to put her forehead to her knee with no apparent difficulty. When I commented that such a move seemed impossible, except for a young person, Brent told me that that staff member had only been doing the yoga exercises for six months and was not as young as she appeared.

Her example was mildly encouraging, but such flexibility seemed out of the question for me. Then, at age sixty-nine, I could barely bend enough to bring my head and knee within twelve inches of each other, either right or left side. Brent said, "Don't give up. Do this exercise regularly, and within six months you'll be able to do it too." At this writing, at age eighty-five, I have to report that despite long-standing efforts, my body has not loosened to that degree. However, I can also report that nearly continuous efforts in the direction of flexibility has stretched my body so that I can almost touch my forehead to my right knee, but for the left, I find my body just won't bend that way.

Doing exercises every day intended to create and keep flexibility does not mean that that is all these exercises do. Repetition is the key to almost any change. Even though yoga *asanas* are not strenuous, they do, in fact, strengthen muscles if they are done regularly.

When my own children were young, there was an oak tree in the backyard that had an overarching branch, just the right height above the ground for a rope swing. The branch, however, was only about three and a half inches thick.

The branch was quite limber, just barely strong enough to handle the weight of my oldest. Since it was the only place available to put a swing, I used it. I fastened the ropes to the branch and cautioned my children to use the swing one at a time so as not to put excessive weight on the branch and break it. They swung happily on it. About a year later, the repetitious flexing from the action of the swing going back and forth had caused the tree to increase the size of that branch all the way back to the place of joinder with the main trunk. The augmentation was far beyond the amount of annual growth that branch would have had from natural wind-whipped flexing.

In a year, the tree had strengthened that branch to a potential that would hold all three young children without threatening to break. The repetition of flexing nearly every day, simply from the play of the children, had made demands to which the cells of the tree responded. The exercises suggested here will do the same thing for the muscles you involve in these actions.

Does this rule of cells responding to demand apply to all cells of older folks as well as younger ones? It is clear that the studies of seventy—and eighty-year-olds, who changed from sedentary lifestyles to doing exercises for an hour a day five days a week in six weeks, produced bodies that experts in aging decided reduced the biological age of all members of that group by at least eight years and some up to twelve years.

Consider. We replace nearly 100 percent of all the atoms and molecules that are the building blocks of the cells in our physical bodies each year. Within two years, we have replaced every part of every cell, and some authorities now think that within about thirty months, all the replicating cells themselves have been replaced at least once. Every time we breathe in, we take in 10^{22} of molecules of oxygen that ultimately circulate in the blood and are used by the body to (among other things) make new cells. So why shouldn't the new components of muscle tissue, ligaments, skin, even bones, make our cells as flexible as we want them to be?

One of my own personal rules for doing the yoga stretching exercises I do is that there is no rush. I started out doing each exercise five times, and the fifth time would always be easier and the flexibility more pronounced than the first. But I am not in a race with anyone, certainly not with myself. The flexibility that I have is enough for me to navigate this planet easily and feel good about it.

I feel no need to become an accomplished yoga practitioner. I feel no need to please anyone but myself. And that's easily done. I like what has happened. I like what is happening.

Yoga *asanas* themselves are described in stick-figure positions at the end of this book—illustrations that will help you imagine the body positions that, for me, are most helpful.

The first illustrations are about enhancing circulation. Arterial and venous, as well as lymphatic circulation, are helped by gently squeezing the body, starting at each extremity, and working toward the heart, squeezing in a slow and easy spasmodic rhythm. The lymphatic system of the body seldom gets the attention it deserves. But it, almost as much as the arterial and venous systems, is responsible for maintaining good health. This first routine, paying attention to circulation, will help your body keep all its fluids flowing.

The rest of the illustrations are of Hatha yoga positions. There is a flow here too, but the flow is of easily moving from one position to the next, stretching and opening joints in order to keep your body flexible. Remember to hold the position, to allow the muscles and ligaments to stretch and be comfortable in the stretch. To change muscle memory, a new position must be held for at least fifteen seconds. To simply open a joint, a five-second hold will do.

One thing that has jumped out at me from recent reports of the benefits of exercise is the frequency with which walking is recommended as the simplest, most effective way to keep in reasonably good trim.

In the central parts of many smaller European cities, the streets are narrow, the shops crowded together, parking is difficult and time consuming, and many people live within walking distance of what is designated as *centre ville* or city center. It is not that Europeans would not drive as close to their destination as we like to do if they had a reasonable opportunity to do so. But they do not. The central parts of most of these cities are not vehicle friendly.

While visiting these cities, hotels and B&Bs were so situated that I found walking was preferable to extricating the car from the parking area and looking forward to crowded streets, delays at traffic lights, and generally unpleasant driving conditions.

There are exceptions, of course. Major cities that are the capitals of countries are often graced with broad boulevards and spacious plazas. But there are parts of those cities, as well as of most of the oldest cities, like Rome and Athens, that are crowded, congested (and thoroughly lovely to this American), and where one must walk if one is to get to any particular destination.

So in Europe, I walked and found that what in contemplation seemed like a long way was, in actuality, usually pleasant and interesting.

In Rome, when the concierge said the walk to a restaurant my son Tim and I had chosen for dinner would be about half an hour, I thought, *Let's get a taxi.* But the evening air was pleasant and the directions concise and clear, so we walked. The walk seemed not long at all, though it took nearly the full time predicted, and there were so many things we would not have seen or experienced from a car. And the exercise left me feeling really exhilarated, something I have never felt after riding to my destination.

Unfortunately, in this country, walking in most cities has been designed out of the many possible methods of getting around. That means for most of us, walking is not a part of living, as it naturally should be. It has to be planned and the place to walk carefully selected for, first, safety and, second, interest of scenery.

Some newly designed cities require new development to have a minicenter with limited access for vehicles so that walking and bicycle riding are encouraged. Living in proximity to the minicenter is also encouraged by zoning laws and development restrictions.

Austin, Texas, where I lived for nearly twenty years, abandoned a middle-of-town airport for a larger one on the outskirts of the city. Plans for the changeover of these six hundred acres were developed with the intention of promoting a lifestyle that included walking and bicycle riding to and from work and shopping, which is more in harmony with the earth and our own bodies.

The reason to mention this is that while yoga *asanas* are excellent for the purposes they have, of keeping flexible and fit, walking is also an excellent way of keeping one's body healthy.

Back problems are helped significantly by walking. Circulatory problems, digestive problems, and eliminatory problems all are greatly helped by regular walking. It is a real shame that walking has become something we have to do to stay healthy, when, for millennia, walking was something we did normally, every day, uphill and down, which promoted good health as a beneficial side effect. Intentionally choosing to walk up two or three flights of stairs is also good for the legs, lungs, heart, and circulation.

Sexual underperformance, both in males and females, can be helped by vigorous walking and by doing deep knee bends or squats, all of which exercises the perineal area where our sexual parts and glands are located. Good circulation and muscle tone there is as important as in the heart or any other part of the body.

Other useful exercises include Kegel exercises for women to tone and tighten the vaginal walls. Similar muscle-tightening exercises for men that encourage good blood flow into the penis can extend quality sexual experiences into advanced chronological years. The recommendation is to tighten and relax muscles in the perineum, that floor of the pelvis between the anus and the sexual parts of both men and women, and do the cycle of tighten-relax in multiples of ten. Do it while driving, while waiting for a red light to change.

Keeping all the internal muscles of the body in good condition is important, but these muscles play a particularly important role in both the emotional and the physical parts of your lives. Sex is important, and keeping fit for the task is an obligation both to your partner and yourself.

Eye exercises are not something that most people do. It is only when you suddenly realize that some abnormality has interfered with vision that you will start to exercise your eye muscles.

The tiny muscles that focus the clear lens in the front of the eye can lose some of their ability to help the eye to focus. They do this by tightening and relaxing the lens for near and distant vision. These tiny muscles control the shape of the lens, and as our work becomes more sedentary and we stare for longer hours at computer screens and TV monitors, they seldom get a real workout.

As they relax and forget their jobs, we can lose the ability to focus our vision, distant or near or both. There are simple eye muscle exercises that are almost guaranteed to help with both near and far vision within about a week.

To help train your eyes to focus better, take a newspaper with subheadlines that you can read easily up close and have a spouse or partner move that paper away from you just to the point where you no longer can clearly read the sub headlines. Measure that distance. Then pin the paper to a wall, in good light, that same distance from a comfortable chair. Spend three minutes each morning in that chair focusing on that print that was just beyond your clear-distance vision. In a day or two, you should be able to read the subheadlines. Then increase the distance a few feet each day until you are able to read the subhead twenty or more feet away.

Close vision can be helped by using the print on the side of a wooden pencil, the print that usually tells the manufacturer and the hardness of the lead. The print is fairly small but, in good light, is usually readable at arm's length. Keep the light bright; there is no reason to try to do the impossible. With your eyes focused on the print, bring the pencil toward your nose until you no longer can read the letters. These two exercises will strengthen those tiny lens control muscles and should greatly improve both distant and near vision.

The next eye exercise will also help with both distant and near vision. These can most easily be done in bed first thing in the morning. With these, you should also notice improved vision within a week.

Imagine that you are looking at a compass. In order, you will look up and to the right (NE) and then down and to the left (SW) and then NW and then SE and then E and then W and then N and then S. The secret to success with all exercises intended to improve muscle tone and flexibility is to hold each position for a slow count of fifteen. Muscle memory lasts for about that long, and to change the muscle memory, the new position must exceed the memory time of fifteen seconds.

Flexibility is really key to greater use of all parts of our body. There is another way to keep major joints more open. This is quite easy and can be done before getting out of bed in the morning.

Stretch arm and shoulder joints by taking one wrist in the grip of the other hand. Pull your arm sideways at ninety degrees to your body, hold five seconds, and release for five seconds, allowing both arms to be by your side. Do the same, making a forty-five-degree angle above your head relative to the centerline of your body; rest and then do the same thing directly above your head. Repeat stretching the other arm.

Roll both legs up, holding your shins, pulling both knees up as though trying to make the shoulder and knee on each side touch. Hold five seconds and release five seconds with legs stretched out. Repeat three times.

Pull right leg up, left hand on right knee, as though trying to make the right knee touch the left shoulder. Relax the lower leg and foot. Hold five seconds, release, and relax five seconds. Do three times and then do the same with the other knee.

One hand on each side of the back of the head, pull the head forward gently, as though trying to make the chin touch the chest. Be very careful with this one. Do not force your neck. Consciously make the neck muscles relax. Hold five seconds, relax five seconds. Do three times.

These stretching techniques are intended to open joints in the morning that may have become stiff overnight. It also can make a big difference in your energy level if you spend a minute of two breathing deeply before getting out of bed.

Breath like a baby; let your stomach extend and balloon out as you breath in, forcing air into your upper lobes only after the lower lobes are fully inflated. Hold the breath for a count of five to allow the alveolar sacs to absorb all the oxygen available in each breath. Toning (see "Toning," #42) is particularly good for developing strong and capacious lungs.

Exercise such as walking, weight resistance, or anything that gets the heart rate up to about 120-130 bpm is usually safe and effective and helps the body do its work of clearing out arteries that have become less flexible or narrowed by accumulation of plaque. Lifestyle changes are also necessary with this remedial exercise.

Just don't overdo and pay attention to your body. Discomfort is a sign to stop. Any chest tightness is a sign to see your cardiovascular physician. Exercise is intended to help create good change. Don't force your body to choose change for which it is not ready.

You will change. It is better if you choose changes that will be good for you.

Wheresoever you go, go with your whole heart.

Confucius

#38 Using Energy to Heal

It's hard to believe that something we hold in our hands, examine with our senses, and call solid—because we have instant sensual confirmation of the property of solidness—is actually simply a collection of tiny pulses of energy.

According to scientists and others who delve deeply into the question, what all the universe is made of are elementary particles, (things than which there is nothing smaller). They have named these quarks, leptons and gauge bosons. In ascending scale, these combine to form electrons, atoms and molecules that make up all the material world as we know it. What I have gathered from the basic reading I have done about this is that quarks and their cousins, the base components of everything, from the hardest rock to the most ephemeral gas, are simply specks of energy.

This energy is not simple and undifferentiated. All energy is informed. That information defines how these energies combine, aggregating to form what we call pure substance and also combining with other energies to make all the substances we recognize as our material world, the world we can touch and experience with our senses.

Regardless of what it seems to be, your body, composed of seventy plus trillion cells, with about 200 different varieties of cells represented, is composed of energy in varying forms but nothing more than energy. Even though your eyes cannot see and your senses cannot experience these bits of energy as energy, the mind can understand the concept.

Energy is not the whole picture. Information is what makes the basic energy become concrete in the myriad of forms we see, we hear, we touch, we understand. Information is energy too, but it seems to be different from the energy that forms the basis for all other aspects of our universe. One of the things experience teaches us is that information can be changed.

What is a rock can be made into iron. What is heated can pass though stages of being seen by human eyes as red and then white and then x-rays, and on and on until we run out of names to give the highest of energies generated by the highest of temperatures, the highest of which we have not yet developed instruments to measure.

The thoughts we generate in our brains are composed of units of energy too. Electroencephalograms used by physicians to graph brain waves are able to detect the level and frequency of thought energy. However, these units of thought energy are evanescent; they are created, exist, but then seem to have limited lives and dissipate when their usefulness is over.

Human thought, generated by the activity of our brain cells, is a combination of energy and information. We have from credible sources, doctors trained in Western medicine, reports that in India and Tibet, some humans can make themselves into masters of their own minds and bodies to such a degree that these people can control the cells of their own bodies.

One reported case was of a man who allowed himself to be buried in an airtight box for more than twenty-four hours, after which he emerged in a deep somnambulant state but gradually recovered his faculties until he became normal again. He had induced in himself a state of hibernation, effectively stopping his own metabolism and reducing oxygen requirements to near zero for more than twenty-four hours. These and other reported acts of self-control seem amazing.

Unusual feats such as this show that control of the energy and function of one's own cells is possible. While such extreme examples make us wonder how that could happen, lesser examples of control of the body are before us frequently. For example, those who break dependency or addictive habits are by their thoughts, controlling cells that want to continue receiving the addictive substance.

Control of one's cells offers to any human the ability to use his or her own energy to do many things, including heal themselves of the effects of injuries.

When our bodies develop malfunctions (illness, disease, injury), the energies in that portion of the body involved are somehow disarranged or interrupted. We understand the basic units of energy that make up the cells remain always the same. Therefore, it must be the information that is somehow skewed.

In physical injuries, it is easy to understand that external forces have influenced the information that controls the way cells hold themselves together. Bacteria, viruses, and other pathogens that create malfunctions of the body's cells can also be thought of as external forces (also information and energies) acting upon the information that creates the cellular structure of our bodies.

As these external forces become smaller and smaller in size, they become more difficult to detect. Yet scientists using powerful microscopes tell us how they work. These invaders change the information that is critical to cell performance, either by attaching to the exterior surface of the cell or by directly invading the cell and changing basic cellular instructions. In each case, performance (information) is in some way changed or disrupted.

Examples of injury grossly demonstrate that when the original information that created both cellular structure and cellular function is changed, the whole body-functioning information (for lack of a better term) is also changed.

Reestablishing information that has been skewed by misinformation back to its original energetic information is what healing is all about.

We each have the power to do that for ourselves. With our minds, we can generate energetic healing by visualizing either or both an attack on invaders and strengthening of the original information about function.

Our hands, also, seem either to have a natural energy that help our cells realign to their original and true information, or perhaps, our hands are really simple conduits of energy from outside the body, carriers of energy, rather than transmitters of their own energy supply.

An example of energetic healing is found in the statistics that were accumulated at a children's hospice in Austin, Texas, some years ago (Center for Attitudinal Healing). They treated children who had diagnosed terminal cancers. The caregivers were able to induce cures in some of these youngsters by having them visualize their body's immune system as Pac-Man-like soldiers who marched through their bodies, finding, attacking, and gobbling up cancerous cells.

This did not work with all the children, but the rate of cure was significantly above the average for the types of cancer being treated. Other traditional modes of treatment were kept in place for all children, and visualization was the only variable.

An example of hand energy is Reiki, a form of energy healing. In traditional Reiki, the hands of the practitioner are held in close proximity to the body of the patient-subject over the area needing treatment. Where possible, the injured member is positioned between the hands in order to receive a flow of energy through the injured area.

The purpose is to induce universal energy (the literal definition of the word "Reiki" in translation from Japanese) into the area where the body's own energy pattern has been disrupted. The ultimate purpose of healing is achieved when the body's own energy pattern is restored to its normal condition.

Universal energy needs to be condensed and focused. Initiation ceremonies are intended to prepare the body and, especially, the hands of the practitioner to do this. Practitioners are initiated into Reiki in a ceremony conducted by a Reiki master through a series of meditations, incantations and a ceremony similar to *laying-on-of-hands.*

Laying-on-of-hands is a venerable tradition, predating Reiki by millennia, and signifies acceptance and initiation into a group that has particular attributes or powers. Hands are universally thought to have special energies and laying-on-of-hands should be familiar to all Christians because it is ubiquitously used in baptismal ceremonies. Both Catholic and Episcopalian communicants are accepted as having declared their belief in the Trinity by the Bishop laying his hands on the head of each of those "confirming" their faith, preparing them to receive sacramental bread and wine.

In Reiki, the ceremony prepares the initiates to become efficient receivers, concentrators and transmitters of healing energy, a force that is believed to be universally present but diffuse.

A personal note: I have been initiated as a second-degree Reiki practitioner. Though I have seldom used the power for anyone other than family members and family pets, I did have an experience involving a secretary at my law firm. She had fallen the evening before and said an x-ray showed a slightly displaced fracture of the ulna, just above the wrist. The arm was lightly wrapped, as the physician wanted to allow the natural swelling to reduce normally before splinting.

With her permission, I held the injured area lightly between my hands. At about the third minute of treatment, we both heard and felt a snap in the wrist area.

The next afternoon, she told me later, the swelling had gone down; and her doctor was ready to apply a splint. Comparing x-rays, he told her the fracture was now undisplaced, in excellent position, and that a simple wrap, without splinting, would be sufficient.

My experience with Reiki over some twenty years as a first and then second-degree practitioner has been that the power to condense and focus energy seems to have diminished with lack of use and over time. During the first years, offering Reiki energy to another would cause my hands to literally buzz and tingle. After a few minutes, the palms would become red. Those I was treating would report they felt heat, and the areas treated would also tingle, as though from a light electrical charge. Now my hands feel the energy, just not as strongly.

Use of this healing power may also be instinctive. Think of the times when you have injured a part of your body. The first impulse is to grab and hold the injured part. When our neck hurts or our lower back is stressed and painful, what is the common human reaction? Why, we put our hands on our necks and we put our hands on our hips or lower back. What we don't usually do is hold our hands there until enough energy is transmitted though our hands to help calm or heal the part that hurts.

Five minutes seems like a very short period of time until one is asked to hold still for that long. Five minutes at a time seems to be generally agreed among Reiki masters as the appropriate time to feed energy into the area intended to be healed. When next you have a small cut, bruise, strain, or sprain, try holding the injured part of your body for five minutes and feel the results. You will be surprised at the flow of natural energy-healing power through your own hands.

The body doesn't heal instantly. More than one treatment is necessary, even with the dramatic flow of energy that a Reiki master can generate. Expect results over several treatments, just not immediately.

Another healing technique that I have recently discovered also involves energy. "Holographic healing" is the term a doctor of chiropractic in Savannah applies to her skills. Dr. Cathy Mickler's explanation to me was consonant with my own understanding of my body.

Each organ and other vital parts of my body have a unique frequency of vibration. So does every bacteria, virus, parasite, fungus, and pathogen that might disrupt normal cellular function. The first part of her examination of me was to discover if any frequencies were abnormal—that is, different from the frequency signature of a healthy organ. To do this, she used a combination of kinesiology and her own unusual ability to see energies that emanated from my body. Her explanation to me was that she treats the energy before it manifests in the physical structure of the body.

Discovering an invasive pathogen, she used a device to induce the appropriate frequency into tiny pills that, when absorbed sublingually and flowing into the fluid systems of my body, were intended to disrupt the energy (frequency) of the pathogen and effectively remove it or kill it.

On the first visit, she discovered I harbored both bacteria and viruses that were not causing any overt symptoms, but when I took the little sublingual pills she formulated for me, I really felt quite a dramatic change in my well-being. At the next visit, she said those pathogens were on their way out of my body, and the treatment continued until they were gone.

Dysfunctions of vital organs and systems in my body received the same attention and treatment regimen, again with good results.

Dr. Cathy Mickler focused her attention on the ultimate core of my energetic being. Finding both pathogens and dysfunctions, she treated each with energies of specific frequency, first to disrupt and remove the pathogen then to restore the appropriate frequency to the vital organ or system in my body that was troubled. Her approach to healing fit exactly with my understanding of what my body is and how it could be healed.

She is one of all too few healers that I have discovered who understand they must see beyond the physical aspects of the body in order to find and then treat the basic cause of dysfunction, using the signature frequency of pathogens or body systems to remove the pathogen or heal a system by resetting its proper frequency.

By changing the inner attitudes of your mind,

you can change the outer aspects of your life.
—Proverb

#39 Meditation

Meditation is surprisingly easy, notwithstanding what you may have heard or read about it. It can be an experience of such complete and utter satisfaction that you will smile whenever you think about it, and you will want to go back to that experience again and again.

In answering questions about meditation, I have realized that the general perception of meditation is that it is somehow an activity of the unusual person. It is true that pictures of meditators in India, Tibet, in other countries where Buddhism and Hinduism are dominant religions offer an austere, even ascetic, concept of what meditation is and how it is done. In the United States today, teachers of meditation offer widely diverse approaches to what is a very simple and, as it feels to those who meditate regularly, a very easy and comfortable human activity.

In the late nineteenth century and into the 1920s, various writers and cultural leaders became interested in the ancient wisdom of India. Some went there and wrote of their observations and experiences with the yoga masters, mostly in northern India, the Himalayan foothills, and Tibet.

Many returned to write chronicles of the lives of these extraordinary yogis, mostly men but a few women. There were detailed many seemingly miraculous activities—for example, manifesting solid tangible objects at will; appearing at two locations many miles apart simultaneously, with credible witnesses at each location confirming a tangible, continuous presence; instances of mental communication at great distances; and so on.

Other Westerners went to live with the *rishis* (teachers) and yogis (those who achieve contact with the universe through action) and returned to write of their experiences. Yogis themselves came to this country and, through lectures and writings, offered detailed accounts of how a spiritual life was lived in India. All of these writings and teachings included descriptions of how the yogis and *rishis* would go within and shut out the world around them as a way of reaching an inner state of personal power.

Some spoke of going into a trance. There is little to differentiate a trance from the state one achieves in deep meditation. However, the common understanding of "trance" is that one has lost control of oneself. In meditation, one never loses control of oneself or the awareness of self. In fact, meditation is the means by which it is possible to obtain an awareness of the true self, that eternal spirit which is the essential part of each of us.

The broad attention given to Gurdjief in the early 1920s was evidence of a widespread desire in this country and in England to awaken the spiritual side of our existence. Mass motivators of the early twentieth century, like Gurdjief and poet/artists like Kalil Gibran, offered a very different way of addressing the spirit than was then (and still is) used to promote the teachings of large Christian denominations.

A later renewed interest in meditation, as a means of escaping the turmoil of the tangible, real world, came along about the time when Flower Children were offering baskets of flowers to soldiers facing them with bayoneted rifles during the many protests against the Viet Nam War.

Maharishi Mahesh Yogi (1918-2008) was a brilliant Indian electronics engineer with great personal charisma and organizing talents. Turning from the business world and a career of engineering projects, he set about to engineer the world in the direction of peace and harmonious living.

Maharishi translated and added his own commentaries to the Bagavad-Gita, an ancient epic narrative attributed to Lord Krishna, composed of often arcane language and apocryphal stories of battles between good and evil, of human triumph over adversity, and parables of man's relationship with society and governance. He also brought forward for Western world attention Vedic texts basic to the four—or five—thousand-year-old tradition of ayurvedic healing. He developed a theory that the mental energies of large groups of people meditating with a common purpose (to bring peace to the world) could influence the course of action of both world leaders and the world population and convened several meditating groups to prove that theory. The pragmatic results of practicing this theory tend to establish that massed and focused group energies really can influence society.

Meditation in the past seems to have been a very individualized activity, personal to the practitioner. How to meditate was taught by master to student. Inevitably, variations and ideas of correctness of how to achieve a meditative state developed and were written about by those Western writers who investigated the subject.

The use of a mantra, however, is nearly universal. A mantra is simply a mind-tool, which is the Sanskrit definition of "mantra." A mantra usually consists of one or a group of sounds repeated mentally or chanted quietly but audibly. The objective is to focus the mind and remove mental distractions. One may achieve that result by staring at the flame of a candle or focusing on one's breathing, paying attention to the inflow and outflow of *prana*, to the exclusion of all other thoughts. One may simply allow the activity of the brain to bring up all the thoughts that demand attention until there are no more thoughts and the mind is then quiet.

Maharishi (M'harshi) was not shy about his mental and spiritual powers. The name he chose for himself indicates his self-regard. *Maha* means "exalted" or "highest"; *rishi* means "teacher" or "leader."

In 1958, Maharishi came to the United States, bringing his concepts of how to achieve a better life. Among the many extremely beneficial things he introduced was a particular meditation technique he claimed as his own, transcendental meditation (TM), which he copyrighted in the United States.

He systematized the teaching of this meditation technique, creating a standard for all his disciples and TM teachers to follow. He also operated on the principle that a gift is not as highly regarded as things we pay for. Maharishi established a uniform high charge for teaching TM because he wanted TM to be the gold standard of meditation. Creating TM teachers remains a substantial source of income for his organization. The teaching of TM remains one of the most important civilizing forces of Maharishi's legacy. I'm told that in every major city in the United States and in most college towns, one can find a TM teacher. The world has responded to his teachings, and at the present time (2009), the extensive organization he created reaches, literally, throughout the world from its headquarters in the Netherlands.

In talking about meditation, allow me to digress slightly to define terms that are used and thought about, very loosely it seems, by most of us. For example, the term "mind" seems straightforward and useful, referring to that portion of a human being which thinks. It is also useful to separate "mind", the abstract, from "brain," the concrete part of each "self" which thinks.

My dictionary defines mind with one-third of a very large page devoted to synonyms, including "the seat or subject of consciousness," "the intellect," the "thinking or perceiving part of consciousness," and so forth. All of these terms are abstract.

"Brain," on the other hand, is defined in concrete terms as "nerve tissues, fibers, cells, neurons, ganglia, dendrites, etc." Those brain cells that control countless autonomic bodily functions seem not to be involved with the mind that thinks and that, in meditation, we quiet.

Cells that are part of voluntary thought and the acting-out process of thought manifesting into action are sort of in-between . . . part mind, part not mind. And there are clearly other parts of the cellular structure of the brain that do involve thinking and perceiving. Somehow they seem to be involved in what is "mind."

We are able to measure, quite finely, brain activity, both autonomic and volitional. Recent experiments measuring thought energy have been remarkably successful, even precisely marking the site of specific brain cells involved in specific single thoughts.

There is no doubt that the human brain generates an electrical field from its activity, both voluntary and autonomic, measurable by electroencephalography (EEG) and other graphing devices. These are useful in the medical specialty of neurology to help determine if there are brain electrical disturbances that would indicate injury or other abnormal conditions of the brain.

EEGs have also been utilized to show the pattern of brain activity during meditation when they exhibit a smoothness and regularity of brain electrical activity, different from the normal waking-brain tracing. These meditative tracings are also very different from the EEG tracings taken when the brain is disturbed by anger or other emotionally charged mind events.

When events that we call "mental telepathy" occur, the brain must be working and may constitute the sending apparatus, but the mind is the perceiving part of us that tells us that a thought has been received.

When we meditate, it is the mind that is spoken of as the part of us that is involved. We quiet the mind to meditate. When we remain aware of ourselves during the meditative state, it is the mind that is staying aware.

At that stage, our autonomic brain cells seem to quiet and slow their activity. Heartbeat, respiration, and brain activity all are slowed dramatically and demonstrably (by EEG) during meditation, but our bodies continue to function. At the same time, mental activity slows until, when we reach the state of no thoughts in the mind, we reach a state of awareness of self and awareness that we are a part of and one with all of the rest of the universe. Being able to connect with the universe of all matter, at a cellular level, may be the way yogi masters do what appear to others as miraculous actions. And meditation, the method by which we make a mind connection to our own bodies at a cellular level, is the less dramatic means by which we each can influence the world we live in.

During the intense competition between the United States and Russia for domination of the world's peoples and resources, which threatened to develop into a fighting war at frequent intervals, Maharishi set about to quiet the conflicts and induce a condition of peacefulness to the world. His means was through teaching transcendental meditation to great numbers of people worldwide and having them meditate in large numbers at the same time with the same intentions to create an energy field for peace.

His concept of how to effect more peaceful relations between hostile countries was and is based on having a stated proportion of meditators to the population in one (not necessarily both) of the areas involved. He taught that if at least 0.001 (one tenth of one percent) of the general population focuses their meditation on peace, with the intent of influencing events generally toward that goal, that percentage of the population, through meditation, can create an energy field strong enough to influence events to move in the direction on which they focus.

The concept of teaching people to meditate (using the TM technique) and bringing meditators together to meditate in groups to create a group mental force field for the purpose of creating a calming effect upon the world was put into practice and has been underway for about thirty years, not only here in the United States, but also worldwide.

Maharishi's ideas of using meditation to influence political action involve what is now a very large group of disciples who learned TM. Literally, hundreds of thousands of people have been taught transcendental meditation. Although the practice of group meditation for world peace does not seem to be as frequent now as in the past, for many years, the ideas of Maharishi were followed; and there were regular group meditation sessions to influence the world to be peaceful.

One hesitates to think of how much more warlike the world would likely be if TM meditators had not used their TM energy for peace. But another way of looking at it is to compare the world now with thirty, forty, fifty years ago. We are, demonstrably, more peaceful, though the peaceful millennium is not yet.

One can think of all the usual political, geopolitical, and economic reasons for the breakup of Russia and the end of the cold war. The influence of something as subtle as a mental force field is not subject to the kind of evaluation we apply to observable phenomenon. And there are legions of people who feel threatened by the idea that the mental activity of one person or a group of persons can influence behavior of others, either specific or general. But it is true; we each have the ability to control the physical world around us. Some advanced yogis and *rishis* in India reportedly can exercise quite deliberate and specific control over their own bodies as well as over the environment in which they existed.

Maharishi and Deepak Chopra, both reaching back to their experience with and knowledge of Vedic teaching in India, assert that control of our world is possible using the energy of the mind. With meditation, one's intention can be made one's reality. One has only to begin meditating with clear mental focus on one's intention, reaching within to the cellular level of oneself and without, to the universe, with the intention of creating one's own world, to experience the fulfillment of those intentions. This is what we can each do using meditation.

Meditators have focused on narrower issues than world peace with some statistically convincing results. In Washington DC, during a time of escalating violence on the streets, when crimes against persons and property were rising to intolerable levels, a group of over four thousand TM meditators from around the world went to Washington, gathered together, and held regular sessions during which they meditated, intending to influence the behavior of the local populace to become less violent and less criminal. During that time, the Washington DC police reports show that there was a statistically significant decrease in violence and in crime against property and persons.

I met Maharishi in 1974 when I lived in Houston. A friend, Gould Beech, had become an advance person to set up meetings as Maharishi travelled across the United States. At six foot two, I towered over him. He had not at that time adopted the name Mahesh Yogi, which I'm told means "supreme teacher." He was then and remained, during his long life, an extraordinary human.

Barely over five feet tall, at our meeting he chose to be seated on a slightly raised platform on a heavy oriental rug, with flowers on both sides of his position. His speaking voice was thin and high, and he had a disconcerting speech pattern that included a sound like "eh" vocalized on a rising inflection, which he used frequently to punctuate and space his thoughts.

I thought then that Maharishi's presentation of himself was a bit overproduced. But his message was clear and very attractive. Peace was attainable. The process of moving the politicians of the world to seek peaceful solutions to all problems could be initiated, directed, and hastened to completion by the power of meditation. It was a great and engaging idea. I was engaged.

I had a brief introduction to him by Gould and then attended his lectures on the power of meditation. I was impressed with the idea that I could join a group that might influence the world in a direction toward peace. Offered the chance to learn TM, I remember paying a very small fee for the private lesson that included being given my mantra. For me, it was the single sound "om," repeated until the mind quieted.

Meditation as a daily practice for me lasted less than two years. I meditated less and less frequently until 1994. In June of that year, when I was stressed to the point of thinking about leaving this world, I went to Deepak Chopra's Center for Mind Body Medicine, then in Del Mar, California. There, meditation was a part of the daily routine. We meditated singly in the mornings and in group meditations before evening meals, half an hour each time.

Deepak Chopra teaches what he calls primordial sound meditation, PSM. Simply put, the mantra given to each new meditator derives from their birth date and time. Classic Vedic texts set out mantra sounds and combinations of sounds for each of seventy-two time periods during the twenty-eight-day lunar month. I was taught PSM for a cost of $350.

Deepak Chopra wants this to be available to as many people as possible, while still asking for reasonable value in exchange for the discipline taught. As so many have learned who try to give away useful information, there seems to an important aspect of exchanging energy for energy. Money, in this case is the energy exchanged for the energy of information and discipline. As Maharishi believed, we seem not to value as highly things we get for little or no energy exchanged.

When I sit down to meditate, I find a comfortable chair that supports my back and lets my feet rest easily on the floor in front of me, slightly apart. I put my hands in my lap, palms up (you can't be tense with your palms up, try it!). I take three or four deep clearing breaths through my nose to oxygenate my body. At the same time, I allow all of me to become comfortable in the position I have chosen.

I then relax my whole body. At the beginning of learning to meditate, that process took several minutes. Now I find that I just tell my body to relax, and it does within less than a minute.

A good practice is to start with the toes on one foot. Tell those muscles to let go, relax, and then work back up to the top of the leg, focusing on each set of muscles in turn, mentally talking to them and feeling them let go of all tension. Do each leg, then each arm in turn. Then continue with the trunk of the body, the neck, face, and head muscles until the whole body is free of tension. If a part of the body feels still tense, tighten those muscles for a few seconds and then let them relax. They'll feel nicely calm after that. Pay attention to where your tongue is in your mouth. If it's pushed up against the roof of your mouth, let it drop and relax.

I start mentally saying my mantra and continue saying it over and over, but my attention may be drawn to an itch on my hand. Saliva collects in my mouth, and I need to swallow; a back muscle feels cramped, and I need to move to be comfortable. And there is a spot on my left cheek, just below my eye, which often develops a sort of intense tingle while I am starting to meditate.

My old friend Joe Nichols, a professional psychic in Austin, Texas, described the itch that demands to be scratched as the body starts to descend into a light trance as "meditation lice." Demands of my body for attention are natural. One has only two alternatives and they're both okay. Scratch the itch, swallow, move the body, and make the body comfortable because that is the path to complete relaxation. But not the only path.

The second alternative is to focus easily but purposefully on the mantra and find that soon the body relaxes into the program, and the demands for attention just disappear. An intense itch on the skin, if consciously ignored for a minute or two, will leave and not return. The feeling that comes with not giving in to pesky little imperious demands of the body is very empowering.

I usually create a contest with myself to see just how much self-control I really have. I consciously calm that side of my face demanding attention, softening muscles I have previously relaxed, making them even more flaccid. Usually then, the tingle intensifies instead of disappearing, as though my body is saying, "Ignore me, will you? I'll show you!" But then, when I resist the powerful urge to scratch and when I refocus on my mantra, I soon become aware that the body's demands for attention are gone. My mantra, my mind tool, worked. Distracted by a mindless repetitive sound I hear only in my mind, the mind has isolated itself from transient nerve stimulations which the physical body creates as a part of the process of quieting down.

We are all so action oriented and live our lives "on the go" that the state of repose, except in sleep and even then sometimes, can feel unnatural. Some nerve endings are slow to settle down. Some seem to just sort of rebel and continue to discharge their energy, refusing to quiet, requiring attention of some kind.

The choice of attention we give those little meditation distractions is important to our long-term conditioning. Physically scratching creates an immediate satisfaction but is a temporary response only. The way to create a satisfactory relationship between the physical body and its master and mentor, the mind, is to constantly remind the body who is really in charge. When we do that, the routine of quickly settling into the relaxed condition necessary for meditation is easily achieved.

Sometimes when I close my eyes, random thoughts ping-pong around in my head. My mind races on, heedless of my desire to meditate. Sometime I fall asleep while meditating and wake up after twenty or thirty minutes with a stiff neck. Although one doesn't move out of the chair and the physical functions of the body slow dramatically, meditation is a journey to see the self and to make contact at the most basic level with the universe.

The three possible outcomes of that journey are each okay.

You may find your mind won't quiet. Thoughts keep overriding the mantra, and after twenty or thirty minutes, you end the journey and come back to the present. That's good because these thoughts that kept demanding attention needed to be attended to. The very act of thinking them is enough to discharge some or all their energy and they disappear. Those thoughts will not interfere with the next meditation.

The second potential is to fall asleep. Your body's physical demands for rest overrode the mantra and your mind's attempts to meditate. If the rest was needed, the body is better off for the rest.

The best possible outcome is that the mind relaxes, the mantra continues until all thoughts are gone, the body stays in a quiet state, and the mind is alert and reaches a state of knowing itself. Contact with the universe is established, and all things are possible when that happens.

Meditate about half an hour once or twice a day. Twice a day is ideal, and if one is in a healing mode and meditating to enhance the healing process, then twice a day should be routine. Meditating for over half an hour frequently leaves one momentarily quite disconnected from reality; there is a tendency to be ungrounded when one comes out of the meditation, and one may have to consciously become grounded again.

Meditations should be in places where there will be no sudden sounds, like telephones ringing. The first time that causes a shock to your system will likely be the last time you'll meditate where that can happen. Coming back from a meditation should be gentle. Two to five minutes of horizontal time on a couch or bed is my favorite.

Meditation does not require absolute silence. I have learned that meditating in an airplane can be a very satisfactory meditation experience. Traffic sounds, the sounds of birds, or children at play, if not too raucous, should not interfere with your ability to quiet your mind and go deep inside.

Meditating is a way to get in touch with your guides, those energies that you may have been told were guardian angels. We all have them. We don't all know about them or may deny their existence. But the next time something in your life happens which unexpectedly saves you from a problem that seemed certain or when an event you had been wanting to happen really does happen, thank your guides. They had something, maybe everything, to do with that.

Seldom will any meditation be just like the previous one. Each experience will likely be different. When there is a purpose intended to be accomplished by meditating—for example, to create health in a part of your body which lacks health—as you begin the meditation, put your attention on that part and express your intention silently but clearly to your body, your expectation of change. There is no need to strain at the intention. Clarity is more important than force of will.

Simply putting attention on the part of the body needing health energies is sufficient. Intention and attention are the two operative words of creating your own world as you want it to be through meditation.

Meditation is your way to reach the gap and to inform what is there with your own energy, which is, in turn, the way to influence the universe to move in the direction you intend. Meditation is your way to reach deep down into the essential energies of the universe and direct those energies in a way you intend. The energies of the universe are boundless. There is no rationing. We can each attract to ourselves those things we most deeply desire. We merely have to put our intentions into a form that will get results. That is what meditation is all about.

Even when you have invested great time and energy in developing your

skills and knowledge, creating who you think you want to be,

life is flexible. You can change your mind. You can change direction.

You never ever lose the option to be in the future, different than you have

been in the past.

—GPD

#40 The Gap

Meditation is not an activity. It is a nonactivity.

When we try to explain meditation and what can happen when we meditate, as Alice said of her experiences through the looking glass, things get "curiouser and curiouser."

One of the most curious is that, while meditating, we may find and enter what Maharishi Mahesh Yogi and Deepak Chopra term "the *gap*."

We are not generally aware there is a *gap* as a consequence of how our brains process the information that comes to it through the senses. We think we see and hear a continuity of sight and sound. But what is really being received by our senses is a series of discrete pulses of vibrational energy. Our brains interpret the sensory information we receive as continuous because the primary function of all our sensory perceivers is with survival. We need to know what is around us; what is not around us can be ignored. The *gap* is both around us but not around us. It is somewhat like the concept of zero—essential but essentially in the mind.

But seers and psychics know the *gap* is real, as do quantum physicists.

The gap *is the interval between vibrations.*

The universe and all its parts pulse or vibrate constantly, without ceasing. Some vibration frequencies are within the perceiving range of our human senses, and we send these on to our brains for processing. Other frequencies are too low (like the vibration of the earth) or too high (such as radio frequencies) for us to detect with our human senses. But we have developed monitoring devices. These devices, which both monitor and measure, tell us that not only is everything in the universe vibrating, but also that the frequencies of vibrations are not the neat continuous sine waves that monitoring screens portray for us.

Energy that we can and do detect is actually in the form of impulses so nearly contiguous we perceive them as a flow. Frequency, as a technical term, assumes a continuous sine wave and describes the maximum energy level of each pulse per unit of time. Continuity of flow without variation of energy level is a concept we intuit. In fact, every action is composed of a series of subactions, which our senses fail to discern, but which experiments in quantum mechanics tell us exist.

Time is discontinuous, yet we experience it as continuous. Light and sound are each composed of discrete pulses of energy at a particular vibrational frequency that we interpret as a flow. We analogize it to things that our eyes see as continuous. "Time is a river flowing," says the poet.

Thoughts are pulses of energy that are also discontinuous.

Between the pulses there . . . are . . . gaps.

It is this *gap*, this interval, this nothingness that both precedes and follows each change in position of everything in every action. In the *gap*, there is no energy; there is only information. The *gap* is where intention can be sent to inform the next pulse of energy. In the *gap*, everything is potential. Where everything is potential, intention can shape and form the action that follows. The *gap* is the place from which the next pulse gets its direction. It is this *gap* that both Maharishi and Deepak Chopra describe as the goal of meditation. This is the transcendent place of TM. This is the *gap* of PSM.

When we reach the *gap* with our meditation, we can place our intention in that space, change the information that is ready to direct the next pulse (action), and influence actions that follow. We can use our energy to change the direction of the flow of action—in a word, the future.

In the ordinary flow of our lives, we have no need to detect that *gap*, and we do not. But seers and thinkers for millennia, by focusing their attention on what is real and what is maya (or illusion), have told us that the *gap* exists and that it is where intention can modify the next action. It is worth repeating that the *gap* is where you can send your intention to modify information and thus change your future.

In the *gap*, information that already exists creates a high probability that the action following will continue the course of the action preceding. It is however only a high probability, not a certainty. If we influence the probability amplitude of information in the *gap*, we thereby change the actuality of the event immediately after.

A marble rolling down an incline has a high probability (a certainty according to Newton's first law of motion) that it will continue to roll in the direction in which it is going unless acted on by some outside force (to change its direction or speed of travel).

At each nanosecond of its movement, there is a high degree of probability that it will continue on the course and with the speed of the preceding nanosecond. But a variety of things can intervene to change the information about what the next action will be. Gravity, the change of angle of incline, and friction can each energetically change the information and thus influence the course of events.

Or one can reach down and pick up the marble, a dramatic and visible change of information about what the next action will be.

You can, by going into the *gap* with your intention, do the equivalent of reaching down and picking up the marble: you can change the information about what has a high probability of happening next. The information that will compel the next discrete action is what you can reach and modify with your intention, creating a personalized next action in your favor.

In the *gap*, energy is at rest, but information is at work. Information is what controls the next discrete energy burst. What happens in each next pulse of energy is based on probability only. In the *gap*, the information that will control the next action is formed *but can be changed*. It has probabilities, but not certainty. What it does have is the potential of *all* possible next actions, which is why you can influence the information and the next action.

At each *gap*, the possibilities for reforming information are essentially boundless. When new information is introduced into the *gap*, the change organizes the energy potential differently than would have been predictable from the preceding actions. Predictability is modified as the next pulse of energy (action) diverges from the stream of the past action in response to the new information.

The beautiful thing about the whole process is that we mortals do not have to know anything at all about how it works in order to make it work. The two fundamental things we do have to know are simply that (1) we need to put our attention on what we want to influence and (2) we have to put our intention out to the universe. We do that by finding and entering the *gap*, using our minds, in meditation.

To modify information in the *gap* does not require mental sweat. It does require clarity.

To be effective, information placed into the *gap* by your mind must be precise and certain. It can be in the form of mental imagery or simply directions that narrowly define a desired result. To transmute intention into information in the *gap*, the intention must be narrow, focused, and well-defined.

The process is quite simple. A good way to teach yourself to put information into the *gap* of your own meditation is to visualize the result you intend as you begin your meditation. With practice, you will find the most effective visualization process for you. Later, as this becomes deeply embedded into your meditation routine, other ways of placing information into the *gap* will present themselves.

I used to think that people who prayed for an event to occur or for something they really needed to come to them were fooling themselves. I have since come to realize that I was the fool for not recognizing what they knew: no matter that they called it prayer, they were focusing their attention and intention, and the universe was responding.

A simple, useful example of how the universe works that confirms our power to affect events in our favor is something I've heard referred to as the "parking prayer." Starting out for a destination known for a limited supply of parking places, a request to the universe to provide a parking place has never failed to provide one for me. And I've talked to others for whom the advance request for a parking space works infallibly.

But you do not need to limit your intentions to providing parking spaces. Nothing is outside the scope of what you can influence; everything is within the scope of your personal powers. It works in all areas of your life if you focus your attention and intention. A widely quoted saying is "Pray and duck," a common recognition of the sequence of getting what we pray for, which is not always what we really wanted. *Thus, there is a need for extreme clarity.*

Good health is the most important aspect of your life that you can influence through attention and intention. Relationships get a little more complicated because of competing (and probably conflicting) intentions pushing information to influence the outcome.

This may be why we so often say, "I'll leave it up to God (or the gods, universe, etc.)." We often are not really sure that we really want what we think we want and so retreat to a position (or assertion) of noninvolvement in the outcome. So we end up not having to accept the responsibility we really do have for what occurs.

You have the ability to affect your own body in ways you probably never thought possible.

In the space of twenty to thirty months, not only many of the cells of your physical structure that can divide and create baby calls will have done so, but also all the cells—even neuronal cells, cardiac muscle cells, and others that do not frequently replicate (roughly about 18 percent of all of our body cells)—will have exchanged all their oxygen, nitrogen, carbon, sulfur, and other gaseous and mineral component molecules and atoms many, many times over.

It is truthful to say that at the end of any given twenty-four-month period of time, your body will be effectively composed of 100 percent different total components than at the start of the twenty-four months. At every age, at any age, aware of and entering the *gap* of your own cellular energy frequency, you have the capacity to make yourself over.

To change yourself at a cellular level, you need to only change the probability amplitude of the information in the *gap* between the existence of a single cell and the existence of its child cells, the new cells created as each cell completes its life cycle, divides, and then dies. You do this with meditation.

You have the ability to heal and renew those cells that do not divide and die. That also happens as a result of meditation. Your cellular body is so used to taking orders from your brain, and your brain is so used to and attuned to receiving directions from your mind that by simply putting attention on the expected result and directing a pure uncluttered intention that your organs or cells or systems heal, it will happen.

The *gap* is real. It is available to each of you. If you have a desire to change the direction of your life or any part of it, the *gap* is where you can do that.

Just a reminder:

The thought is the mother of the deed.

—From Sanskrit wisdom

#41 Wrinkle Resistance from Sulfur

Looking good is much a matter of keeping fit. Woman or man, we all have a streak of self-approval that needs to be satisfied about how we appear to the world. We do feel much better about everything when we feel good about how we look. That doesn't mean looking handsome or pretty in the usual sense. When we take care of our physical selves, the inner glow that people see and we feel makes the traditional idea of beauty not very important. Natural good looks, unique to each of us, comes from the energy we project when all our systems are go.

Even so, wrinkles are no fun to have, not least because of the underlying structural abnormalities that wrinkles reflect. At about age twenty, for many of us, the smile lines that we ignored for so long will start developing into permanent creases, wrinkles that we'd rather not have.

What causes us to wrinkle? Cells that make up our skin are continuously being born in the lowest layer of skin, then are pushed up though the middle layer to the outermost layer, the epidermis, from which they are constantly being sloughed off (the process may take as long as a couple of weeks). With all those bright, shiny new cells in evidence, why isn't our skin the same as a baby's skin? Why do we wrinkle?

In a few words, the underlying collagen beneath the layer of skin is subject to becoming more fibrous, with strings of tissue cross-connecting and becoming less flexible. This stiffer and less-pliable understructure shows in the more pliable, more flexible, and younger cells of the outer skin above. Your skin cells can be baby soft like you're two weeks old, but you still look wrinkled. Your skin isn't really old. It just looks old. Sorry. That's the way our bodies are constructed.

Theories of general aging place transitory damage to the DNA in individual cells high on the list of what causes our organs to function less efficiently and for us to run down as our chronological years increase. What is generally accepted as fact, however, is that damage to the DNA will usually put replication on hold until the damage is repaired or the cell dies. The replication process requires that there be a full set of chromosomes available to the cells about to be born for the process of replication to progress to conclusion. When the DNA is damaged, the chromosomes usually are also impaired.

There are colonies of cells located all over your body. They relate to the whole body sort of like the political divisions we have invented, like how county and city relate to larger political entities. These colonies have the power of life and death over individual cells in their immediate vicinity, determining when additional cells are needed and pronouncing a death sentence on damaged cells.

It seems logical that if cells become less functional because of damaged DNA and cannot reproduce, new baby cells from undamaged cells will be called for to replace the damaged cells. And for those new cells, good nutrition is a must. But not all damaged cells accept community orders to go away. Some just hang around, damaged, unable to replicate, but still unwilling to die. These damaged cells seem to play some part in causing wrinkles. That's a part of a natural process too.

For those cells that do replicate, without that good nutritional broth as an environment, there are some investigations that support that new cells—however faithful the new DNA is to the old—if born into a marginal environment, simply duplicate the toughened exterior envelope of the parent cells and start off their cellular life partially compromised.

You want to keep in mind some basics about nutrition and cellular health. For all cells, sulfur is an element vital to a flexible, permeable exterior envelope, the skin of the cell. Flexibility is as essential for each individual cell as it is for the organism as a whole. All parts of the body are in constant motion. Cell moves against cell; groups of cells move against other groups of cells. Organs never stop working.

Easy permeability is critical if information messenger molecules circulating in the blood, after attaching to their receptor sites on the exterior of the appropriate target cells, are able to quickly deliver their message or be taken into the interior of those cells to trigger needed cellular processes.

Sulfur is found in all growing things. Much of the sulfur in the world comes from a cycle of evaporation into the atmosphere from algae in warm waters. This sulfur returns to earth in rain and is taken up into the fibers and roots of all growing vegetation.

Sulfur is not as readily available to us as once was the case. We eat much less of green leafy vegetables, and the time from harvest to table allows vital sulfur components to be lost to evaporation.

Animals that graze on grass have sulfur in their flesh, and we get that benefit when we eat that meat. Eggs have high sulfur content in the yolk. Sulfur can also be absorbed into the body through the skin.

Sulfur springs and baths—once common in this country and around the world, as places to go to "take the waters," to soak in warm sulfurous waters, to drink with one hand while the other hand held the nose—all provided the body with sulfur, which the food of an increasingly urbanized society does not.

Sulfur springs have been noted to have been used by humans as far back as human recorded history extends. Experience must have taught us that soaking an injured extremity in the waters of a spring containing mineral compounds of sulfur promoted healing. Now we know why. Sulfur is essential to the well-being of new cells. New cells are created at every injury site to replace the damaged and dead cells that result from the trauma of injury. Sulfur is needed by these new cells to be vibrant and healthy, and in any injured area, sulfur in abundant supply promotes rapid healing. Sulfur is as essential for good maintenance of existing cells as it is for the creation and well-being of healthy baby cells.

Before his death a few years ago, my uncle Jim was a practicing chemical engineer, with the expected engineer's bias of viewing any folk wisdom with skepticism. He asked me one time what possible benefit could come from soaking an injured part of the body in an Epsom salt bath. In his mind, as he expressed it to me then, soaking in Epsom salt merely put money in the pockets of the manufacturers of Epsom salt without providing any benefit to the user.

I knew then that Epsom salt is merely the common name for the crystalline form of magnesium sulfate. However, at that time, I did not know of the body's need for sulfur, both for good cell maintenance and, particularly, for cell repair (or the body's need for and rapid utilization of magnesium ions, for that matter). And I did not know then the extent to which the skin acts as an organ that facilitates the transfer of many things into and out of the body, including sulfur in a form the body can use for repair of injured cellular tissue.

Since the body excretes excess sulfur after about twelve hours, persistent attention to keeping a constant level of sulfur in the body is essential to maintaining sulfur in our blood.

There are two ways to ensure a constant and adequate supply of sulfur: (1) a large serving of green leafy vegetables at least once every day as a minimum or (2) MSM.

MSM (Methylsulfanylmethane) is an inexpensive sulfur product, available in crystal form, which can be dissolved directly into water or aloe gel. Or mix crystalline MSM in a 5:1 ratio with crystalline vitamin C and then add water. Apply this to the skin in any place where sulfur is particularly desired for the benefits it provides, such as on and around any cut or abrasion where you don't want to leave a scar or on your procreative parts.

MSM is also available commercially in capsules, caplets, colloidal solutions, and lotions. It is frequently offered in a mixture with other substances and herbs. None of it is expensive. MSM was discovered by large animal veterinarians treating racehorses. MSM-soaked poultice bandages applied to injured tendons and ankle and hoof lesions prompted much faster and more complete recovery in these injured animals than had previously been possible.

From the racetrack to the local nutritional supply store took only a very few years. Some adventurous surgeons are using MSM to speed healing of surgical wounds. The results have been very impressive, many wounds healing with little or no scarring.

MSM in capsule form is a regular part of my daily supplemental nutritional diet, and I recommend it to you for all the reasons you've just learned, including delaying the onset of wrinkles.

"The most beautiful things in the world

cannot be seen or even touched.

They must be felt with the heart.

—Helen Keller

#42 Toning

One of the things that I came to understand—first, because of my work as a lawyer in representing people who had injuries caused by others and, second, because of my marriage to a woman who was supersensitive to energy and health needs of the body—is this truth: each of us is responsible for the health of our own body.

The commercial world of medicines and patent medicines, of medical machinery for hire and hospitals for profit, of doctors who took lessons in how to optimize their income by systematizing their routine for seeing patients are all really fairly recent. The for-profit medical world would now have us believe that nothing healthy can happen until we pay them for some pill or treatment. It really isn't the case at all.

Some doctors have always been entrepreneurs, charging what they could. But many provided great quantities of free or almost-free care because at heart they were healers. Hospitals used to be operated by organized charities or religious orders or, sometimes, by counties and cities, where there was concern for the health of the citizenry. The change from medicine being available to all, either because of the goodness of heart and charity of doctors or society or organized charities has been recent. Within the past forty years, for-profit medicine has become the rule, and it has had the effect of changing how we reflexively think about health care.

There have always been natural healers, those with extraordinary talents that they put to use for the good of their fellows. Natural potions, salves, nostrums, methods of healing the body that natural healers found worked were what people turned to when they were poor, when they feared what medical doctors might do would harm rather than help, and when they had exhausted whatever the medical community tried to do that hadn't worked. It was all a matter of taking the responsibility to find what would work with one's own body. Because not withstanding we all have bodies that are pretty much the same, we are all really, really unique. What works with one may not work with another. What I want to tell you is about a method of producing health and healing that is little known but quite effective in many respects.

During 1987, a window of learning opened for me about concepts of self-healing that are outside the usual. At that time, I was married to Peggy. She was, and still is, one of the most unusual people I have ever known. Her personal energy field was so powerful that she could not wear a battery watch. It could not compete with the natural energies she emanated, and all the quartz watches she tried stopped after only a few days on her wrist. She finally bought a Swiss balance movement watch that wound by the motion of her arm.

Peggy and I had both been recently initiated into second-degree Reiki. Our inquiries led to informal lessons from a friend skilled in body scanning, meditation, and other self-exploration fields. Peggy felt her healing powers very strongly and began practicing Reiki professionally. We took over a little house next to ours to use as an office and therapy studio. She developed a following and soon had an active Reiki practice.

A man who declared himself a Russian émigré came to her Reiki office one afternoon, intent on persuading her to include *toning* as a therapeutic tool. To that end, he offered to teach us what he knew about this procedure. His declared purpose was to make the world aware that toning could work miracles in everyone's health. If only people would learn and practice this simple self-healing technique, he proclaimed, it would be an effective cure for a variety of bodily malfunctions.

He needed a place to teach. He was candid that he also wanted to use our client base to start his own practice thinking, logically enough, that anyone interested in Reiki would likely be open to another nonordinary healing experience.

Full of his subject, Boris (not his real name) had even written a short treatise about toning, which he pressed on us. I still have a copy. He also gave each of us a pitch pipe to get the right note an important, though not critical, aspect of toning. It was the round sort that all teachers used to have when I was a child in school. I still have that too.

His premise was that each organ of the body—having different cells, structure, and function—has its own individual, specific energy signature (i.e., frequency of vibration). To be well and healthy, the cells of each organ should vibrate at their specific frequency. Illness or other deterrents to good function change the frequency. Ergo, restore the frequency and restore good health.

String theory, advanced by theoreticians in an effort to explain how all matter works, posits that all matter is composed of vibrating energy. It is simply the frequency of the vibration that differentiates matter. If Boris knew this at that time, he did not say. His understanding of toning was apparently developed out of his own work with his own body, experimenting with the tones he produced and pragmatically determining the effect they produced.

Toning intends to induce the natural frequency vibration of the cells of the various vital organs within the body, using the vibration of one's own voice. When the cells of those organs are tuned to their natural frequency, an essential condition for the health of that organ and, by extension, the whole body, they will rid themselves of whatever disease is troubling them and be restored to a condition of good health.

Open-mouthed tones can be loud and seemed, to me, to do more for the surrounding area than for me individually. But closed-mouthed humming tones really did make my upper body vibrate, down to my pelvis. With some higher-pitched tones, I could feel vibration down to my knees.

Tibetan monks have learned the art of making their voices create multiple overtones by manipulating the placement of the tongue, jaws, lips and by changing the configuration of the cheeks and throat. It is called throat singing. Toning uses similar techniques to create overtones. The broader the range of vibrations one generates, the more likely one is to send forth to the body the unique vibration signature of each major organ.

Vocal tone quality is influenced by the size and shape of your sinuses, the many small cavities in our facial bones, which are not under your control. What is under your control, in a major way, is the size and shape of the cavity created by your throat and mouth. Vocal cords vibrate, which in turn causes the air in the throat and the mouth to vibrate. By changing the shape of mouth and throat, pure tones can be changed to pure tones plus many possible overtones. Overtones—vibrations above, below, and around the pure tone—are what toning aspires to have us create with our vocal chords.

When you hum a note, with teeth and lips closed, place your hands on your face and feel where the vibration is greatest. Now while keeping lips closed, continue to hum, but slowly drop your lower jaw. You will feel the vibrations increase dramatically in your nose and around your eyes. Now hum and hold your hand on your upper chest. You will feel the vibration there. Your heart and lungs are vibrating too, underneath the breastbone. Experiment with the shape of your mouth cavity. Open your throat more, tilt your head back to lengthen your throat, move your tongue down, up, place it forward, to the back. Open your jaws wide, still without opening your lips.

Each change will create a different tone in your head. With just a little practice, you can learn to place the sound. The first placing should be into your ears. Trying to yawn while toning will teach you how to do this. With practice, you will be able to tell when a sound is causing different parts of your body to vibrate. Practice in placing the sound will allow you to massage all your internal organs.

Different pitches and different shapes of the mouth and throat influence the relative strength of the vibration at the heart level. Move your hand around as you tone to find where, in your body, different tones resonate most strongly.

Though we are each different, our cells have basically the same structure. They should react to frequencies the same way in everyone. The recommendations of Boris are at the end of this story. To find for yourself what notes and tones are best for each of your organs, you can communicate with your own body using muscle testing. If you do not know this technique of self-communication, you can find out more in my e-mail about *kinesiology* (#48 in this book).

After Boris went away, toning remained dormant in the back of my mind. I was healthy. I felt no need to tune myself up, so to speak. Then came an episode of chest pain, which required two stents, a subsequent bout of atrial fibrillation, and medication to keep that under control. At the time of the first signs of serious problems, my body was approaching seventy-six years of age. That's probably quite a long run without serious problems. Autopsies during the Vietnam War showed some soldiers as young as twenty-three had advanced coronary artery blockages.

Only recently has my internal message machine reminded me that toning might be a good thing to do. I smoked from age fifteen to age forty-nine and in the last years smoked heavily. I quit totally in 1974 and have not smoked since. So far, I have no signs that smoking has done more than slightly reduce my total lung capacity and likely caused some degree of atherosclerosis.

It is distressing to learn that stopping smoking did not stop my risk of smoker's problems. Occasional exposure to the harmful effects of the secondhand smoke has continued my status as one of moderate health risk due to smoking. Recent studies, incidentally, have established that people exposed to secondhand smoke are at risk for the same health problems, including heart attack and death, as those who smoke and assault their lungs intentionally.

Atrial fibrillation is often a lifelong condition. Luckily, mine resolved after about two years of medications and a determination to not be afflicted with this. A rhythm irregularity continued intermittently after the atrial fib resolved. About a year ago, an episode of high blood pressure put me on a mild medication for that. Other medications to ameliorate cardiovascular problems have been prescribed occasionally.

These past risk factors plus an abhorrence of taking medications for any purpose caused me to start toning again.

For ten minutes, right after waking, I sat cross-legged and upright and toned. With lips closed, but playing with the sound by changing the shape of mouth and throat, I toned for ten minutes. My body at first didn't like the idea of breathing deeply, and toning started a couple of coughing episodes. But shortly, my lungs expanded. I found that I could breathe into both the upper and lower parts of my lungs and fill them to capacity.

Each breath and tone takes about fifteen to twenty seconds. I start at the note my body wants, then go higher, one pitch level at a time, until I reach my upper limit, three to four tones on each note. Then I go as low as I can and finish out the ten minutes on low notes.

To find out if toning was helping reduce my blood pressure, I took the pressure each morning before and after toning. The results have been quite astounding to me. Over two weeks, the first BP reading dropped from 137/72 to 116/60. The second reading changed from 107/52 to 98/48. BP readings during the day have stayed about 135/75—for me, a normal range. My lung capacity felt greatly improved.

By the way, I am convinced there is not any such thing as coincidence, serendipity, or any of the other descriptive words we use to describe things that happens to us that we do not expect and are often marvelously good for us. Forces we do not understand seem to control much of what happens.

What we see, hear, get in the mail can be exactly relevant to what is happening to us in other parts of our lives. People show up when they are most needed; we take a different route home and see something that we needed to see. It happens a lot.

Toning seems likely to be more useful at this time in my life than when I learned of it. But if I had started a regimen of toning then, perhaps later problems of circulation and lungs (probably caused by years of foolish smoking) would not have developed. The appearance of Boris is just another example of the way important information showed up unexpectedly in my life. Often too, the information seemed unimportant and unnecessary until later events prove quite the opposite.

When you hear friends talk about putting first things first, think of this. I am not sure where I heard it first or where it originated. Everything we do has a precedent. This says it nicely. GPD

Watch your thoughts,
> *for they become words.*
Watch your words,
> *for they become actions.*
Watch your actions,
> *for they become habits.*
Watch your habits,
> *for they become character.*
Watch your character,
> *for it becomes . . . your destiny.*

—Proverb

#43 Massage

When someone you know comes up and rubs your shoulders, it really feels good. Not only the touch of someone friendly, but the pressure on the muscles; the subtle adjustment of the body under the hands of another always feels good. Want to know why?

Every massage provides more benefits than you know, even the unprofessional shoulder rub from a friend. But a really good massage guarantees abundant and varied health benefits, present and prospective. It's hard to believe that something that feels so good could also be so good for you, but massage is one of those unexpectedly beneficial actions we should all know about and take advantage of.

The skin is the largest organ in the body. Stimulated by rubbing, it produces hormones, information-messenger molecules, interleukin, interleukin II, interferon, and a whole panoply of the body's natural pharmaceuticals.

One of the very useful neuropeptide substances that the skin produces is vasoactive intestinal polypeptide (VIP). VIP is found in the brain, the intestines, and, most interesting of all, the skin. Massage seems to stimulate the production of VIP, which, when released, becomes a trigger for many really beneficial consequences in and to the body as a whole.

As an information messenger, VIP sent into the circulatory system by massage causes blood vessels to dilate, increasing coronary blood flow by 15 to 20 percent.

VIP is a molecule that occupies the same receptor site as the HIV virus. In theory, VIP released into the bloodstream will block HIV from getting into T cells.

At an informal after-supper get-together that I attended while at his clinic in Del Mar, California, Deepak Chopra briefly mentioned the type of full body massage, which Ayurveda calls the Abhyanga massage, used on AIDS patients in a veteran's hospital setting. These patients felt better, functioned better, and had less side effect responses to medications being taken at the time than those who did not get the massages.

Massage on patients other than AIDS sufferers seems to promote their quicker recovery. Tests have shown that after an ayurveda massage, the level of human growth hormones (HGH) elevates. HGH, normally produced by the pituitary gland, really drops off dramatically at about age sixty-five. Studies indicate that after age sixty-five, about half the population is partially or wholly deficient in HGH.

Fortunately, the pituitary can be stimulated to produce HGH, even in those over sixty-five. In a colony of old rats (twenty-six months, nearly ready to pass on), a severe caloric restriction for two months induced GH secretions to return. Rats are not people, but the results are used to support the argument that, in humans, HGH reduction need not be a permanent condition.

A recently developed supplement, HGH-Plus, includes a variety of nutrients and amino acids that are intended to stimulate HGH production in older humans.

Touch is a very important part of human interaction, and we seem to have lost some of the information about just how important it is. Babies in the preemie wards of hospitals who are stroked, even when the nurse has to insert her arms into sleeves built into the sides of the incubators to touch the babies, go home weeks earlier than those who are merely fed, changed, and left alone in their Isolettes.

When a dog licks its puppy, there is an immediate elevation of growth hormones in the puppy's bloodstream.

Rabbits being fed a high-cholesterol diet to gauge the effects on the heart and circulation all died as predicted except one small group. Investigation showed that the lab assistant in charge of that group, before each feeding, took the rabbits out of their cages, then cuddled, petted, and fondled them all. These rabbits had only a slight rise in HDL in their blood, whereas all the other rabbits not cuddled, petted, and fondled died. Anyone for petting and being petted?

Our physical bodies all come equipped with an internal pharmacy, which is always on the job. It makes the natural pharmaceuticals that are needed in response to the information carried by messenger molecules that are constantly in motion, circulating around the body in the bloodstream. There is always the right dose of the right substance at the right time with no side effects.

These natural pharmaceuticals are proteins, the formulae for which are carried in your genetic codes. One very big reason to be sure that the nutritional broth from which all cells derive the food they need for good health and function is that your cell's walls need to be flexible and permeable. Information from messenger molecules needs to be able to pass freely and quickly through the cell's outer envelope to get to the nucleus, the command center, where all information about what is needed and how to make it is stored in the genes.

Sulfur, the fourth-most-prevalent mineral in the body, is necessary for the cell wall to be both permeable and flexible. MSM (Methylsulfanylmethane), a form of sulfur the body can absorb readily and use, has become, within the past twenty years, a must-have supplement for everyone—you included.

Information-messenger molecules are sent on their way by a variety of different stimuli. As we've noted, touch can start a process of hormone and peptide creation that affects other parts of the body. Other senses are also part of the complex of messenger molecule production, as is the mind.

With the simple thought that "I'm thirsty," hormones in the brain set us out to search for water. At the same time, messenger molecules alert the kidneys, heart, and lungs to hold moisture. An antidiuretic hormone is produced to make sure that water loss is kept to a minimum. From a thought, the body is mobilized to respond.

Hormones also are produced by the body in response to stimuli we may not even know about through our senses. Melatonin, for example, is produced by the pineal gland, which responds to light in both visible and invisible parts of the spectrum.

As mentioned, after a massage, the concentration of interleukin in the body elevates, and the concentration of free radicals goes down. Interleukin is a powerful modulator of the immune system and stimulates T cells to produce interleukin II, known to be a potent viral fighter and thought to be important in fighting the AIDs virus.

The information about massage of AIDS patients in a VA hospital I mentioned earlier developed from a program Deepak Chopra, renowned writer, lecturer, and one whom I regard as my personal guru, initiated with a VA hospital in California.

As a trained endocrinologist in Western medicine, Deepak knew the great benefits massage provides. Thinking that soldiers in the hospital would both enjoy and benefit from massage, he set up that program to have massage therapists visit the hospitals and give a massage twice a week, for a period of six weeks to a group of service men suffering from a variety of illnesses.

By all standard medical measurements of health, those who received massages healed more and healed more quickly than those who did not participate in the program.

The lotion that most massage therapists are taught to use to lubricate the area being massaged has value to the person being massaged only in the effects the lubrication has in allowing therapist hands to move easily across the skin of the one being massaged.

Other than as a medium for assisting the hands to slip over the skin, the lotion has no value to the massage therapist, either. If the therapist you select for massage does not know the benefits of sesame oil, particularly oil that has been processed using curing processes I developed, take your own supply of cured sesame oil with you to the session. The processes I developed are available from skindharma.com and youthingstrategies.com. Caution them to use it very sparingly.

Therapists are used to slopping it on the commercial lotions because those have drying properties that make them disappear.

About one quarter ounce of sesame seed oil is all that is needed for a total body massage. By the time the full massage is done, that marvelous oil will have totally absorbed. You will not be or feel oily; and your skin will be more soft, pliable, and radiant than you can believe.

Just a word here about the extraordinary benefits of this oil: sesame seed oil has a long history of use by humans, the first recorded use having been among the Vedic people of northern India nearly three thousand or so years BCE.

It is the only natural oil that the body accepts and allows to circulate in the bloodstream. It is extremely useful when applied daily to the skin in a self-massage. Sesame oil absorbs into the skin quickly, attracting and attaching to toxic molecules in body tissue and carrying these toxins along in the bloodstream to be dealt with by the waste removal system of the body. Information about more great benefits of sesame seed oil is in another e-mail (#35 Sesame Oil).

But back to massage; the really great thing about stimulating your skin to produce all those wonderful beneficial effects I told you about earlier, is this: *your skin doesn't care whose hands do the rubbing.*

What that means is this: the self-massage I described to you in another e-mail (#36 Morning Routine), may not provide the same sybaritic rewards as a professional massage, but the physical response of your skin cells will be the same, even when your hands are the ones doing the work. Your own self-massage is very rewarding, and the price is right. So give your cells all the benefits a good skin rubbing will bestow and do it every day.

It is our own choices that have

most frequently been

the direct cause of

who and what we are.

—GPD

#44 Sweet Breath

Who doesn't remember at least one experience in school, where some child had breath so bad you had to stop breathing for a moment to move away into fresher air? Bad breath is an indicator of a problem somewhere. It can come from a sour stomach, a sinus infection, or just poor dental hygiene. You may not know when you have it, but if friends back away when you talk to them, be alert. Something in your system is broadcasting a warning. Pay attention. Don't be afraid to ask. If there is a sinus infection or another condition that you were unaware of, you can't start fixing it until you know about it.

You all know from school health classes that bacteria gets into our body through many avenues of entry, but the nose and mouth were emphasized in my grammar school in New York City. Keeping the mouth clean was important too, from a social acceptance standpoint. One did not want to have "morning breath" or the foul smell that came from the mouths of kids that didn't brush their teeth and had bits of rotting food still caught between teeth.

It all sounds disgusting. And it was. And is. But bad breath can come from many causes. Keeping the mouth and breath clean is not merely a socially relevant habit; it is also a serious health issue that should not be downplayed. The good news is that gingivitis and excess bacteria in the mouth can be managed with minimal effort and cost.

What I didn't know then was that unpleasant breath can also result from indigestion, from a systemic disease of the body; bad breath can be from poorly digested or particularly malodorous food and comes from the stomach before it exits the lips. Sinus infections are well-known creators of bad breath. But most often, it is from conditions in the mouth: poor dental hygiene or gingivitis, bleeding gums.

Gingivitis is a more serious problem than many people realize. Bleeding around the gumline indicates a bacterial infection has started. Infection is undermining and separating the tough elastic tissue designed to adhere tightly to the roots of your teeth. The purpose of that seal is to isolate the roots of teeth from the contents of the mouth and protect against pathogenic bacteria having an easy entry into the bloodstream via this potentially deadly direct pathway.

Blood coming from the gums indicates that you are vulnerable to whatever bacteria may happen to be in your mouth. If bacteria can migrate down along the margin of the tooth, in the space created by the separation of gum from tooth, your whole body, through the blood circulatory system, is exposed to whatever bacterial soup is in the mouth

The heart is the most vulnerable organ to opportunistic bacteria that enter the circulatory system through this means. The arterial system feeds blood to the teeth, as well as to all other parts of the body, and the venous complex carries blood back to the heart: a veritable blood highway for bacteria that can enter the body this way, straight to the heart.

The condition we are addressing here is that generated by bacteria that has collected around the juncture of the gum and tooth surface. When it causes bleeding gums, it has progressed much too far for health and safety. That condition should be regarded as a warning to take action to protect the body against a bad, potentially fatal bacterial invasion.

Gingivitis is caused by bacteria; plaque is caused by bacteria. The mouth is, literally, full of bacteria, most of it useful and only some not. But the some that is not can be truly dangerous to your health. Every means possible should be taken to avoid allowing such bacteria to establish a presence elsewhere in your body. For this reason, it is well worth the effort to control the bacteria that causes gingivitis and plaque, both of which are major problems for many people.

One natural and really positive method of preventing gingivitis is to regularly use a mouth rinse of a light organic cold-pressed seed oil. All vegetable and seed oils are antibacterial, but vary in potency. The best for this purpose is sesame seed oil, followed closely by safflower oil, grape seed oil, and extravirgin olive oil.

Swishing a light organic cold-pressed oil around in the mouth for at least five minutes each morning will accomplish cleansing the mouth of bacteria that would otherwise cling to teeth and hide at the margins of the gums and in tiny folds and crevices of the interior walls of the mouth and the tongue.

Using seed or vegetable oil as a mouthwash takes only about one teaspoon of the oil per day. Before taking any water into your mouth, taking medications, brushing your teeth, or cleansing the mouth with any prepared mouthwash, take about a tablespoon of oil, swish, and chew it as though it had substance. Allow the oil to move easily in the mouth, all the while being conscious that you want the oil to reach between teeth and into every part of the mouth.

You will find that mucus from the sinuses will naturally migrate into your mouth to mix with the oil, as will mucus from the back part of your mouth and throat. After about five minutes of this, the oil will have changed color to milky white. It is now loaded with bacteria. Dispose of this bacteria laced compound into the toilet or into the basin while running very hot water to be sure it goes down the drain without presenting a threat to your plumbing.

Rinse your mouth with hot water. Brushing teeth, gums, and tongue with a medium-bristle toothbrush and mild toothpaste completes the cleansing process.

At the Maharishi Institute for Management at Fairfield, Iowa, a study and control group of sophomores and juniors from the college found that after six weeks of regular swishing, the gingivitis bacteria count in the mouths of the group using the oil was reduced by more than 80 percent. The control group had no change.

A medical authority in the Ukraine has published a paper that asserts that twenty minutes of this effort, using safflower oil every day for two weeks, will cure basic ailments that afflict the body—not just in the mouth, but general systemic illnesses. My own knowledge of the comparative efficacy of seed oils leads me to recommend, for this purpose, sesame seed oil would be a better oil to use.

When shopping for an oil to use as a mouth rinse, look for cold-pressed oil. Using oil with natural enzymes undiminished by heat is important. Enzymes are killed by heat of over 115 degrees Fahrenheit, and you want to have all the natural enzymes in the oil available to assist in bacteria control while using the oil as a mouth rinse. Cold-pressed means seeds, fruits, or other natural food products are put into a press, squeezed, and the resulting oil collected without any heat applied to increase the production. Cold-pressed oil (often called expeller pressed) comes to you with all the natural enzymes ready to do their work purifying your mouth.

Most vegetable oils are tortured by manufacturers in their intent to derive every last drop of available oil from the raw product. Extreme heat of up to 250 degrees Fahrenheit cooks the seeds and kills the enzymes; in addition, a powerful petroleum solvent is often used, to be later removed by a partial vacuum, which, unfortunately, frequently does not completely remove all the solvent molecules. You don't want to put even a trace amount of this solvent in your mouth. Other process uses various chemicals along with heat to extract oil.

An equally important marker to be sure to look for is *organic*. Under the present USDA rules, *grown organically* means that no artificial fertilizers and no pesticides, fungicides, nor herbicides have been used to grow the crop involved and that none have been used on the earth where the crop was grown for two years before the present crop was seeded into the ground.

This does not guarantee that the plant will not have taken up some agricultural toxins as a part of its growth, but it brings that risk to the lowest potential in today's agrichemically driven world.

Because of poor and wasteful farming practices over the past 150 years, fields where food crops are grown have become depleted of minerals essential to your good health. Soils are also nearly empty of the natural bacteria plants depend on to assist in the uptake of nutrient essential to healthy plant growth.

Organically grown, unfortunately, does not certify you are getting nutritionally healthy farm products. It only means that you are not being subjected to farm products that contain residues of poisons used in the business of farming.

Those chemical residues are in amounts the FDA and the USDA consider to be poisons that humans can tolerate. Eating or, in the case of oils, taken in though the skin, chemical residues of farming are said to be without serious damage to the body. Well, maybe.

This policy is based on the idea that the body can tolerate and the human liver can detoxify some quantity of poisonous chemicals that in larger doses would be deleterious or even fatal to human health. No distinction is made about the size of the body or the fragility of the immune system of people eating or using these foods.

Nor is any consideration given to the greater vulnerability of pregnant women, nursing mothers, infants, children, or frail elderly. All are presumed to be able to accept, and their bodies detoxify chemical poisons in foods, the inevitable result of growing food crops with the primary assistance of chemical poisons.

As mentioned, the best oil for mouth swishing is sesame seed oil. It has the greatest antibacterial components, is the lightest of oils, has a nice nutty taste, and has the most potent anti-inflammatory healing properties. It also becomes lighter in its viscosity as one swishes it in the mouth. Sesame seed oil is also the oil with the longest history of human use without bringing health problems to the user. It has been in use since discovered in northern India by the Vedic people, about four thousand years ago. In all the medical literature, there is only one documented case of an allergic response to ingesting sesame seed oil.

Oil sellers have recently started to market seed oils in plastic, which has been shown to leach components of the container into the contents. Recent tests have shown plastics marked 5 and 7 (on the bottom of the container) are the most likely to leach into the contents of the container. A glass container will not leach poisons into the oil and is preferable.

Along with the process of swishing, there really is nothing that will take the place of regular use of dental floss. Flossing is necessary to ensure the mouth has no residual fragments of food, even after brushing. Swishing will not likely dislodge all fragments of food or completely neutralize the bacteria that cause plaque to form on your teeth. Everyday use of dental floss is also an essential part of good care of your teeth.

Your dentist will be amazed at the health of your gums and at the absence of plaque and dental caries. They will remark on the excellent condition of your mouth but will probably raise their eyebrows at your explanation.

For your spouses, partners, girlfriends, and boyfriends, your mouth will be sweet and clean every day. Your breath will have taken on a new fragrance of good health. For yourself, your health will be protected as nothing else will protect it from harmful bacteria in your mouth.

> *Admittedly, there are events in each life that happen*
>
> *over which you have little or no control;*
>
> *but the vast majority of both small and large things in your life*
>
> *are under your partial or full control.*
>
> —GPD

#45 Weight Control

Weight control is something that is a current topic of consideration among nearly all age-groups, and I assume yours as well, though you are all still quite youthful. Diets are sometimes well thought out and effective in controlling body mass, but along with instructions about eating (dieting), I hope you will also pay attention to how your body performs. To say we are each unique is to say the obvious. But it is worth emphasizing because the diet that works for one might not—probably will not—work for all.

When you think about adopting a controlled diet, particularly if the goal is weight control or body image revision, before you act, think about what I am about to offer as advice and also read my e-mail on Kinesiology. Make sure that before you invest money and energy in an eating plan, it will really enhance your well-being.

Several common habits affect your body's ability to maintain a constant and healthy body avoirdupois. The human body has had pretty much the same general operating format for more than a million years, counting our simian heritage. During all that time, there has been no light except from the moon and stars to brighten the night. Our digestive systems developed in accord with the circadian rhythm of day followed by night. Morning was the time to start the day—often very early, at first light or the break of dawn. Hunter-gatherers for eons, human's quest for food, as with our animal and other kin, was never ending.

Although there has been an aggregation of humans into cities and the first light of dawn sees most rushing to work rather than foraging for food, our systems have stayed pretty much as they always have been. To stay healthy and with at least normal amounts of energy to meet the day, we should pay attention to how our bodies work—how they have always worked.

The Swiss have a word for the first meal of the day. "Breakfast is golden," they say. Then they add, "Lunch is silver, and supper is lead." This pithy observation emphasizes the circadian rhythm of our nature. Early-morning food is metabolized soon after eating, and the energy that flows through us from this sets us on our paths with a hearty, vigorous step.

By lunchtime, the stomach has emptied, the body has expended energy in whatever tasks we have assumed, and those energy depletions cause us to want more food. It is worth a small diversion to take a look at what happens to the food we take into our bodies.

What follows assumes a meal that fills the stomach about three-quarters full. The stomach turns food into a semiliquid mass, infused with either pepsin or hydrochloric acid, and sends that mass further along in the digestive process. It takes about three hours for this process to complete if the stomach starts out relatively full. As the chum passes though the rest of the digestive system, fiber and nutrients break down into smaller and smaller components. Nutrients and minerals pass through the stomach lining and are absorbed into the blood for distribution as needed. Fiber keeps on going to form a mass in the lower colon, where the body adds toxins removed from body tissue and extracts water to be reused where needed. Fecal matter is excreted, more food is taken in, and the process repeats.

After eating, the body sends copious quantities of blood to the whole digestive tract to assist in the process of turning solid matter into usable nutrients and to absorb those nutrients into the bloodstream and carry them throughout the body.

By lunchtime, breakfast food is still moving through the digestive system: from the stomach to and through the small intestines, the duodenum, then the ilium, followed by passage through the jejunum into the colon. In descending order, those segments compose the lower digestive tract. This decreases the supply of blood to the body generally, brain included—all of which affects and, to some extent, temporarily diminishes energy available to the whole body. And the body usually feels it.

It is no wonder that after lunch, we often want a postprandial nap.

To digest protein and much fiber, the body's need for hydrochloric acid is critical. The cells of meat protein particularly require acid to liberate the useful molecules of protein from the connective tissue of the meat and permit the further processing of those molecules into usable nutrition.

When, as a part of a meal, we drink a carbonated beverage, the CO_2 that creates the carbonation is an alkaline substance that reacts with the hydrochloric acid to form a salt that is not useful in the digestive process. CO_2 neutralizes the acid the body needs to metabolize food. As you might guess, this interferes with digestion in a very substantial way.

You'd think having carbonated drinks with the meal would make us thin from lack of nourishment. But the opposite is true. CO_2 is such a potent interference with digestion that much of the food that goes into the duodenum is not broken down into usable components.

Sugar, of course, is the major part of most soft drinks. Coca-Cola and Pepsi-Cola have eleven and twelve teaspoons of sugar per twelve-ounce bottle respectively. That's a whole lot more sugar than your body can use as energy, so it turns the excess into fat. The body is very efficient at turning sweets into fat molecules and placing them in convenient places for retrieval in times of food scarcity, another heritage action of our bodies. This is another very efficient way we accumulate fat. If fat accumulates on your hips and around your stomach and you drink CO_2 beverages with your meal, that's a good place to put the blame.

We should keep in mind that famine has been a constant threat to human existence, until very recently, all over the world. The human organism developed efficient means of preparing for and keeping the body alive during periods of low food availability. Fat accumulated in large quantities in various places around the frame was insurance against days of little or no food intake. Until very recently, in Africa, a woman's accumulation of fat was accepted as a normal and appropriate advance storage of nutrition pending the famine everyone knew could happen at any time.

We have evolved to safeguard, as much as can be, the passing on of genes from generation to generation. Women are much more important in that process than men. So it is that women tend to be prone to fat accumulation. It is an evolutionary matter.

We scarcely think of famine as a threat to our way of life in the developed world. However, climate warming (the preferred term is now climate change), now threatens us with the potential for famine. Agricultural pests, formerly kept at low levels by frigid winter temperatures, are advancing into areas of the world that once were warm enough to grow one crop, but too cold for overwintering pests. These pests are now flourishing. In a monoculture society, where we plant huge areas of land in single crop arrays, the potential for mass destruction of food crops by insects that can multiply and become unstoppable in very short periods of time is a real threat.

In the meanwhile, most agree thinner is better. Thinner provides less stress on the body structure, including internal organs that do not do well when encased in fat. Getting thinner and maintaining that condition is not only a matter of what we eat, but how efficiently we metabolize the foods we do eat. That, in turn, depends on the genetics of one's heritage. Some of us are very efficient at extracting the most nutrient value possible from every scrap of food. These people need less food than those whose systems are not so efficient. This, again, is evolutionary.

Other factors that impact the results of food intake are your blood type, your frame size, your habits of eating, your allergic reactions to various foods (allergies that we know about and those that involve low-level reactions not readily apparent to the person who is allergic), and others that are more technical that this brief essay warrants exploring.

Raw vegetables (except root vegetables) are better at providing nutrients for everyone than cooked vegetables. The reason has to do with the vitamins, enzymes, and nutritional content that is lost to heat and/or absorbed by the water or steam in which the food is cooked and then discarded.

Enzymes die at about 115 degrees Fahrenheit. We need them to fully digest the food that contains them. Our own bodies supply enzymes to perform that service up to about middle age; but like almost everything else, the body's ability to supply all the enzymes we need starts to decline, and as it does, our ability to get full value of energy from the foods we eat also declines.

Notwithstanding, cooked foods are more easily digested, particularly by older folks, and more of the available nutrients may be metabolized. In many cultures, Indian and Chinese, for example, very little food is eaten raw. However, in the United States, increased attention to disease prevention from contaminated fertilizer or water has created an agricultural culture both knowledgeable and careful about clean growing conditions. Generally, raw foods in the United States are safe and can be made safer with washing in mildly chlorinated water.

In order to allow the body to process the food and empty the stomach before going to sleep, the evening meal should be light and eaten before seven o'clock. Soup or porridge at night is easily digested and nourishing.

The reason to eat light at night and never after about seven o'clock is twofold: As mentioned above, the stomach takes about three hours to empty. Going to sleep with an empty stomach is important because the repair of body tissue and cells damaged by toxins and stress starts at about eleven o'clock in the evening and continues for about three to four hours. The body needs all its supply of blood to be involved in this, bringing nutrients, oxygen, hormones, and other repair molecules to needful cells.

If the body has to spend blood energy digesting, particularly meat protein, which takes longer and more energy to digest, the body will be stressed and not able to do its repair work efficiently. One of the most likely causes of adding fat to the body is eating meat protein after seven o'clock. The American habit of having a steak for dinner is counterproductive to maintaining your body's natural weight.

If you find that eating heavy meat, like beef or pork, after seven o'clock in the evening leaves you still feel slightly full the next morning, it is because your body has allowed the meat to stay, mostly undigested, in your stomach overnight. Not a pleasant thought.

This all is a part of your circadian rhythms. Your body is evolutionarily programmed to do certain things at certain times because that is the way, over millennia, human cells prospered. Of all the parts of us that we should not try to control or interfere with, the evolutionary, natural flow of activity that the cells have developed to achieve and maintain their own good health is most important to our whole body's good health.

Establishing a natural weight for your body type is a matter of eating right, getting enough sleep, avoiding toxins like tobacco and alcohol, and being good to your cells. Given a healthy diet and reasonably healthy physical routine, your body will shed unnecessary pounds; and by simply turning away from soft drinks, eating light at night, and taking in lots of raw vegetables, you can find the weight with which you and your body can be comfortable.

It's not that some people have the will power and some do not.

It's that some are ready to change and others not.

—James Gordon, author

#46 Changing Your BMI

None of you are fat. Partly that is a matter of genetics. But partly, it is a matter of economics. Recent studies have established that many, many people living at or below the poverty level are obese. Why? Simply because they are constrained by their lack of income to buy food that is cheap. Cheap food is most often full of calories but not so full of nutrition. Also, the inner city, where poverty is most prevalent, has few of the stores that one finds in the suburbs. Fresh vegetables are hard to find, often nonexistent, in the inner city.

So obesity is not simply a nutritional matter. It is that, but poverty is the main driver of our present obesity epidemic.

If you are not fat (obese) but simply a bit overweight, changing your body mass index (BMI) to less than 25 can be an important step on your path to better health.

You can figure out your BMI with this formula: weight in pounds divided by height in inches squared multiplied by 703.

Once you've determined your BMI, use the following chart to determine where you fit in:

Below 18.5: Underweight
18.5-24.9: Normal
25-29.9: Overweight
30 and above: Obese

In 2009, one of the pressing health concerns of the United States is the weight of many of its citizens. More than half our people are considered overweight enough that their weight is a medical, rather than a physical, condition.

Children, who used to grow up active and slender, with nutrition providing added muscle and sinew, now, starting as young as three years of age, often lead sedentary lives; and the nutrition they take in turns to fat, rather than contributing to energy, muscle, and bone growth.

Statistically, the Nemours Foundation reports that "one-third of all kids between the ages of 2 and 19 are overweight or obese. So younger people are now developing health problems that used to affect only adults, like high blood pressure, high cholesterol, and type 2 diabetes."

According to the US Center for Disease Control, in 2008, thirty-five states had more than 25 percent of the adult population with a body mass index equal to or greater than 30, the point at which an adult is statistically obese.

Only one state, Colorado, had a population where less than 20 percent of the adult population was considered obese.

In three states, Alabama, Oregon, and Wisconsin, more than 30 percent of the adult population was obese.

If we include those adults who are considered simply overweight as distinguished from obese, the CDC 2008 total leaps to 67 percent of US population.

Sugar, in one form or another, is in nearly 100 percent of prepared foods sold in the United States. As a part of our agricultural policy Congress and each administration for nearly seventy years has acted to make sure the citizenry has had abundant food at prices they can afford. The objective was not purely humanitarian. Policy makers wanted to be sure the population, after paying for their essential food supplies, still had abundant dollars for other things. The financial ability to purchase manufactured goods, an activity that has been widely reported as "powering the US economy," was a very important consideration.

Corn is one crop that has been heavily subsidized to accomplish those policy objectives.

Corn has a high percentage of starch that is the basis for the derivative manufacture of high-fructose corn syrup.

HFCS has been an ubiquitous component of nearly all US commercially manufactured foods and drinks that require a sweetener as a part of their recipe. Recently, some manufactures of food and drink products have announced their change from HFCS to sugar or other sweeteners.

Slate, an online magazine, has reported, "The ingestion of glucose, a . . . basic sugar, is known to stimulate the release of body chemicals that regulate food intake. Fructose, on the other hand, does little to suppress your appetite, and it seems to be preferentially associated with the formation of new fat cells. A growing body of research has led some scientists to wonder whether the increased consumption of fructose over the past few decades might be responsible for rising rates of obesity."

Although the corn lobby has been quick to denigrate any study that links obesity to corn products, the move to other sources of sweeteners than sugar or HFCS can only be viewed as having healthy consequences for consumers.

Sugar from either cane or beets as well as HFCS are both composed of nearly identical proportions of fructose and glucose. Fructose is almost twice as sweet as glucose and it is what distinguishes sugar from other foods that are rich in carbohydrates (potatoes, bread), carbohydrates that break down in the digestive process into glucose.

Fructose is metabolized primarily by the liver while the glucose from sugar and starches is metabolized in an entirely different way involving nearly every cell in the body. The difference in sugar (fructose plus glucose) and other carbohydrates that break down into glucose and other nutrients, is that sugar puts a direct and substantial burden on the liver as well as challenging the pancreas to produce insulin to regulate and modulate the effects of fructose body wide.

While the sugar in soft drinks, ice cream, cakes and candies is substantial and puts an extra burden on the body's ability to keep in balance, some fruit juices create an even greater problem: juices such as apple juice, go right to the liver to be metabolized. This, if the quantity of fructose is too great or the liver is already burdened by other needs of the body, requires the liver to short circuit the metabolic process and immediately turn the sugar into fat.

If there is a level of sugar intake that requires an amount of insulin to balance it that is more than the body would ordinarily produce, the condition of hyperinsulinemia (overproduction of insulin) results.

This causes the sudden crash in energy that many report after eating ice cream or other sugar-rich foods. But the problems don't stop there, because the hyperinsulinemia sets up a condition in the body that interferes with the production of energy derived from cellular conversion of fat into energy.

Fat that would otherwise be utilized, diminishing the body's store of fat and reducing the BMI of the body involved, is halted. The fat stays where it is—on hips or belly or thighs or wherever. And all because of too much sugar for the body to handle as it is set up to do.

So reducing sucrose, fructose, and other sweeteners in the diet is an extremely important part of encouraging the body to burn the fat that it has, as an energy supply, and to also burn the fat that is consumed, inevitably, as a part of the traditional diet of the American household.

Research that is both ongoing and expanding pretty well establishes that sugar is in many ways poisonous to the human body. In small amounts, the effects are too small to be identified and recognized except over long periods of use. The connection between high sugar intake and insulin imbalances are well established. Now, researchers in cancer causation are finding more and more links from insulin malfunctions to both the stimulation and the nourishment of cancerous cells.

It is not only at home that we must be diligent in watching what and how much we eat.

Restaurants compete for business by offering more and more food to their customers, thinking, correctly, that the offer of a lot more food for what appears to be very little more money will entice customers into their establishment.

The economics of this strategy are irresistible. Assume a dinner of average size priced at $12.95. Food cost is about 40 percent of that or $5.20. Increase the food amount (and cost) by

10 percent or $0.52 and the price charged to the diner by $2.00 (to $14.95, not a high price) and we see that for an investment of $0.52, the patron gets more than he can eat and the restaurateur gains an increase in net income per meal of $1.48.

But those extra calories, beyond what is needed for our (mostly) nonmuscular work, multiplied by many meals, means lots of stored body fat that will contribute to the overweight condition of many diners.

Dinner plates have increased in size over the past thirty years. In 1970-1980, most dinner plates were eleven inches in diameter. Now they are twelve and twelve and a half inches in diameter. That extra space on the plate forms an invitation to the home chef to fill up the plate with just a bit more food at every meal.

Deepak Chopra has a practical method of meeting the challenge of too much food on his plate: he listens to his stomach. When his stomach tells him it is about three quarters full, he stops eating.

Ayurveda, the ancient Indian system of keeping healthy, says there are six tastes distinguishable in foods that humans eat: sweet, sour salt, bitter, astringent, and pungent. If all of these six tastes are satisfied, the diner is satisfied; she doesn't leave the table still hungry, even with a meal that fills only three quarters of her stomach.

Ayurveda has developed *churnas*—table condiments of various spices—each *churna* delivering a spectrum of the six basic tastes so the diner will feel satisfied when her stomach is nearly full and not overeat.

Eating the heavy meal in the middle of the day when the digestive fires burn the most intensely and eating light at night is another strategy that ayurveda strongly suggests to keep one's weight at an optimum number. Having soup first at noon meals also contributes to a feeling of satisfaction and limits the desire to overeat.

Limiting the intake of red meats, particularly beef and especially pork (even though some cuts appear less than red), is also recommended. Beef is fed on a mostly grain diet. The natural diet is grass and browse. Pharmaceuticals are used in huge quantities to keep animals that are herded together in relatively small pens and are required to stand in their own excrement from getting too many diseases. That is not the way beef for the table should be raised.

Pig raising is worse by magnitudes. Turkey is better for us in many ways than chicken. Fish and shellfish, if you happen to live near either coast, are good even though heavy metal contamination has become something of a worry, except for fish from the arctic regions.

An occasional juice fast, where nothing but fruit or vegetable juice is taken in as nutrition for a day or two, is both cleansing for the system and soothing in the sense of relieving the body of the task of digesting heavy proteins. It is surprising that such a "fast" does not leave one hungry and is exceptionally good for the overall health of the body.

A salad mix of raw vegetable is excellent and not only for the enzymes that raw vegetables provide. Our bodies do produce enzymes, but sadly, as the years go by, and particularly after about age sixty, the self-supply of enzymes tends to diminish. Nutritional supplements of all kinds are needed. The raw salad can be an excellent substitute for store-bought enzymes and tastier by far.

A particularly good salad includes organic carrots, celery, zucchini, yellow squash, green string beans, black beans, asparagus tips, broccoli crowns, cucumber, cauliflower, apple, walnut pieces, raisins, and anything else that might come to hand. Cut the veggies into half-inch cubes and douse the mix with fresh lemon juice, herbed vinegar, and tasty extra virgin olive oil. Add some squares of a hard cheese, such as Asiago, and serve with strips of avocado on butter lettuce. You won't believe how good such a salad is. Stick with organic as much as possible. The superior taste and freedom from agricultural toxins are worth the little extra that organic may cost. And it tends to reduce your BMI.

Digestion and metabolism of the food you take into your body are of paramount importance to your cells. Food that is not well-digested cannot be fully metabolized and is really just a pool of fat particles waiting to attach to your body in places you'd rather they didn't.

As our systems need more and more special care, the availability of nutrients in the food we do eat is a more and more important consideration. Well-cooked food, with the fibers already partially or fully broken down by the cooking, are more available to the food processing systems of older folks than undercooked or raw foods, even though raw foods do contribute lots of good things we need.

The low-fat crazies would have us eat cardboard if they could, without butter. But we need fats. Eating butter is not the criminal act some nutritionists tell us it is. But moderation is important. With oils, cold-pressed means that powerful solvents (petroleum based) are not used, and the seeds or other sources of the oil are not subjected to high heat in the extraction process. Solvents and high heat both tend to cause oil to change its nature from the pure sweet goodness that it naturally has. Pure nutritious oil to cook with and to put on food is a part of a healthy diet.

Recent tests have shown that the flavor of oil disappears when it is used to fry or sauté. Flavor remains when used in vegetable or other mixes in the cooking process and when used on raw foods or after cooking. So for the sake of economy, save your really good oil for the table and use pure but not so flavorful oil at the stove.

Using care to choose what, when, and how much you eat can change your weight, BMI, and, ultimately, your health. It is worth saying again; you are what you choose to be.

It is so hard when I have to and so easy when I want to.

—GPD

#47 Headaches

As students, you have had lots of experience with stress. Not only is it stressful just to grow up, but school, schoolmates, teachers, subjects, not to mention parents and siblings, also all caused stress of one kind or another. Often, that stress, concentrated in the shoulders or neck and because of the way the body works ended up as a headache. The many causes of headaches will not go away in your lifetime. But there are ways to manage the stresses that causes them, and it is not hard.

You may already know this, but it is useful to touch on the mechanisms involved. When neck and shoulder muscles go into tension, or even spasm, from stress, both externally and internally imposed and trap the nerves that traverse or end in that area, that constriction interferes with the free flow of energy on those nerve pathways. The tension also restricts the blood flow that, in turn, reduces the amount of vital oxygen to those cells. The body responds to these insults, telling you that things have gone awry. The message comes in the form of a pain in the neck or pain in the head that can lay us low.

Shoulders have concentrations of nerves. The brachial plexus is a concentration of muscles and nerves just above the center of your collarbone and just an inch or two from the point where the shoulder meets the neck with one on each side. When one of these brachial plexus becomes tense and in spasm, you can feel the area turn into a knot about the size of a half walnut, just under the skin.

The tension and resulting spasm that cause this condition can come from either or both mental or physical stress. Bending over a desk or hours at a computer will cause physical stress from a long-held position in which your muscles are kept tense. Combine that with mental stress from the brain effort of the work and the shoulders will tense. That translates into more physical stress, and that causes the brachial plexus to swell and let you know it is unhappy. The resulting headache is usually across the back of the skull and up behind the ears. In most cases, you were not aware of the stress and tension until your body sent the signal saying "stop!"

The physiology of the condition is very clear. The neck has a pathway of nerves that, generally, come out of the spine in both directions laterally, follow the hard baseline of the skull, and curve upward past the back of the ear, over the ear, to each temple, branching out then to serve all portions of the face. These are the nerve (energy) pathways of acupuncture, acupressure, and shiatsu massage; where they intersect or branch are the *marma* points of ayurveda.

Chinese acupuncture describes the condition of nerve constriction as a congestion of energy. Nerves are somewhat like electric wires we are all acquainted with. There is a central communicating fiber that, when healthy, is encased within a sheath, the myelin, that protects it externally and lubricates the fiber internally, allowing for minimal twisting and stretching. When the sheath is pinched, the nerve fiber may be crimped as well. The fiber either cannot move at all or, when moving, is irritated. In either case, the message sent to the brain can be either one of pain that, in the case of a pinched nerve, can be excruciating or discomfort, which can range from extreme to mild.

The brachial plexus on either shoulder can knot up from tension in the shoulder muscles, holding oneself more or less rigid when subjected to the often extreme demands of present-day living. At times, these complexes of muscles and nerves can become almost too tender to massage. However, bunched-up muscles need to be smoothed out if the nerve pathways are to be opened to their full potential. Tangled muscles tighten on nerves that, in turn, send a message of stress back up to the brain that cause other nerves that serve the neck and forehead and eyes to send facial muscles into tension, and a headache is started.

Tension and stress headaches can usually be controlled in advance by daily vigorous massage of the nerve endings that are thickly concentrated in three easily accessible parts of the body—the outermost edge and internal ridges of both ears, the web of flesh between the thumb and forefinger, as well as the palms of both hands and the soles of both feet.

All the major organs of the body have nerve pathways that end in the feet, the ears, and the hands. Massaging those nerve endings with daily morning massages seems to keep open the pathways of those nerves through the body, preventing constriction of energy and the pain such constriction can cause.

"Reflexology" (foot massage) is a term common to most. A good reflexologist knows the points on the soles of the feet where specific nerve pathway endings connect to both internal and external parts of the body. Massage therapists know of these nerve pathway terminals in the outer edge and adjacent cartilage of the ears and in the palms of the hands. Having no professional to do this, these terminals have to be massaged by ourselves.

Acupuncture aims to keep these pathways open and free-flowing, using exceedingly fine wires inserted into the nerve pathway or intersection to drain off accumulated or congested energy. The objective is to open the nerve pathway to its normal free flow of nerve energy and information.

The Japanese healing art of shiatsu uses both pressure-point therapy and massage therapy. Shiatsu is also based on the objective of keeping nerve pathways open. Shiatsu uses both focused firm pressure and long stroke massages over nerve pathways, intersections, and endings to relieve pain and promote good health.

Acupuncture derives from Vedic healing traditions that predate Chinese acupuncture by nearly two thousand years. Vedic healing tradition is most commonly known today for the generally accepted identification and location of the seven major chakras of the body. Maharishi Mahesh Yogi (1915-2008) and Deepak Chopra are primarily responsible for bringing and promoting knowledge of Vedic healing to the Western world.

Vedic healing teaches that there are *marma* points that correspond exactly with acupuncture nodes used by practitioners of that art. Vedic healers believe there are innumerably more *marma* points than the points used in today's acupuncture healing.

How does one use this information to relieve and prevent headaches?

We live in a stressful world. The tensions of living and the pressures associated with fast-paced professions and occupations in which accuracy and speed are accepted requirements of participation mean that our bodies require preparation for the day, every day, not to mention relief each evening from the assaults to the body by the day's normal and usually stressful events. We must take the time to focus on relieving this disease imposed upon us by the simple fact that we are living in a stressful world.

Pressure on the knot that arises at the brachial plexus will help keep those nerve pathways open, if not actually free-flowing. Place one finger right on the top of the point that hurts the worst and press, the firmer the better, holding that pressure for a slow count of twenty. Because the area is usually too broad to be served by one pressure-point (shiatsu) treatment, search around and find all the areas that hurt and repeat the single finger pressure treatment.

Fifteen seconds is the usually accepted time for pressure to cause muscles to relax and nerve pathways to be freed, thus the slow count of twenty to be sure it has been at least fifteen seconds. One treatment will usually not be enough. Repeating this several times during a day may be necessary to break down the tangle and free up the nerves and ease the pain.

Heat applied to the brachial plexus (as with a hot washcloth) also will help to relax those muscles and free up entrapped nerves. It is also likely that there is inflammation at the site that can be helped with some mild anti-inflammatory, a so-called NSAID (nonsteroidal anti-inflammatory drug) such as Ibuprofen.

Nerves that radiate outward from the spine along the lower edge of the skull can become trapped in tense muscles of the neck. They also respond to pressure and firm rubbing along the nerve pathway. Follow the nerve up behind and over the top of the ear to the temple, the forehead, and around the eyes with repetitive gentle massage. Gentle but firm rubbing in a circle as you move from the occipital ridge, up behind the ears, and then to the temple and forehead is recommended.

But the preventive method of clearing nerve pathways, massaging ears, hands, and feet every morning, and making sure to firmly but gently press and rub all the areas where the nerve pathways are known to terminate is the most effective way to make your days go more smoothly and to preempt the headache cause—the blockage of nerve pathways by muscle tension that is an inevitable part of our modern life.

I routinely use either plain ayurveda sesame oil or sesame oil with selected essential oils every morning, on my whole body (see "Morning Routine," #36). Alerting the nerve endings in my ears, hands, and feet that the day is beginning and that I will pay attention to their comfort during the day has meant that since 1995, when I learned of this technique from Deepak Chopra, I have not had one headache. My earlier experience with the stresses of preparing for and participating in court trials meant frequent headaches and frequent resort to Excedrin or other OTC pain relievers. No longer do I need that relief. So I highly recommend this simple process, which takes less than three minutes total, as an everyday routine to keep healthy.

Do you want to know who you are?

Don't ask.

Act!

Action will delineate and define you.

—Thomas Jefferson

#48 Kinesiology: A Different Language

What if I told you that you have the inherent ability to have a conversation with your cells?

I know that you all understand that you, the one who inhabits your body, have an obligation to make sure your body has all the basic supplies it needs to keep healthy, energetic, and fully functioning. You all learned in biology that the many urges you respond to during each day—to eat, to drink, to sleep, to eliminate wastes—are prompted by communications your cells send to your brain about what your body, both specifically and generally, needs you to do to help it function efficiently. Communication from your cells to your brain is going on all the time.

Sometimes there is more urgency than at other times; for example, when there is an imbalance in hydration and you feel an acute thirst, sometimes there is merely a hint of a need, as when your cells need vitamin D and send your brain internal memos (messenger molecules carried by the blood) that prompt you to think that going for a walk on a sunny day would be a good thing to do. As with so much of life, paying attention to what is going on around you—in this case, in you—is vital.

Your cells not only initiate communications, they respond to questions. With that, a conversation is possible, and that's what this e-mail is about.

You've probably heard stories of seemingly unusual requests of pregnant women for food items that may be out of season or available only when stores that usually carry those items are closed. These anecdotes, often funny, are recognized wisdom that the body does speak forcefully to us about its needs, at least under some conditions.

When the fetus' needs have depleted the mother of some important mineral or other nutrient in her body, her own cells let her know about this by calling up a memory of food rich in that particular nutrient. Cellular communication to her mind-body that an essential nutrient is in short supply is translated into a desire for that food.

Cells communicate their needs in ways calculated to get them what they need. Cells invoke the cycle of action, memory, desire, intention, and then, again, action to satisfy their needs, coming into the cycle at the point of desire.

Hunger is a cellular request for replenishment of our general energy supply. Any calories will do temporarily, but too often we reach for the quick fix—prepared and, often, sugar-laced foods. These not only don't bring lasting hunger satisfaction, but the negative effects of the insulin swings brought on by sugar intake also lets us get way down energetically and, for some people, emotionally as well.

Our cells do communicate with us in their own ways. As we become more and more sensitive to our body's needs, it is possible to tune in to those expressions of need as the cells send messages to our consciousness. As the example of the pregnant woman illustrates, these messages frequently come in the form of desire for a particular nutrient.

Memory of a prior action that satisfied a cellular craving focuses mind-body attention. Intention to satisfy the need follows memory. Memory becomes desire. Desire stimulates the self to perform the remembered satisfying action. When needed nutrition is found and taken into the body, our cells have available what they asked for.

Cellular demand for satisfaction may be as strong as thirst or as subtle as a vague desire for a plate of pasta or shrimp, which cellular memory predicts will bring it the nutrients desired.

These simple examples illustrate how our cells are able to and do communicate their needs to their controller, the you who is neither body nor mind nor a combination of body-mind. The you who is the decider and ultimate controller of the mind-body receives and interprets cellular messages, putting cellular needs into, first, attention and then intention (desire), followed by action, with, hopefully, satisfaction of cellular needs the final result.

But listening to our cells only when they communicate by prompting us to action so strongly that we cannot avoid paying attention, only when their internal signals cannot be denied, misses the great opportunity that kinesiology affords.

You can ask your cells questions and get answers that very reliably tell you what your cells and, therefore, what your body needs.

Kinesiology is the name of the skill that has developed to describe both the vocabulary and the process by which there can be meaningful two-way communication between the external world and the internal world of your cellular nature. It is the language of cells made understandable.

George Joseph Goodheart Jr. (1918 – 2008) was a chiropractor who founded applied kinesiology. He died on March 5, 2008, at the age of eighty-nine. Applied kinesiology, now shortened to simply kinesiology, is the practice of evaluating the relative strength of certain muscle groups to the presence of any energy. Energy, in this definition, is anything external to the body being tested. This easily testable concept is that, in the presence of an energy that contributes to the well-being of the body, musculature will be relatively strong. In the presence of any toxic or deleterious energy, musculature will become relatively weak. It is the cellular response that is being evaluated. In most instances, the weakness or strength is readily apparent.

As with any aspect of life, there is some skill involved in doing this. Practice will make understanding cellular answers more accurate. More subtle information can be accessed.

The profession where it is most often used is chiropractic, whose practitioners are often rebels by nature and, thus, more willing than the average allopathic physician to utilize processes like kinesiology.

As with most written descriptions of actions, words are not nearly as effective in conveying a meaningful understanding of kinesiology as just a few minutes with one who is experienced in using it as a tool would be.

If you have a chiropractic healer as one of your health-care providers, you have probably experienced how they use this form of body communication to pinpoint problems they intend to treat.

If not, a call to almost any doctor of chiropractic in your area will provide information about where some hands-on training in kinesiology is available. If you want to use kinesiology to communicate with your body, you want to really learn this language of the cells.

The most important result of learning from someone who knows about kinesiology, someone who is trained and experienced in the skill required to interpret the body's responses, is the confidence it will give you that there really is a cellular language that your body already knows. With this means of communication, your body will freely offer information that you, the choice maker, need to have about what is useful and what is harmful to your cellular structure.

If you want to know whether anything pertinent to your life is beneficial or harmful—e.g., food, drink, environment, habitation, current or contemplated activity, or whatever—your body will let you know honestly, forthrightly, with no fibbing, and no withholding of communication. Your body really is your very best friend in this regard with, literally, inside information about the life you and your body have in common. No one else has the information; nothing else can tell you what your cells can tell you.

Learning this language and how to use it in dialogue with your body is important beyond finding out which foods are good and which are harmful. You will likely find some foods harmful, even though those foods may not make you obviously ill.

Everyone fools himself or herself about all sorts of things. Habits that are very harmful to our cells, such as smoking or drinking alcohol, we excuse ourselves for doing, usually because we are addicted to the use of these substances to a greater or lesser extent. But ask your body if a habit is harmful and your body will tell you the truth.

To understand how cells in your body express themselves through muscle strength or weakness, try this (this will require a partner).

Stand with your right arm stretched out horizontally to the side. Have your partner in this learning event press down on the top of your hand with just enough force to overcome the resistance your arm has to this moderate pressure.

Don't break a sweat trying to hold your arm level. Just hold it straight out with an easy resistance to the downward pressure. Obviously, you can resist the actions of your partner and foil the intent and interfere with the subtlety of this learning event. So don't do it. Try to understand the way your body will speak to you in this way.

What your partner (and you) will be testing is the relative strength of the resistance of your muscles as you move into the next part of this process, where your body will be asked to communicate with you. Once the first level of resistance is established, it is important to maintain this same degree of subjective resistance throughout the next steps. Both your partner and you will be interpreting the degree to which your body will maintain that same muscular strength against the same external pressure as questions are posed or substances are tested.

Take a pack of cigarettes or a spoonful or pack of white sugar crystals in your left hand and hold that against your body. Mentally, ask your body, "Is this substance in my left hand good for my body?"

With your right arm outstretched and keeping the resistance the same as before, have your partner press again on the top of your right hand, using the same downward pressure as before. You will find that your ability to resist the pressure is dramatically less. You may not be able to resist the pressure at all. Your arm may just collapse.

What is happening? Your muscles, your cells, are responding to the specific energy frequency of the sugar and telling you that

that frequency is disruptive to your cells and negative for your well-being.

As I have pointed out to you, thoughts are energy, and this energy has power. You do not even have to put anything into your hand for your cells to react.

Simply think about something as dangerous to your well-being as a cigarette or just think about the smoke of tobacco; the thought is enough to cause your cells to react. Visualizing anything and asking your cells for a response will tell you if that something is not good for you.

Questions do not have to be about something concrete. Testing whether a relationship is beneficial or harmful is an example of exploring the emotional content of your being by kinesiology.

There are literally no limits to what your body will disclose to you regarding what it has experienced in the past and what, at the deepest nonconscious levels of your brain, it predicts will be beneficial or harmful effects in the future.

The energy of your brain is not local only. That is, the energy of your brain is not confined to your body. The energy of everyone's brain is sufficient to be detected by machines I'm sure you have heard of (EEG or electroencephalogram) created for that purpose. This machine measures the electrical output of the neurons in your brain. The occasions when we pick up the thoughts of others, or they pick up ours, are examples of nonlocal brain energy. The phenomenon is so common that we have long described it as mental telepathy. Often that happens at a great distance, proving that there are no physical limits to the distance our thoughts can travel.

In asking others about this, I have never talked to any adult to whom this has not happened. It seems to be a universal phenomenon although not one most of us have learned to control and use at will. Exceptions come to mind of yogis in India.

Accessing the knowledge of your cells is possible and is a most useful part of knowing about and being able to use kinesiology. Test this for yourself. Clear your mind, and establish a baseline of resistance with either arm, tested by someone you trust. Ask your helper to imagine some toxic substance without telling you what it is. Have them then test the muscle strength of that same arm again while they are thinking of the toxin, and you will find the result will be the same as if you had imagined that toxin.

Our minds are capable of receiving information that we, on a conscious level, cannot access and do not "know" in the usual sense of that word. But we can access and learn of this inner knowledge because we are all connected to each other, and each mind is connected to the universe.

The next step in this is to learn a method of muscle testing, which does not require a partner.

Make a circle with the thumb and little finger of the left hand; interlock it with a circle made with the thumb and forefinger of the right hand. To establish a baseline of resistance, pull the right-hand-finger circle through the left-hand-finger circle at the point where the left fingers meet, while you are mentally saying, "My name is" . . . and thinking your name. The resistance will give you a baseline for what your cells understand to be truth.

Now say, mentally, "My name is Mickey Mouse" while doing the same procedure. When you think the truth, your left finger circle will be strong. When you think the lie, your right-finger circle will easily break through the left-finger circle. The loss of strength when you think the lie will be repeated each time your cells detect that you are thinking a lie.

Again, the object is to allow your muscles to create a strong, circle, to not allow a breach of the circle. Gauging the strength of the resistance at the beginning will create a baseline for comparison.

Stay open to receiving information through the relative resistance of breaking the closure of your left-finger circle as you pose mental questions you want answered. In this process, your finger muscles are messengers of communication from your cells and your subconscious.

Try this at any restaurant, particularly if there is nothing on the menu that immediately stands out as something "you" want. If there is an immediate "knowing" of what you want to eat, your cells are speaking to you, and the choice will be clear.

Often though, we look at a menu, not really knowing what we want. Testing each item by merely focusing on that item while using the finger-circle kinesiology just described will give you good information about what your cells think of the nourishment in each food evaluated.

Using this technique, you can dialogue with the intelligence of your body about allergies, medicines, supplements, foods, exercise, relationships, and anything and everything that is of concern to you about your own health and well-being.

Caveat: mentally state your question simply and clearly. Do not ask more than one thing at a time. Examples: "Is this . . . good for me?" or "Will . . . contribute to my well-being?" Simple declarative statements will work equally well. Example: "This . . . will contribute to my well-being." What you are testing in this manner is the truth or falsity of the statement. Therefore, a baseline of truth is needed. Saying or thinking your name, while testing your muscles, will give you a baseline of what is true.

In the United States at least, reliance upon manufactured medicines will only increase in the future. You should test those that may be prescribed for you (or if you are given a sample packet) to see if your body thinks they will be beneficial—i.e., will help cure or alleviate the problem from which you suffer. Almost certainly, your body will regard them as toxic, as poisons to be avoided. Most medicines created by big pharmaceuticals are synthetic combinations of chemicals designed to kill something. Yet if you hold one dose in your hand and think, "Will this one dose (pill, tablet, etc.) contribute to my well-being?" your cells may have a favorable response.

As you become more experienced in this, you will find ways to ask questions about the present and the future that work well for you. Most answers your cells give you about the future will tell you only what is predictable at the moment of asking. External events are always changing what the future will actually be.

Asking questions of future events also requires focus and specificity. At my age, a practical question involves the likely time of death. Having a will and instructions about life support are important to have finished in advance of the need. That particular event is actually dependent on so many future unknowable variables; no answer will bring information one should rely on. Still, recent gene studies indicate that longevity does seem to be programmed into the genetic code of our cells. It is a bit odd and a little discomforting to think of our cells as having an expiration date, but that is what science is now postulating.

Consequently, a question that asks, "Will I be alive on (for example) January 1, 2050?" will get a definitive response. By narrowing the date window asked about, you can obtain knowledge that will disclose what your cells know at that moment of your genetically programmed longevity.

As I have said before, all of life involves choice making. As we choose, having more information is better than the alternative. To make good choices, you need reasonably good information. Your body will tell you the truth about you. But you do have to ask.

Your body is in a constant process of change.

Every choice you make

influences what that change will be.

—GPD

#49 Investing or Making a Living?

Mary and I were at a white-tablecloth restaurant some time ago, dining with two friends, and had an experience that surprised us all. We have talked about it since as a mark of the casual times we are now living in. It also indicated that the purpose of the restaurant owner was not to serve his patrons well but that his purpose was to sell food to make money. In other words, we were in the establishment of an entrepreneur who had invested in a restaurant for profit, not as a way of making a living or a way of life.

We came to that conclusion from these events: the food we had ordered was delivered to the table by a pair of young servers, each suitably garbed and each carrying a medium-sized tray with two plates of the food we had ordered.

They came to the square table at its point, between our two friends. Trained servers make note of the position at the table of each diner, as they order, so that the food each ordered can be distributed quietly, efficiently and without having to ask, who had ordered what. The first indication that we were dealing with untrained servers was that they found it necessary to ask who had ordered the first dish the lead server removed from his tray.

When Mary answered affirmatively, instead of moving around the table to her side to place the food in front of her, from the right side, as is customary, the server reached across the table, shoving her plate past the face one of our friends and then asked Mary if she would take the plate and put it at her place. My dinner was then served the same way, from the same place, the server asking me to accept my plate of food in midair and place it on the table in front of me. Our friends, being next to the server, had their food served to them directly and, more or less, as expected.

There are a lot of reasons why this would be bad manners anywhere. In a fairly high-toned restaurant, with quite high prices, it was unexpected.

What it said to us was that the young men who were serving us had no formal training as servers nor had the owner of the restaurant thought it necessary to make sure their employees knew even basic procedures for serving efficiently and with care for the diner.

But the ultimate conclusion was that the owner of this establishment was in a business he (or she) did not know and therefore had not known how to train his staff.

The business was being operated because the location, the menu its chef had prepared and the high prices charged, almost guaranteed a handsome profit, no matter the quality of service.

This was a business created simply to make a profit. It was not a service offered to the public, by which the owner would make a living, perhaps a very good living, by providing good food and good service, at a reasonable price, to a public that needed such a business.

This difference speaks to the prevailing idea of "entrepreneurship" currently in vogue in this country. We are plagued by money hungry citizens who just want to invest in a business that will make money. The idea of hard work, careful attention to the product and the service, of finding a need the public has and filling that need in order to make one's living, for generations the touchstone of American business, has gone. Replacing honesty and hard work has been a love of money that makes those with a little money want to make more by investing. It doesn't seem to matter what the investment is. Anything that is likely to make a good profit seems to do.

I tell you this because making money, while important, should not be the prime objective of your life.

It used to be said, "Take care of your business and your business will take care of you." That was based on observation that those who took the risk of opening their own business, who were careful about the quality of products offered, who trained employees to take care of customer needs, who provided services that went beyond what the customer expected and who charged what were considered fair prices, would prosper.

It is still the case that businesses that follow these simple rules do prosper.

There is a big difference between the operating rules of a business established for the owner to make a living and the make-a-profit-quick rules that are the all too frequent principles that presently prevail in our country's businesses, large and small.

I've mentioned that the truly enlightened person makes decisions based on what is best for them in the long term; short term versus long term pleasure is the dichotomy that requires careful thought and even more careful decision making. It has ever been so. Described by Socrates and reported by Plato more than two thousand years ago it still distinguishes the smart business person from the not so smart.

To continue the restaurant example, using only the freshest ingredients likely requires more attention to detail and is likely more costly. Training the wait staff and maintaining service quality certainly requires more time and energy than allowing each server to follow his or her own ideas of proper service.

Yet, with this example, it should be quite apparent that investing the time, energy and attention to detail with the intent of serving the best food and service to the public that could be managed is likely to bring greater rewards economically than economizing on ingredient quality and allowing untrained servers to represent the restaurant.

You may find that working in another's business is more comfortable for you than having your own. Be sure to look for an employer that does things the old way. Those who pursue profit, simply for the sake of profit, will fire you without a thought for your welfare. It is all simply money to them. While the man who is in business to make a living will more likely not hire you until he is sure he can keep you as an employee for as long as you want to be employed.

No matter what the task, it pays to always reach for the smooth part of the handle.

—Thomas Jefferson

#50 Is the Glass Half Full?

Whether one sees a glass as half full or half empty is a cliché. Though it is an oversimplification, the question does reflect what is grossly observable in the personality traits of most people. There are those who, when faced with a decision to move into unknown territory, ask why. Others faced with the same situation ask why not.

I was blessed with a mother whose own growing up had been one which allowed her spirit to bloom and develop an outlook on life that remained optimistic in nearly all circumstances. Even when my father was hospitalized for nearly two years with tuberculosis, she cared for the needs of my brother and me with unflagging enthusiasm. She was the one who taught me to put emphasis on the "why not" aspect of life evaluation.

The woman who mothered me came into my life when I was just three years old. Florence Wells, Flo, an elementary school teacher with the New York City school system, married my dad about two years after the death of my birth mother. She was a marvelous combination of tall, blonde, and well built with a strong, healthy sense of herself. She brought her optimism about life into our home. Although the Depression was no kinder to us than to other local families, she always had a good-humored outlook about the future.

Her own childhood had been spent in Hampton Bays, Long Island, a small community about seventy miles from New York City. Her father had owned the local drayage business that, in the early 1900s, was horse powered. Her stories of youthful freedom and adventure, of riding horses from her father's business over the back roads and along the shores of nearby Shinnecock and Peconic bays were a part of our nightly story time.

She brought to that marriage and to her happy practical assumption of my care and nurturing an approach to life that could be summarized as "Let him do it. He'll soon find out if he can or not."

She told me later, when my letter came to them announcing that I had had all of farm life I could stand for one summer and was off to join the Ringling Bros., Barnum & Bailey Circus and would write to them again about where I was, that she told my father to relax and see how I managed the experience. She was willing to let me try, assuming that the circus, while not the usual environment for a sixteen-year-old boy, could be a positive experience.

And so it was. In the nearly three weeks that I worked as a circus hand, I made friends; had self-appointed protectors; thrilled to riding circus wagons from the train sidings to the circus lot in small and large cities and towns; mingled with performers, animal trainers, clowns, freaks, and workers; worked hard; risked dangers without ill effect; and generally had a terrific time.

One of the most important things I learned is that I had protection from sources I never knew. Not only did my boss, Scotty Horsebrough, an old-time circus hand, watch out for me, but he also told the porters in the sleeping car where I shared a bunk with Scotty to make sure I was not robbed, not molested, and not interfered with in any way. And they did.

The men who were the professional electricians while I was with Ringling were all gay. It was during WWII, and they had not been drafted, so they were able to do the work they enjoyed. A sixteen-year-old inexperienced boy as I was then could have been raw meat to a group like that, but I wasn't. I was seriously propositioned a couple of times early in my circus experience and offered money for oral sex, but one particular young electrician stopped that cold. He told me later he had told the others that I was too young and to leave me alone. After that, I was not propositioned nor was there ever any hint of any sexual invitation in my daily work around this group of openly gay young men.

Innocence is, in most cases, a protective shield. Horror stories exist, and I do not doubt that there are those who take advantage of innocence. But generally speaking, as a species, we act communally to protect the young until they have reached a point at which discretion is assumed.

The overall application of this wisdom has been diluted by population growth. As our numbers increase and we are herded closer and closer together in our living conditions, we seem to have lost some of our natural inclination to look out for each other. As a society, we seem to have lost a lot of what I remember as community caring for each other. That used to exist, and it hasn't been that long ago.

In the community in which I grew up, I can remember women I scarcely knew telling me, "David Nagle, that's not a good thing for you to do. You wouldn't want me to tell your mother about this, would you?" I was a part of the village it takes to raise a child. The village looked after me, and I knew it.

Today, our society has decided that instead of taking care of the children, it is more important that both mother and father work to bring in the money to buy the goods that makes the US economy purr. Neither mothers nor fathers are around as once they were. Children are frequently left to their own childish devices.

The opportunity for the unscrupulous to take advantage of children has increased. The natural protections for the innocent that insulated me have, I fear, mostly disappeared. The circus experience I had sixty-nine years ago might not be possible today without more risk. But risk and the acceptance of risk are always relative.

While the possibility of danger might have increased, young people of today are much more aware of the world than I believe I was at age sixteen in 1941. Life without risk is not possible. Managing risks is a part of living. Living smart means keeping up with the information flow about us and our environment.

The electronic revolution, which everyone over the age of twelve seems to have tapped into today, allows the aware child to have far more good decision-making tools than similar-aged children of even thirty years ago.

With those new tools, even without the village to help in the care and nurturing of young people, we can all have a greater chance of success in nearly every decision we make about all aspects of our lives.

So risk. Get the facts together, take a look around, and risk. If you look at life as a glass half full rather than half empty, life is likely to be much more fun. Life is also much more likely to offer satisfaction in the living if you simply ask *why not* instead of *why*?

See the glass of life as half full!

Then fill it up from there.

AUTHOR BIOGRAPHY

David Nagle is a retired lawyer now living in Savannah, Georgia.

After three years in the US Navy in WWII, he returned to the University of Virginia, graduated in 1950,andworked in radio and TV in Houston, Texas.

He began his study of law at age thirty-one at the University of Houston. A cooperative boss at KPRC-TV  allowed him to work evenings and weekends and go to law school in the day time with a full class schedule. He graduated and was licensed as a lawyer in 1958.

Married while at the University of Virginia, he and his wife raised three young children, the oldest of whom was eleven when David began the practice of law in Houston.

He never represented businesses or corporations but found a satisfying life helping less-advantaged clients in both civil and criminal matters. After thirty-six years of being a trial lawyer, he retired from the practice of law.

An e-mail project grew out of a desire to reach out to and mentor his grandchildren, who had always lived too far away to be a frequent presence in his life. Beginning with stories of family and his own early childhood, the project expanded to include information, advice, and commentaries on many varied subjects, including how to stay healthy and live long.

This book is an outgrowth of that series of e-mails and internet mentoring of grandchildren, who, by the time of the last in the series, had become young adults.

He used writing skills, honed in the legal profession, to make his e-mails interesting and informative to a generation once removed.

Enhancing
Circulation

Asanas

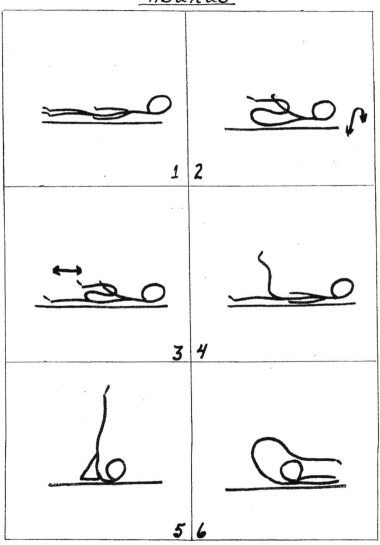

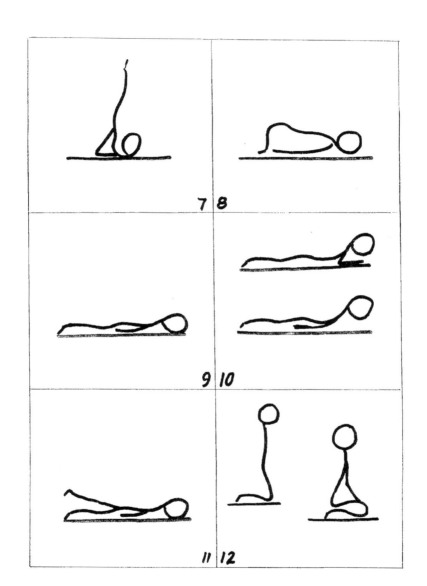

7 8

9 10

11 12

YOGA

ASANAS